WHO IS AN INDIAN?

Race, Place, and the Politics of Indigeneity in the Americas

Edited by Maximilian C. Forte

Who is an Indian? This is possibly the oldest question facing Indigenous peoples across the Americas, and one with significant implications for decisions relating to resource distribution, conflicts over who gets to live where and for how long, and clashing principles of governance and law. For centuries, the dominant views on this issue have been strongly shaped by ideas of both race and place. Who is permitted to ask, and answer, this question?

This collection examines the changing roles of race and place in the politics of defining Indigenous identities in the Americas. Drawing on case studies of Indigenous communities across North America, the Caribbean, Central America, and South America, this unique volume compares Indigenous experience throughout the western hemisphere. The contributors question the vocabulary, legal mechanisms, and applications of science used to construct the identities of Indigenous populations, and consider ideas of nation, land, and tradition in moving indigeneity beyond race.

MAXIMILIAN C. FORTE is an associate professor in the Department of Sociology and Anthropology at Concordia University.

Who Is an Indian?

Race, Place, and the Politics of Indigeneity in the Americas

EDITED BY MAXIMILIAN C. FORTE

UNIVERSITY OF TORONTO PRESS
Toronto Buffalo London

Toronto Buffalo London
www.utppublishing.com
Printed in Canada

ISBN 978-0-8020-9818-4 (cloth)
ISBN 978-0-8020-9552-7 (paper)

Printed on acid-free, 100% post-consumer recycled paper with vegetable-based inks.

Library and Archives Canada Cataloguing in Publication

Who is an Indian? : race, place, and the politics of indigeneity in the Americas / edited by Maximilian C. Forte.

Includes bibliographical references and index.
ISBN 978-0-8020-9818-4 (bound). – ISBN 978-0-8020-9552-7 (pbk.)

1. Ethnicity – Political aspects – America. 2. Indians of North America – Ethnic identity. 3. Indigenous peoples – Ethnic identity – America. 4. Politics and culture – America. 5. America – Ethnic relations. I. Forte, Maximilian C., 1967–

GN550.W46 2013 305.80097 C2013-901825-5

University of Toronto Press acknowledges the financial assistance to its publishing program of the Canada Council for the Arts and the Ontario Arts Council.

University of Toronto Press acknowledges the financial support of the Government of Canada through the Canada Book Fund for its publishing activities.

Contents

Preface

The original impetus for this project came from a very particular context of concern. My research in the Caribbean alerted me to the extent to which notions of "purity," "blood," and lately even DNA analysis came to figure prominently not just as ways of ascribing Indigenous identities, but also as means of claiming them in light of widespread, categorical assertions by colonial rulers and scholars that these peoples had vanished. To my surprise, similar politics of identity were being instituted in North America – indeed, the interest in DNA studies had spread from the U.S. to the Caribbean, and in North America as well I found a concern with blood, purity, and the stigma faced by "Black Indians" who were being rejected as claimants to Cherokee citizenship. In Canada, at least some band councils, such as that of the Saint Regis Mohawk Reserve, have blood quantum requirements of not less than 25 per cent and issue their own tribal ID cards. Also in Canada, one can repeatedly hear or read some Euro-Canadians referring to this or that public figure as "not a real Indian … he looks white," the kind of statement that references phenotype, is framed by stereotypes, and applies "mixture" as if it were a diluting factor which one can just as easily encounter in Australia or the Caribbean. If race, blood, and even DNA were so prevalent, could we find similar concerns spread out across all of the Americas? If so, why? If not, why not? Are race, blood, and DNA essentially the same thing? These were the very first, seemingly very simple questions that led to the emergence of this project.

This book has now been years in the making and has gone through many different stages of development and transformation, each time seemingly with a different combination of participants. Since its inception in 2006 as a session comprising two panels held at Concordia

University under the auspices of the Canadian Anthropology Society (CASCA), and as another session in 2007; through to the development of a grant application for a seminar funded by the Social Sciences and Humanities Research Council and held in Montreal in 2007; and then through two stages of submitting chapters from 2008 through 2010, the project overall has included a total of as many as twenty-one scholars from across the Americas and from across the disciplines, only some of whom appear in this volume. In particular I would like to thank and acknowledge the advice, support, varying degrees of participation and interest, and correspondence of individuals who were involved at different stages of the project, including Kimberly TallBear, José Barreiro, Phil Bellfy, Marisol de la Cadena, Alice and Dennis Bartels, and the late Melissa Meyer who sadly passed away in the middle of this project's development. We also benefited from the participation of Indigenous scholars, who comprised half the number of participants in the overall project. With an immense amount of research and writing taking place in the United States, there was often a tendency to have greater American representation than Canadian, Latin American, and particularly Caribbean. The result of this struggle, the constant revision and reinterpretation, we hope will offer some critical insights into the processes of making "race" out of (or against) Indigenous identity and the role of "place" in debates about Indigenous identity.

Indeed, the project first began as an effort exclusively focused on race, motivated by the recognition that there were no volumes that, treating the Americas as a whole, provided an overarching framework of the ideas and applications of race in the definition of Indigenous identity. This was the basis for the first gathering in 2006, "Indigeneity and Race: 'Blood Politics' and the 'Nature' of Indigenous Identity," which was organized under the auspices of the Canadian Anthropology Society's annual conference and held at Concordia University on 13 May 2006, as well as the second coming the following year dealing with Indigenous cosmopolitanism and transculturation. The major themes were developed in our symposium, "Who Is an Indian? Race, Blood, DNA, and the Politics of Indigeneity in the Americas," involving fourteen participants and hosted at the Clarion Hotel in Montreal from 2–5 August 2007, with the support of the Social Sciences and Humanities Research Council of Canada. However, as a result of the discussions held at the symposium, we came to the realization that race alone could not be the exclusive subject of our concerns in addressing how people have historically answered the question, "Who is an Indian?" The role of place, land, territoriality, and resistance to neoliberalism figured prominently in a number of the papers presented there, to the extent that we concluded that both race and place should be our dual framing concepts. The previous concern with DNA, represented by as many as four participants, largely diminished and then vanished altogether, especially when we no longer had the same participants as in earlier stages of the project. This is not to say that DNA debates are absent in the volume as a whole, but rather that they no longer structure the volume as a central focus, which in any case would still be more relevant to the North American situation than elsewhere.

I would like to acknowledge the generous support of the Social Sciences and Humanities Research Council of Canada (SSHRC) for funding our Montreal seminar fully, allowing us to meet all of the travel and lodging expenses of our participants, as well as the generous support of the Department of Sociology and Anthropology at Concordia University in helping to subsidize the production costs associated with publication. I am also thankful for another SSHRC grant which helped to pay for the preparation of an index for this volume. Finally, I am especially thankful to the University of Toronto Press for its early interest in awarding us an advance contract, and for its exceptional patience in dealing with our multiple delays in what for me has been the most prolonged project that I have yet undertaken.

Acknowledgments

This has been a project long in the making and that fact is the basis for thanking the contributors to this volume for what has usually been their extraordinary patience, understanding, and especially their endurance. At the University of Toronto Press, I have to particularly thank Douglas Hildebrand, the acquisitions editor for the social sciences, for his outstanding care in helping to revive a project that passed through a change in editorial staff at UTP, and for guiding it through some of its most critical stages. Had it not been for his work, there is no chance that this project would have seen the light of day, and I warmly thank him for his patience as well. I am grateful also for the work of our managing editor at UTP, Leah Connor, who supervised the production of the work as it neared its final release. The copy editor, Beth McAuley, did a tremendous job of combing through chapters, with a keen eye for even the tiniest detail that needed attention, while saving us a great deal of time with her extensive copy editing. The cover designer, Ingrid Paulson, is to be thanked for meeting the challenge of producing a visual representation of a topic that is fraught with tension and controversy, and for doing so in such an elegant and stimulating manner. The indexer, Allison Diaz, who has produced a number of indices for me in the past, must be congratulated yet again for closely reading, digesting, and rendering such a useful index as this one. I cannot neglect to thank the Social Sciences and Humanities Research Council of Canada for a grant which entirely financed the symposium held in Montreal in August of 2007, which directly led to this volume, and for partially financing its publication. In addition, the Department of Sociology and Anthropology at Concordia University managed, in difficult financial times, to provide a significant financial donation to cover the costs of production, which cannot be thanked enough. Finally, I appreciate the work of three anonymous reviewers, and one internal to UTP, for their many productive comments and suggestions, and as always any lingering shortcomings should not reflect on them.

WHO IS AN INDIAN?

Introduction
"Who Is an Indian?" The Cultural Politics of a Bad Question

MAXIMILIAN C. FORTE

When they get off the boat, they didn't recognize us. They said: "Who are you?" And we said: "We're the People, we're the Human Beings," and they said: "Oh Indians," because they didn't recognize what it meant to be a human being. "I'm a Human Being, this is the name of my tribe, this is the name of my people, but I'm a human being." But the predatory mentality shows up and starts calling us "Indians" and committing genocide against us as a vehicle of erasing the memory of being a human being ... Even in our own communities, how many of us are fighting to protect our identity of being an Indian, and 600 years ago that word, "Indian," *that sound* was never made in this hemisphere – that sound ["Indian"], that noise, was never ever made! Ever. We're trying to protect *that* as an identity, see, so it affects all of us.

– John Trudell, Lakota poet and activist, quoted in Diamond, Bainbridge, and Hayes, *Reel Injun* (2009)

It is one of the many ironies of the American experience that the invaders created the category of Indians, imposed it on the inhabitants of the New World, and have been trying to abolish it ever since.

– David Maybury-Lewis, co-founder of Cultural Survival, "A New World Dilemma" (1993)

There's tremendous racism in Peru. In Lima, brown people, the descendants of Indigenous people, try to live as white as possible. That's because of the influence of the media and government. If you embrace your Indian-ness, you're shunned. You're less than a third-class person. It's an insult to call someone an Indian. It's the equivalent of calling someone stupid.

– Benjamin Bratt, actor, quoted in Yellow Bird, "What We Want to Be Called" (1999)

The question of my identity often comes up. I think I must be a mixed blood. I claim to be male, although only one of my parents is male.

– Jimmie Durham, Cherokee artist, quoted in Jaimes, "Federal Indian Identificion Policy" (1992)

What does *part* Indian mean? (Which part?) … you don't get 50% or 25% or 16% treatment when you experience racism – it is always 100%.

– Joane Cardinal-Schubert, quoted in Strong and Van Winkle, "Indian Blood" (1996)

Recent years have witnessed growing anxiety on the part of states as they attempt to define, identify, and manage the explosion in Indigenous self-identification that is occurring across the Americas, not least in places where previously no Indigenous population was even recognized to exist, as in parts of Central America and the Caribbean. In confrontation with state policies of identity construction and management, and in tension with popularized stereotypes of what "defines" a person as an "Indian" (to use the colonial and colloquial label that also spread across the Americas), are Indigenous persons and communities. The power to define one's own identity has become a critical feature of self-government and figures prominently in the politics of decolonization. In one indication of this rapid surge in self-identification, according to 2000 U.S. Census data, self-identified American Indians have become the "fastest-growing minority" in the U.S., growing by more than 400 per cent since 1960 (Hitt, 2005; Shoemaker, 1999, p. 4; Nagel, 1996, p. 114). Of the 5.2 million counted as Native in the 2010 U.S. census, nearly 2.3 million identified with one or more of six other "races"; on the whole, the number of American Indians and Alaska Natives identifying with multiple ethnicities grew by 39 per cent in a decade (Fonseca, 2012). In Canada, more than twice as many people self-identify as Aboriginal than are registered as "status Indians." Brazil has seen its Indigenous population grow by more than 300 per cent in fifty years (Warren, 2001, pp. 11–12). In Central America, states have officially recognized Indigenous communities, in a break with previous narratives of amalgamation (Hooker, 2005; Stocker, 2005; Tilley, 2002). The Caribbean has witnessed the resurgence of people claiming the identities of Indigenous nations that were long thought to have been extinct, and some are using DNA testing services to prove their ancestry (Guitar et al., 2006; Martinez Cruzado, 2002). The question of who has a legitimate right to proclaim an Indigenous identity, and by which criteria, has become one of the most divisive issues now afflicting Native North America (Churchill, 2004, p. 60). Proceeding geographically from the north to the south of the Americas, this volume brings to light key case studies in the politics of defining Indigenous identities, with a prime focus on race and place.

"One of the most perplexing problems confronting American Indians today is that of identity," states Hagan, and as he argues (1985, p. 309), the question that is emblematic of that problem is, "Who is an American Indian?" Archuleta makes a similar point – "One of the most provocative issues facing American Indians today concerns the competing definitions of Indian identity" – and notes the questions that often stem from this problem, including those dealing with the "characteristics" that define "Indianness," whether Indigenous identity stems from genetic or cultural affiliation, and whether or not this identity is open to change (2005, p. 1). As Weaver notes, "there is little agreement on precisely what constitutes an indigenous identity, how to measure it, and who truly has it" (2001, p. 240). These are by no means new problems; indeed, what makes them so noteworthy is their long-term historical persistence. In his annual report for 1892, Commissioner of Indian Affairs Thomas Jefferson Morgan addressed the question "What is an Indian?" by remarking, "One would have supposed that this question would have been considered a hundred years ago and had been adjudicated long before this. Singularly enough, however, it has remained in abeyance, and the government has gone on legislating and administering law without carefully discriminating as to those over whom it has a right to exercise such control" (quoted in Hagan, 1985, p. 309). In 1984, the Branch of Federal Acknowledgement planned to "spend millions to try to determine which of nearly a hundred tribes applying for federal recognition should merit it" (Hagan, 1985, p. 309). What emerges from this is that definitions are about not only meaning, but also control, and the power to define the conditions of being of others. In addition, these observations underline how a volume such as this can be both historical and timely (see Fonseca, 2012; Harris, 2011; Olafson, 2011).

Given the battles that have resurfaced over identification, the question of "who is an Indian?" remains prominent and merits severe scrutiny, both for its prominence and for its continual recurrance as a central question that governs Indigenous peoples and their identities. Here are some ways in which questions about definition can and have been posed:

"Who *is* an Indian?" This is a question about "being" and what it means to be Indigenous.

"Who is *an Indian*?" With this altered emphasis, the question instead assumes that there can be a category whose contours and content are knowable and stable, even as it assigns a non-Indigenous term to the identity and thereby hints at a fundamental discontinuity – that is, an imposition by outsiders, an unspoken concession that something is new and therefore is not stable.

"*Who* is an Indian?" With this emphasis, the question can lead to quantitative and statistical answers, like a head count. On the other hand, this last question could also reveal an uncertainty; perhaps nobody is an Indian.

In just these senses alone, these questions about "who is an Indian" imply power, history, taxonomy, ontology, positionality, and science. Yet few people ask whether or not this is a good question, or consider critically what kinds of answers it tends to produce and whether it is a question that *even deserves to be asked*. We seek to problematize this question by taking the routes of race and place, the two primary means used in constructing, circumscribing, and often defending Indigenous identities in the Americas.

With respect to the question of science, as a non-Indigenous anthropologist who has written and taught about Indigenous peoples over the past decade, I cannot help but remember the sharp truth contained in these words of Vine Deloria Jr:

> The massive volume of useless knowledge produced by anthropologists attempting to capture real Indians in a network of theories has contributed substantially to the invisibility of Indian people today. After all, who can conceive of a food-gathering, berry-picking, semi-nomadic, fire-worshiping, high-plains-and-mountain-dwelling, horse-riding, canoe-toting, bead-using, pottery-making, ribbon-coveting, wickiup-sheltered people who began *flourishing* when Alfred Frump mentioned them in 1803 in his great work on Indians entitled *Our Feathered Friends* as real? Not even Indians can relate themselves to this type of creature who, to anthropologists, is the "real" Indian. Indian people begin to feel that they are merely shadows of a mythical super-Indian. Many anthros spare no expense to reinforce this sense of inadequacy in order to further support their influence over Indian people. (Deloria, 1969, pp. 81–2)

Indeed, the question of "who is an Indian" very often resolves into "who is a *real* Indian," thereby introducing various categories of unauthorized indigeneity, or non-recognizable "Indians," which also implies that the nearly divine intercession of some higher authority must be needed to put the debate to rest. This question is one that can often imply a concern for purity and contamination, a desire for control, and the goal of keeping Indigenous peoples in place (or of removing them from their place, and thus removing their indigeneity). It is a seductive approach, in a society that over-values science and technology, for its veneer of "objectivity," though in fact the idea of a "real Indian," an arbitrary construct of powerful interests, could not be any less objective.

When studying this question of "who is an Indian" further, we need to inquire into who is asking and why, and why some answers have been institutionalized and others marginalized. Simply asking the question renders Indigenous identity open to question, and often the questioner is removed from scrutiny, which is one of the problems we sought to address in this volume by turning the "gaze" back on the questioner. The question implies a problem of what constitutes being Indigenous, which can also imply that some have a problem with there being anyone who is Indigenous. Historically, it has been a question typically asked by government administrators seeking to reduce the Indigenous land base by diminishing the number of rightful occupants. However, the question is now asked more often by North American reservation-based Indigenous communities themselves, apprehensive of the increased number of individuals claiming an Indigenous identity, which is another issue we address in this volume. Finally, the question is also asked by scholars critical of "ethnic essentialisms," some of whom see the concept of Indigenous as evocative of "primitive," an outmoded concept that works to maintain social inequalities (see Kuper, 1988, 2003).

Though there is wide agreement that the question posed in the title of this volume is a persistent and prominent one, there is far less agreement as to why that is the case and what the appropriate unit of analysis should be. Regarding this second question, in the view of one of our contributors,

> the question of who is an Indian ... is much larger than that of personal or even group identity – it goes directly to the heart of the colonization process and to the genocidal policies of settler governments across the Americas toward indigenous peoples. The question Who is an Indian? in North America begins with the colonial project of land theft and regulation of Native identity. (Lawrence, 2004, p. 16)

Similarly, Field emphasizes the European conquest of the Americas as the origination of the identity position European invaders called "Indian," thus creating a relational process framed by colonialism, history, and power (1994, p. 231) – while again taking the Americas as the geographic frame of reference. Also looking at the problem through the historical framework of European colonialism, Feagin points to the colonial generation of "sociopolitical structures that have long embedded the practices, ideologies, and institutions of racist subordination in numerous nations," creating a racialized global order (2001, p. 12715) that goes beyond the confines of states and continents. *Who is an Indian* thus becomes a question inscribed with racism from its very foundation. And it is a question that has been inscribed across a vast part of the world: the Americas.

An Overview of Our Approach

Having established an initial framework which characterizes the importance and impact of the problem at the focus of this volume, we collectively and individually address a wide range of questions in our contributions, such as:

- Is the "real Indian" a construct that appears across the Americas?
- Do racial characterizations of Indigenous identity, especially in terms of phenotypical appearance, prevail in places where "Indigenous" has not been defined under the law?
- Are there diverse conceptualizations of "race," both dominant and Indigenous, and how do these confront one another in practice?
- Is the concern with mapping identities a by-product of the resurgence of Indigenous identity politics?
- What issues of power and citizenship are tied up with ways of narrating Indigenous identity in terms of the body?
- What are the historical contexts and political and economic frameworks that work to secure, reproduce, or transform these modes of identifying the Indigenous?
- What options are there for new ways of being/becoming Indigenous under current regimes of certification, classification, and surveillance?
- In the absence of a strong basis in visible racial difference, how do some Indigenous persons go about articulating their own identities?
- How are collective and individual claims to Indigenous identity similar and different?

- How does the definition of Indigenous identity change when it is communicated to different specific audiences?

In addressing these questions, the chapters that follow highlight and examine the interface between the modern state and Indigenous peoples, and they reveal some notable commonalities among states in their approach to the management of identities within. The chapters also speak to how state and other institutionalized discourses of identity are interpolated by Indigenous peoples and become important arenas of struggle, specifically in the debate around the "who is a real Indian?" question. In the process, this volume offers the reader a comprehensive new vocabulary for the study of comparative Indigenous racialization.

Following a geographic line from northern Canada through to South America via Central America and the Caribbean, this volume begins with "Inuitness and Territoriality in Canada" by Donna Patrick, which explores "the question of categorizing indigeneity in Canada by examining the linguistic, political, and judicial processes associated with the notions of territory, ancestry, and belonging that shape indigeneity today," with a focus on the Inuit, situated within a broader analysis of the construction of Indigenous identity in Canada. Her aim is to show "how state categorizations of 'who counts' as Inuit have been resisted by Inuit individuals and collectivities, including the institutions stemming from land-claim agreements and assertions of autonomy." The second chapter, "Federally Unrecognized Indigenous Communities in Canadian Contexts" by Bonita Lawrence, focuses on the Algonquins of Eastern Ontario and the Mi'kmaqs of Newfoundland. Lawrence critically examines the ideological bases and practices whereby the state produces "federally unrecognized" Indigenous communities who are recognized simply as "Canadian citizens." She takes us into an analysis of how the treaty-making process refused to honour some historic obligations to particular Indigenous nations and disregarded their traditional boundaries. As a result, in order to regain Native title to their lands, these nations have to go through a process of gaining recognition, which imposes on them particular definitional criteria, including the stipulation that they have 25 per cent blood quantum. The federal recognition of one Indigenous community in Newfoundland is used as the benchmark to measure other claimants, with, Lawrence argues, the aim of disqualifying them in advance. As she states, "to successfully maintain a system of identity legislation, with its grammar of racial difference, the presence of *some* 'authentic Indians' is the tool through which other Native people can be dismissed as 'inauthentic.'"

The next two chapters deal with case studies pertaining to the United States. In "The Canary in the Coal Mine: What Sociology Can Learn from Ethnic Identity Debates among American Indians" by Eva Marie Garroutte and C. Matthew Snipp, we are confronted with extremely intriguing cases of recognition, authenticity, sovereignty, and self-identification. In discussing the case of the federal recognition of the Mashantucket Pequot Tribe of Massachusetts as a group, examining how they articulate their own identity, and then focusing on the struggles for control over the skeletal remains of Kennewick Man, the authors delineate what may be the start of a generalized sensitivity to the fluidity of ethnic identification in the U.S. The issue at the core of their chapter is the struggle between how Indigenous persons and groups seek to define their own identities in the face of those who would deny their Indigenous identity, and what the bases for such denials tend to be. Theirs is a far-reaching chapter that ranges across issues of government regulation and surveillance; questions of inclusion and exclusion; the political consequences and social impacts of rewards and resources that are attached to Indigenous rights; the "authenticating industry" and the quantification and biologization of Indigenous identity as a measurable substance; and even the commodification and industrialization of Indigenous identity.

While Garroutte and Snipp take steady aim at the biologizing of Indigenous identity, preferring that it be culturalized instead, Julia Coates takes a different line in her chapter, "'This Sovereignty Thing': Nationality, Blood, and the Cherokee Resurgence." This is the one chapter in the volume that especially focuses on sovereignty, nationality, and citizenship, with reference to the ongoing strife around the perceived exclusion of the Black Freedmen from the Cherokee Nation of Oklahoma, where Coates served as a representative of the Cherokee Nation Tribal Council. In contrast with approaches focusing on culture and race, Coates stresses the legal definitions of Cherokee nationality, which are both the product and outcome of the exercise of sovereignty.

The second half of the book shifts away from North America, beginning with chapters that take us to Central America and the Caribbean, then moving on to two South American case studies. Karen Stocker's "Locating Identity: The Role of Place in Costa Rican Chorotega Identity" shows the interplay of competing definitions of an Indigenous Chorotega identity in Costa Rica produced by the state, historical documents, scholars, the tourist industry, and residents of the newly created Chorotega reservation in Guanacaste, thus providing a comparison with the Pequot case in the chapter by Garroutte and Snipp. Interestingly, while place of residence is paramount, an assortment of customs designated as "authentic," plus factors of heredity and "looking Indian," also matter in how the state assigns Indigenous identity. Here we see again a continuum of themes and concepts that stretch across the Americas. Stocker's chapter has elements in common with Lawrence's and my own, especially with reference to the state's creation of special zones of indigeneity in order to minimize and delimit recognition of the Indigenous while imposing or reinforcing a repertoire of strict criteria for recognition that includes race.

In my chapter, "Carib Identity, Racial Politics, and the Problem of Indigenous Recognition in Trinidad and Tobago," I follow three lines of argument in explaining how recognition of an Indigenous presence in Trinidad has been made into a "problem." First, I argue that the political economy of the British colony dictated and cemented racializations of identity. Second, the process of ascribing Indigenous identities to individuals was governed by the economic rights attached to residents of Catholic missions, rights which were cut off from any miscegenated offspring. There were thus political and economic interests vested in the non-recognition of Caribs, and race provided the most convenient justification – a justification that took the form of a narrative of extinction. Third, over a century later, while racial notions of identity persist, current Carib self-identifications stress indigeneity as a cultural heritage, an attachment to place, a body of practices, and a recognition of ancestral ties that often circumvent explicitly racial schemes of self-definition. In particular, I focus on how indigeneity was constructed as extinct in three historical phases: extinction by miscegenation, extinction by localization, and then extinction by recognition itself.

The final two chapters bring us to South America, specifically Peru and Brazil. In "Encountering Indigeneity: The International Funding of Indigeneity in Peru" by José Antonio Lucero, we are provided with an understanding of how international non-governmental organizations and Indigenous actors negotiate the meanings of indigeneity. Lucero focuses on Oxfam America, as it has been among "the earliest funders of indigenous activism." His chapter examines two different moments in the interactive process of legitimation between organizations such as Oxfam America and Indigenous political organizations in Peru, "as actors on both sides of the development encounter shape discourses over the meanings of development and indigeneity across local and global scales." Lucero also takes our discussions to another level by introducing the question of the geopolitics of recognition and, thus, the internationalization of criteria for defining the Indigenous. Jonathan Warren's chapter, "The Colour of Race: Indians and Progress in a Centre-Left Brazil," critically examines the "de facto anti-Indian development initiatives" of the progressive government of Luis "Lula" Ignacio da Silva, finding that such development projects are, paradoxically, "driven by a government that has been the most sensitive to the race question in the history of Brazil." In particular, Warren reveals that in Brazil, the racial question, and, thus, conceptions of antiracism – like much of critical race studies, he adds – simply remove the Indian from analysis, as if Indian subjectivities were entirely irrelevant. A key example of how this has occurred in critical race studies comes from Howard Winant's analysis of racism in Brazil, which singles out Africans. This is odd, as Warren finds, given that as many as a third of Brazilians have some Indian ancestry. Warren's chapter is critical to this volume's contention that "race" is a problem that needs to be studied in connection with indigeneity, not apart from it. His argument is essential, not only for the development of critical race studies, but also for political practice: the antiracist movement cannot be just a Black movement.

In general, we would have liked to include more chapters and present more national cases, even at the risk of producing a volume – or even a set of volumes – so large that most publishers would have turned us away. Having said this, we must recognize that taking the nation-state as the unit of analysis can also be problematic, and in some cases counterproductive, especially when dealing with forces that do not care much for arbitrarily drawn national boundaries. Nonetheless, we did try to obtain contributions on diverse locales, such as Nicaragua, Colombia, and Bolivia, but, for one reason or another, never managed to succeed. We also regret the absence of a chapter on Mexico, which would have provided us with some alternative points for consideration. On the other hand, as it stands now, the volume maintains a geographic balance: half of the chapters deal with North America, and the other half deal with Latin America and the Caribbean.

I would, however, like to briefly address some of the features of the Mexican case that could have been valuable to our discussion (with the caveat that I write from the perspective and with the limitations of someone who is not a Mexicanist). By 1940, anthropologist Robert Redfield reported that in Mexico, "Indian" was no longer a racial category rooted in perceived biological properties, noting also that there was no single definitive answer, either at the official or the popular level, on who was an "Indian": "Nor is it possible to count the Indians as a socially recognized group, as we do with Negroes in the United States, because in most parts of Mexico Indians are not so defined; in such parts everybody is a Mexican and nobody is very definitely an Indian" (Redfield, 1940, p. 132). Race as a category was not employed in the censuses of 1895, 1900, or 1910; it was reintroduced for the 1921 census, then abandoned again in 1930. The reason for this, Redfield suggested, was that "racial differences are no longer of first significance in Mexico." Unlike in colonial times, when there were as many as thirty-two different racial classifications, now it seemed as if there was "one submerged class composed of Indians and mixed-bloods together" (Redfield, 1940, pp. 132, 133). "Indian" had become increasingly "vague," he observed, and while officials continued to speak of the problems of the "Indian," it was as if the word was code for proletarian (Redfield, 1940, p. 133).

In order to identify "Indians" with some degree of specificity, Redfield noted variations across Mexico. His tendency was to focus on all or some of the following: place, language, dress, and material customs (1940, p. 133), but he also noted that there were intangible differences, such as differences in religious belief (1940, p. 136). The new constitutions promulgated since Mexico achieved independence from Spain continually wrestled with concepts of nationality and citizenship, with a marked trend towards erasing race as a category of differentiation (for more, see Lomnitz, 2001). In the 1995 census, "the government counted all persons [aged] five and over speaking an indigenous language as 'indigenous'" (Stephen, 2002, p. 87), manifesting some continuity in the non-racial way of categorizing Indigenous Mexicans. In Article 2 of Mexico's current Constitution, the nation is defined as being "pluricultural," with Indigenous peoples constituting its original foundation; race continues to be apparently absent as a factor in identification of the Indigenous, with a focus instead on language, traditions, beliefs, and so forth.[1]

Yet as Lynn Stephen explained, "concepts of ethnicity used by the Mexican government continue to rely on trait recognition and the certification by experts of indigenous legitimacy" (2002, p. 87) – so that while "race" has exited as a factor, identification of a section of the population continues, grounded in the assumption that these people are different based on certain manifest traits, and with identification contingent on locating these traits within given places. The practice of identification, and the concerns raised about rightful access to collective property, would therefore not diverge dramatically from the other examples found in this book, nor would it mean the absence of racism, even without race (for more, see De La Cadena, 2000).

Why the Americas?

Before continuing, let me pause to explain the geographic scope of the volume, especially as it contextualizes the ways that the chapters are grouped, and the order in which they are presented. The case studies presented in this volume, as outlined below, involve Canada, the United States, Costa Rica, Trinidad and Tobago, Peru, and Brazil. My decision to chart an Americas-wide approach to the phenomenon of race, place, and Indigenous identity was influenced by several important historical and contextual factors, to which the contributing authors also refer at different points in their chapters.

As we know, the first encounters with modern European expansionism occurred in the Caribbean, beginning in 1492, and then spread outwards. The institutionalization of the idea of an Indigenous other – an "Indian" – was not the sole preserve of any one colony, under any one European colonial regime, but rather occurred in all of them. The Americas as a whole witnessed large-scale land expropriations, with the descendants of pre-colonial populations suffering as targets. Across the Americas we find geographic and historical overlaps with respect to the colonial segmentation of labour forces, producing common concerns among the colonizers about how to contain and control Indigenous resistance, and how best to usurp resources in Indigenous hands, by way of producing legal and ideological justifications premised on the construction of an "Indian" alterity that was deemed inferior to Europe.

Early attempts at legalizing definitions of "Indian," "indio," and so on, also occurred across the Americas as a whole, the hemisphere which has the longest colonial history, and where we find the oldest of the modern nation-states to be created outside of Europe. With the earliest attempts at definition, we also find the earliest attempts by states to "manage" their Indigenous populations, and to allocate or deny rights and resources to people based on the facts of their birth. The desire of states to control and manage Indigenous populations necessitated the creation of legible populations, which required the means to categorize them, which in turn involved attempts at definition, whether de jure or de facto, in order to establish boundaries that facilitated governance and, in most cases, the expropriation of resources. A "project of legibility," as Scott explained (1999, p. 80), is immanent in *any* statecraft that "aims at manipulating society." As he explains, legibility requires simplification, which involves the creation of "*interested*, utilitarian facts," facts that are both *documentary* and *static*, and these facts must also be *aggregate* and *standardized*.

Many of the nation-states born out of this colonial framework, and the Indigenous peoples dominated by them, in fact possess overlapping histories with those that were dominated by one or another European power – for example, Indigenous communities in parts of North America, the Caribbean, and the Guianas had experience at different times with Spanish, French, and British colonialists, and in some cases with Dutch colonial regimes as well – so that one cannot demarcate sharp lines of difference between colonial experiences, and it would be analytically questionable to try to do so.

Since the advent of European colonization, key political-economic factors have drawn the Americas closer together in terms of shared historical and cultural experience. One such experience was the widespread institutionalization of Indian slavery, and then especially African slavery, with large African populations on both continents of the Americas. As we shall see, this too is relevant for how Indigenous identity is constructed by colonizers and their successors, in defining and managing who is (not) Indigenous.

Another critical factor that lends support to a more unifying frame of analysis is the fact that the Americas have been subject to U.S. domination, especially in political and economic terms, but also in terms of media, ideological, and educational influences. This dominance, however, has also provided Indigenous people with vehicles and tools for orchestrating Indigenous action and articulating Indigenous perspectives on an increasingly continental and then hemispheric scale. That these factors are important in the discussion of indigeneity was made very evident in the hemisphere-wide actions, protests, and organization around states' commemoration of 1992, the 500th anniversary of Columbus's entry into the Americas. The creation of the "Hollywood Indian" brought into being a pervasive mainstream visual repertoire of what a "real Indian" should look like; these images spread beyond the U.S., especially into the Caribbean, institutionalized in textbooks and in the image of the Carnival Indian.

In the contemporary context, the task of building an understanding of indigeneity on the scale of the Americas is both inspired and mandated by the development, over the past half century, of a transnational

Indigenous political resurgence that has also addressed issues of identification. A number of overlapping and interconnecting organizations have operated, or are operating, to create ties among Indigenous groups, both within large regions comprising multiple nation-states (such as the Andes, the Amazon, the Caribbean and North America) and across some or all of these regions. The hemisphere is home to the largest number of Indigenous-owned and/or controlled media to be found anywhere; likewise, it is home to the largest presence of Indigenous studies programs and Indigenous scholars and activists who correspond and collaborate across national boundaries. This is not to mention shared concerns that defy the specificities of locality, however construed. For example, the problem of "recognition," and the political effects of official recognition of one's indigeneity by the state, shows remarkable congruence across the Americas, in a way that suggests it is a phenomenon peculiar to the modern, secular nation-state and its attempts to "manage diversity."

Multiculturalist policies can also be found across the Americas, from Canada to the Caribbean and the Andes. These in turn arise from political processes these regions have in common. To begin with, most of the modern nation-states of the Americas first began by adopting European and U.S.-inspired liberal constitutions, which established common frameworks (however much denied in practice) spelling out ideas of nationality and citizenship, and which tended to work against Indigenous difference, casting it as a "problem" to be solved through better forms of material incorporation and cultural assimilation. The move from the elimination of difference to the management of difference is also a common pattern that can be observed across the states of the Americas, even if they do not all follow the same policies. With increased international pressure to recognize the rights of minorities, and growing Indigenous resistance, states are compelled to try to balance issues of citizenship with those of collective autonomy, even if merely token acknowledgement is made to ideals of self-determination. Nonetheless, the question of Indigenous self-determination has been directly addressed by diverse states, including Canada, the U.S., Mexico, Dominica, Nicaragua, Costa Rica, Guyana, Suriname, Colombia, Venezuela, Bolivia, and Brazil. With greater recognition of Indigenous rights, however, comes greater concern with identifying who gets to be classed as Indigenous. The introduction of multiculturalist policies and of similar modes of marketing Indigenous difference as a tourist attraction have, together, produced modes of state identification of Indigenous identity which tend to be particularly essentialist and focused on authenticity, continuity, and visible forms of difference. This is the double-edged nature of "recognition" that we find in many case studies in this volume: recognition seems to admit Indigenous difference into national discourse, yet simultaneously also limits and contains it, so that the act of dispossession is never far from the scene.

While ethnographers will tend to emphasize heterogeneity and local social and historical differences between different locations in the Americas, much has already been published, and even more has been assumed, about these differences. In some cases this may have the deleterious effect of justifying the continued (over)production of fragmentary stories and disparate bits of evidence. We instead opted to look at the larger, overarching patterns and historical trends that have produced common questions and concerns, in keeping with the perspectives of transnational Indigenous actors in the Americas, who regularly admit to seeing so much of themselves – their customs, beliefs, and histories of dispossession – in the accounts shared by other Indigenous actors that they encounter in continental assemblies, regional gatherings, and international fora. This, we believe, is what has been especially missing in the current literature dealing with race, and place, in the definition of the Indigenous.

Recognizing a common historical and geographic framework is not the same thing as erasing differences; as has been widely recognized in anthropology, global processes produce varied localized effects, with different class interests in ascendance in different cases, and with diverse actors engaged in different struggles that produce diverse local outcomes. Indeed, had we believed that local differences did not matter, we would not have organized the volume by the different nationalities of the case studies. The intention, as evidenced throughout, is not to deny the existence of differences, which we collectively acknowledge, but rather to avoid so overstating them that we cannot look for a common frame of reference that places these diverse experiences within one dialogical encounter that respects commonalities, where they exist. With an analytical frame rooted in the shared space of colonialism, Indigenous and African enslavement, state-building, U.S. domination, and transnational politics, we suggest that one can arrive at a better understanding of the implications of power in Indigenous self-definition, of the pathways of Indigenous self-determination, and of the common production of this question that is heard across the Americas: "Who is an Indian?"

Why Place Matters

"The question of who counts as Aboriginal [in Canada]," explains Donna Patrick (in this volume), "has long been linked to the question of who owns traditional Aboriginal lands." Patrick's chapter, "Inuitness and Territoriality in Canada," explores the question of categorizing indigeneity in Canada, with "Inuitness" having followed a different trajectory from that of First Nations identities in the rest of Canada, in that the construction of Inuit identity has been guided not just by state policy but by Inuit attachments to both land and language. In Patrick's chapter we learn that "the notion of 'territoriality' operates together with the notion of ancestry" in shaping the identities of Inuit living in urban centres of the Canadian South, as much as those living in the Arctic. With the demise of the "disk system" (more in her chapter about how the Inuit were numbered) and the rise of "Project Surname," the question of who "counted" had to take into account "not only Inuit ancestry itself but also attachments to traditional territories and the linguistic, cultural, and other practices that are integral to 'traditional' Inuitness," argues Patrick, meaning that ideas of race were not ostensibly the dominant mode of articulating Inuit identity, either by the Inuit or by the state. However, this is qualified further, as we shall see below.

What has been the dominant experience for Indigenous populations throughout the Americas has been a confinement to place, at least partly if not wholly informed by ideas of raçe. Designating a special place as the locus of persons with an Indigenous identity can be a way for an assimilationist state – especially one that has historically rejected the Indigenous presence, such as Costa Rica – to create the illusion that indigeneity is minimal and marginal. As Karen Stocker explains in her chapter in this volume, "Locating Identity: The Role of Place in Costa Rican Chorotega Identity," in Chorotega some residents of what later became the reservation opposed reservation status, out of a "tremendous resentment at being the only community in the region officially designated as Indigenous when the whole area had Indigenous roots, and [an] aversion to the stigma attached to Indigenous identity in a country that often projected an image of whiteness and European heritage." The Costa Rican government's imposition of an Indigenous identity on the residents of Chorotega was a convenient way of *removing* that label from everyone who resided outside of that particular place – using the assigned indigeneity of some to reassure others of their Europeanness.

Karen Stocker's chapter, based on ethnographic research carried out between 1993 and 2007, addresses how a wide range of voices – residents of the Chorotega reservation, those who live just outside the reservation, scholars, those contributing to legal discourse and historical discourse, those who have resided or studied in other Costa Rican reservations, and, more recently, the tourism industry – have "defined Indigenous identity in contradictory ways, and in manners that have had varying consequences for those labeled as Chorotega in Costa Rica." She addresses the history and impact of these multiple competing definitions. Stocker traces the ways in which "one set of customs has gone from Indigenous to non-Indigenous, national custom, and back again, as a result of the shifting of discourses around it." Stocker spotlights what she finds to be "a common thread through all of these definitions and interpretations of indigeneity," and that is "the role of place, and how the same concept that mired inhabitants of the Chorotega reservation in discrimination now serves to authenticate its practices."

My own chapter in this volume ("Carib Identity, Racial Politics, and the Problem of Indigenous Recognition in Trinidad and Tobago"), based on four years of ethnographic research and on ethnohistoric research dating to early colonial times, shares some features with the chapters by Bonita Lawrence and Karen Stocker. On the one hand, the state's recognition of only one single organized Indigenous community, in just one of Trinidad's sixteen former mission towns – the Santa Rosa Carib Community in Arima, on the island of Trinidad – makes it seem, however implausibly, that indigeneity was somehow contained and delimited (though in reality it merely reflects the state's bias about how indigeneity *ought* to be controlled and secluded). On the other hand, in articulating their own Indigenous identity, members of the Carib community point to a multitude of factors, beyond but including race, to include a history of residence in Arima.

However, this does not eclipse the fact that places designated as Indigenous can often be racially constructed as confined spaces for only particular *kinds* of people. In Stocker's chapter, it seems that the stigma attached to the place that is Chorotega is the stigma of race. It is interesting to note as well as the close correspondence between a Latin American case (Costa Rica) and an Anglophone Caribbean one (Trinidad) in terms of the presence of race in the articulation of what is publicly identified as Indigenous. In the Costa Rican case, the authorities established a list of criteria that included "physical features ('looking Indian')," and as Stocker adds, "the language of heredity and phenotype is still used locally." In the Trinidadian case, European writers in the nineteenth century, as well as historians belonging to the local elite, had long cast the colony's Indigenous peoples in racial terms, relying not just on notions of phenotypical "purity" but also on evolutionary ideas.

It is interesting to note Trinidad and Tobago as a case that blurs boundaries among different zones of the Americas, containing within its history experiences that resonate with numerous Indigenous situations across the hemisphere. In Stocker's case dealing with Chorotega, Costa Rica, and my own dealing with Arima, Trinidad, we have two former Spanish colonies (with Trinidad also being a former British colony), both exposed to dominant U.S. media images of "authentic Indians." In both Chorotega and Arima, we see similar processes: the designation of a special place of "Indianness" by the state; the adoption of stereotypical American Indian motifs; and a festival and procession in honour of the Virgin, marked by its Indigenous participation. By recognizing only the Santa Rosa Carib community in Arima, the Trinidadian state, like its Costa Rican counterpart, is practicing a form of extinction by recognition: the literal marginalization of Indigenous people to a special zone, resulting in their minimization, and thus the "cleansing" of the rest of the population of any taint of indigeneity (or any promise of further recognition). Yet this process of minimization is also to be found in eastern Canada, as detailed by Bonita Lawrence. In the Central American, Caribbean, and Newfoundland cases we see, despite all the evidence that would render such assertions counterintuitive at best, the emphasis on the notion of total erasure of the Indigenous, reinforced by historical texts and popular discourse that either dismiss the Indigenous presence or so stigmatize it that individuals feel pressured to deny their own indigeneity. In Costa Rica the Indigenous was for very long masked as "campesino" (peasant), while in Trinidad the Carib was long known as a "Panyol" ("Spanish" peasant), and in Newfoundland Mi'kmaqs were labelled "Jackatars." Trinidad and Tobago, like Peru, admits no Indigenous category in its national census. Antiracism in Trinidad tends to exclude Indigenous peoples; there is non-recognition of the fact that most Trinidadians probably have some Amerindian ancestry, and that many thousands have a lot – a situation similar to the one in Brazil, which Jonathan Warren talks about in this volume.

Drawing from broader literature, with respect to the idea of places of race, we can note in the Peruvian example that "modern Peruvian race-making paralleled a political process of place-making as it assigned races to spaces and evaluated these within evolutionary temporal schemes" (De La Cadena, 2000, p. 21). As De La Cadena adds, this is a "racialization of geography," where people were often ranked according to their surroundings (2000, p. 21). In the Canadian case, Lawrence has argued that, in many respects, the state's "regulation of Indigenous identities through legislation is part of a discourse through which crucial aspects of European race ideology were imparted as a world-view to Native people who were no longer in a position to resist such categorization" (2004, p. 38). The removal of Indigenous inhabitants from their lands was tellingly accompanied by policies of assimilation and cultural erasure, to remove them from their histories and identities.

Who *Was* an Indian? From before There Were "Indians" to "Indian" as a Race

Where prior to the European invasion, and into the early colonial period, tribal identities were "fluid, dynamic, situational, and embedded in a matrix of social, cultural, economic, political, and linguistic practices and orientations" (Strong & Van Winkle, 1996, pp. 556–7), the racialized and homogenizing identity that became "Indian" achieved the opposite. As Yellow Bird argues, terms such as "American Indian" and "Native American" are used "to control and subjugate the identities of Indigenous Peoples and undermine their right to use tribal affiliation as a preeminent national identity" (1999, p. 6; see also TallBear, 2003, p. 82).

Racism played a central role in Europe's colonization of what we now call the Americas, as either a superficially biological or a cultural taxonomy that ordered diverse colonial subjects. "Race science," as it emerged into prominence in the mid-1800s and into the early 1900s, "was entangled with and constitutive of the practices of empire … when both the discipline of race science and the political project of imperialism reached their zeniths" (Abu El-Haj, 2007, p. 286). Prior to this time, "race" was often used to denote descendants of a common ancestor (in English), or a stock of animals (in Spanish), which meant that when it was used with reference to humans it tended to emphasize kinship, rather than skin colour or other arbitrarily chosen physical characteristics. On the other hand, it is not a long distance that separates kinship from biological ideas of race, especially as "race was reified as a biologically based descent group, or a permutation of modern peoplehood in the nineteenth century … Philology laid the basis of racial science, stressing kinship and genealogy, and downplaying theology and Christian universalism ... What had been explained by climate or culture came to be explained by innate differences" (Lie, 2004, p. 90). Nor is it a long distance that separates this idea of innate difference from the social constructions of races which developed greatly with the advance of European colonialism: "Colonizers developed racist rationalizations for their destruction of indigenous societies, enslavement of Africans, and other colonial pursuits. This congealed in an *ideological racism* that legitimated oppression and exploitation, especially as the racist ideas became integrated into the general ideology dominant in Western societies" (Feagin, 2001, p. 12711). The social definition of race created categories that defined a person's place in society according to his/her origins, which were inferred by those biological characteristics that were most convenient, a situation some summarize as *racism creating race* (Schnapper, 2001, p. 12702).

As a technology of social control and a means of disciplining a labour force, racism ordered persons by attaching particular forms of labour and particular rights and resources to each "race" (Coates, 2008, p. 208), thereby giving what is in fact a reified and abstract ideational construct a physical and material reality. Racism, especially the "one-drop rule" particular to the U.S. (the rule that only "one drop" of African blood was sufficient for a person to be categorized as Black), worked to diminish Indigenous nations and thus the lands which they could claim, while simultaneously expanding the number of persons who could be held captive as slaves (Churchill, 2004, p. 63). In line with Patrick's observations regarding Canada, Churchill's regarding the U.S., and my own dealing with the Caribbean, Yellow Bird makes the generalizable argument that "the idea of dividing people according to a single racial identity was the invention of Europeans, who socially constructed race to exclude and subordinate peoples who were not white and to privilege those who were" (1999, p. 3). Native peoples in North America possessed their own tribal identities, which were suppressed by European colonialists by labeling them all as if they were one racial group – "Indian": "To the colonizer this made sense because it was economical, efficient, and required little thinking" (Yellow Bird, 1999, p. 3).

As Donna Patrick (in this volume) observes, Indigenous ideas of identity in early colonial Canada "had little to do with race, biology, or ethnicity," and Indigenous peoples in fact demonstrated in practice that they were guided by a "notion of inclusivity" whose existence "has been supported by numerous accounts of Euro-American settlers and soldiers being accepted and adopted into First Nations groups." Numerous scholars would agree with Patrick. As Ward Churchill explains,

> As non-Indians began to appear in substantial numbers across the hemisphere, literally thousands of "White Indians" – mostly English and French, but Swedes, Scots, Irish, Dutch, and others as well – who, diseased with aspects of their own cultures, had either married into, been adopted by, or petitioned for naturalization as member citizens of Indigenous nations. (Churchill, 2004, p. 61)

Churchill pointed out that hundreds of European captives, rather than being executed, had been adopted into tribes and assimilated into them, adopting their ways as their own, and refusing to live once more among Europeans, so much so that that those who "have been a long time among the Indians, will take the first opportunity to run away" (Colonel Henry Bouquet quoted in Churchill, 2004, p. 62). We find similar cases across the Americas, and in my ethnohistoric research on Indigenous peoples of the Caribbean I have found almost identical accounts about the Caribs' European and African "captives." Again, Churchill found that in the U.S., as in the Caribbean, by 1830 at the latest,

> the notion of defining "Indianness" in terms of "race" had been rendered patently absurd. It has been reliably estimated that somewhere between one-third and one-half of all Native peoples still residing east of the Mississippi River were at that point genetically intermixed not only with one another, but with "Negroid and Caucasoid racial stock" as well. This is a genetic and demographic pattern that would spread rapidly westward over then next half-century. There is little if any indication, moreover, that most Indigenous societies tended to view this increasing admixture as untoward or peculiar, much less threatening, in and of itself. (Churchill, 2004, p. 63)

Michael Yellow Bird pointed out that "historically, and even in contemporary times, Indigenous Peoples in the United States and Canada have not regarded themselves as one monolithic racial society" (1999, p. 2).

Race Matters: Who Is the "Real Indian"?

In many parts of the Americas, so-called racial identity shifts have underscored the mutually reinforcing processes of Indigenous demographic and political resurgence. Today, the question of who is a "real Indian" seems to have much more force as a means of either validating or disqualifying claimants to Indigenous identity, as significant numbers of people in various parts of the Americas are self-identifying as Indigenous, as pointed out in the statistics presented at the opening of this chapter.

The question also unsettles the settlers. Lawrence argues that the "white need for certainty about the parameters of Indian 'difference'" is the root of casting Natives as racially other (2004, p. 4). Similarly, Sissons argues, "Indigenous racial impurity has been regarded as ... threatening to the natural order and a cause for colonial and post-colonial concern" (2005, p. 38). Others note that long-established norms of racialization are now under fire, and that many lives stand to be affected by both the maintenance of and resistance to these norms, in material ways that can affect the whole society (Garroutte, 2003; and Garroutte & Snipp in this volume).

Issues of membership and self-identification are increasingly caught up with experiences of Indigenous resurgence across the Americas, as states, and Indigenous communities themselves, try to encourage, cope with, or even challenge the influx of "new claimants" to Indigenous identities. While Indigenous identity was never free of bodily associations, there appears to be a revitalization, indeed an industrialization, of previous modes for fixing Indigenous identity in physical substances (blood, genes, phenotype). Indeed, both the revitalization of concerns with mapping Indigenous identities and the resurgence of Indigenous identification are seen as part of the same process of transformation, where various forms of "de-Indianization" are coming under challenge and undergoing reexamination as part of what some call the "post-traditional condition" (e.g., Warren, 2001).

Both race and place are ways of making the Indigenous visible and, paradoxically, are also ways to minimize indigeneity when they are used as objectified markers of authenticity and when certain political and economic interests wish to place limits on the kind of growth described above. Race and place provide the empirical support for the regulation of identities. This regulation has arguably reached an extreme level in the U.S. cases we studied, a level closely matched by Canada.

In the U.S., "American Indians differ from other twenty-first-century racial groups in the extent to which their racial formation is governed by law" (Garroutte, 2001, p. 224). The intent behind such regulation, and the assumptions on which it rests (which have acquired the weight of law), become apparent with reference to the "problem" of "mixture."

"Racial mixing" presents both a problem and an opportunity for the state and the economic interests it defends. While some will argue, with some justification, that "conceptions of 'race,' 'mixed race' and social status are historically, geographically and culturally specific, and hence do not travel easily" (Ifekwunigwe, 2004, p. 5), which would render generalizations across the Americas problematic, on another level these generalizations are justified. Even some of those making the case for specificity find themselves arguing that "the global processes and erotic projects of slavery, imperialism and diaspora(s) have created similar shifts in the local making, management and regulation of status and power as articulated through the everyday discourses and practices of 'race,' 'mixed race' and social hierarchies," and noting that the "three pillars" – European expansion and colonization, slavery, and the colour code for determining status – certainly have "traveled" (Ifekwunigwe, 2004, p. 5). Here I want to briefly review some of the salient points about "race mixture" and indigeneity in the Americas, from a number of cases.

In Canada, Métis, like its Latin American counterpart "Mestizo," stemmed from concepts of "miscegenation" or what in French is called "métissage" – and both Métis and Mestizo ultimately depend upon a concept of race (Fredrickson, 2005, p. 103). How "race" is put into practice, of course, varies with time and imperial regime. With the British conquest of the French in Canada this meant that the Métis, who under the French might have been absorbed into the mainstream French population, were now excluded, given that the British worked with a narrower conception of what it meant to be white or European (Fredrickson, 2005, p. 105). On the other hand, in the Maritime provinces, "there has been no tradition of 'Métisness' ... You were Indians or white – or you simply had no name for yourself" (Lawrence, 2004, p. xiv). While Patrick (this volume) argues that we do not see in Canada a dominant discourse about the biopolitics of Indigenous identities to the same extent that we do in the U.S., she admits that a "'covert' or de facto blood quantum" has been part of policies governing Aboriginal, and in particular First Nations, peoples. As Lawrence has argued elsewhere, in Canada "Indianness" can be legally assured through a variety of means, such that Aboriginals of mixed parentage neither see themselves as being "mixed-blood" nor are classed as such by the state (Lawrence, 2004, p. 12). However, Lawrence also finds that the dominant culture is permeated by an assumption that "Indianness will *continue* to die with mixed-bloodedness and urbanity" (Lawrence, 2004, p. 12). Let us not forget that assimilation policies in Canada, combining race and place with patriarchy, sought to remove Aboriginals from their lands and their status as Aboriginals. Starting in 1869, Indian status was removed from Aboriginal women who married non-Aboriginal males, forcing them to become members of their husbands' communities (Lawrence, 2004, pp. 33–4). Likewise, and we will discuss this further below, non-Aboriginal women could marry into and reside on Aboriginal reserves. The result of these processes is the creation of a large body of "urban mixed-blood Native people" who "by definition do *not* live in those few sites recognized by the federal government as Indian land" (Lawrence, 2004, p. 8).

In the U.S., Thomas Jefferson leaned closer to the French model of integration via miscegenation when he declared: "You will become one people with us. Your blood will mix with ours, and will spread with ours across this great land" (quoted in Churchill, 2004, p. 64). Jefferson's policy for dealing with American Indians was "to let our settlements and theirs meet and blend together, to intermix, and become one people. Incorporating themselves with us as citizens of the United States, this is what the natural progress of things will of course bring on" (Jefferson quoted in Biolsi, 2007, p. 407). In Biolsi's view, this notion of integration via mixture, of assimilation that is both cultural and biological, is the foundation for "imperialist nostalgia" about the "traditional Indian" – the not-uncommon belief that "real" or "authentic" Indians, "have disappeared or are 'fast disappearing,' and that 'mixed bloods' or 'assimilated Indians' – which is to say, *living* Indian people – are inauthentic Indians" (Biolsi, 2007, p. 404). If the Indian-white line was meant to disappear, the Indian-Black line could disappear even more expediently, especially since the basic operating principle in both cases is the same: that the Indian must disappear. The "one-drop rule," where it took only "one drop" of African blood for one to be classed as "Black" in the U.S., was designed to expand the number of Africans (who could be owned and enslaved, thus increasing capital), while minimizing the number of Indians if they mixed with Africans (thus increasing the amount of land that could be expropriated by whites, also an increase in capital). The process was not reversible, of course, because the intention was elimination: "a drop of 'Indian blood' has almost never been enough to make one legally Indian" (Biolsi, 2007, p. 411).

The dominance of the discourse of racial (phenotypical) purity found in the U.S., where Indigenous peoples are concerned, owes a great deal to the invention and subsequent elimination of these various racial lines. Eva Marie Garroutte and Matthew Snipp, in their chapter in this volume titled "The Canary in the Coalmine: What Sociology Can Learn from Ethnic Identity Debates among American Indians," devote considerable attention to debating the racialization of indigeneity. As just one example of the kinds of interests vested in the non-recognition of "mixed" American Indians, Garroutte and Snipp point to Donald Trump: as a competitor against the newly recognized Pequots, who had plans to open a casino, he volunteered an answer to the question "Who is an Indian?" in phenotypical terms: "They don't look like Indians to me. They don't look like Indians to Indians," further injecting his racial bias by calling them "Michael Jordan Indians." This is useful in showing how one of the most common ways of assigning Indigenous identity in the Americas is by appearance, and – in places where racial discourses prevail, such as the U.S. and Caribbean – by a specific type of appearance: phenotype (Garroutte and Snipp, this volume). In other settings, the anxiety pointed to by journalists such as Hitt (2005) is that of looking too white – the issue is not dissimilar, since it amounts to "not looking Indian enough." Hitt found an acute degree of "ethnic apprehension" among participants at a pow-wow that he visited: "outmarriage, or exogamy, has created a contemporary population that doesn't look nearly as 'Indian' as the characters of our movies and HBO westerns" (Hitt, 2005).

My understanding of the increased drive, in the U.S., to regulate and formally delineate the biological substance of Indigenous identities is that it stems from the following factors: (a) a racial paranoia driven especially by a fear or loathing of Blackness, building on nineteenth-century scientific racism; (b) the struggle to maximize individual enjoyment of limited material resources; (c) the compulsion to defend indigeneity as difference: not everybody can be Indigenous, simply because if everybody is Indigenous then nobody is Indigenous; and, (d) efforts by various governments to define Indigenous peoples out of existence, using miscegenation as a convenient means of assailing Indigenous persons who do not sufficiently conform to what might otherwise be judged mere childhood fantasies of what the "real Indian" is supposed to look like.

In the case of Trinidad, we will see what Biolsi called the "imperialist nostalgia" in histories written by Europeans and local European elites expressed very clearly, in the view that miscegenation results in extinction. This leads to one basic formulation of what it means to be Indigenous/Carib in Trinidad: *the only real Carib is a pure Carib; the only pure Carib is a dead Carib*. On the surface, one might think that the result of "mixture" would be the *expansion* and *growth* of indigeneity – but the concept of race interrupts and prevents that, by asserting fixed, biological boundaries and notions of purity as a defining feature of indigeneity.

In the case of Peru, race has been redefined away from connoting innate biological differences, and towards accentuating cultural differences. Since the early part of the twentieth century, "Peruvians ... have tended to define race with allusions to culture, the soul, and the spirit, which were thought to be more important than skin color" (De La Cadena, 2000, p. 2). This might be an example of "racism without race" (De La Cadena, 2000, p. 4), a "new racism" that ranks peoples as superior and inferior based on intellectual and moral qualities, thereby accomplishing the same basic task as the "old" racism (or current racism as found in North America and the Caribbean). In Peru we find that the current, dominant usage of the term Mestizo involves "a Spanish and Indian racialized cultural mixture, evolving from 'primitive' Indianness into a more 'civilized' stage, and eventually incompatible with indigenous ways" (De La Cadena, 2000, p. 5). In this context, Mestizo might identify "literate and economically successful people who share indigenous cultural practices yet do not perceive themselves as miserable, a condition that they consider 'Indian'" (De La Cadena, 2000, p. 6). Nonetheless, as De La Cadena argues, this connection between race and culture in Peru has a longer history, "one that can be traced back to colonial beliefs about 'purity of blood' (referring to Christian descent)" (2000, pp. 6–7). She stresses that there is "implicit agreement that 'whiteness' – in its local, not necessarily phenotypical, version – is ultimately superior and Indianness represents absolute inferiority" (De La Cadena, 2000, p. 10). Thus, while the overt biological connotations of race were diminished, it was not the concept itself that was rejected (De La Cadena, 2000, p. 19).

If cases in Canada and Peru can show us how race is modified and qualified by place and culture, the Brazilian case shows how race can be entirely divorced from indigeneity, but in ways that demand that we re-draw the connections. Jonathan Warren's chapter on Brazil, titled "The Colour of Race: Indians and Progress in a Centre-Left Brazil," explains that Brazilian Indians are removed from the racial question in

Brazil: "race is reduced to a question of blackness." Indeed, throughout Latin America, Warren sees that Indigenous peoples are "not considered germane to race matters," and quoting Peter Wade he adds: "the virtually unquestioned assumptions [prevail] that the study of blacks is one of racism and race relations, while the study of Indians is that of ethnicity and ethnic groups." Warren also shows that phenotype is present in Brazilian estimations of "authentic" and "real" Indigenous identities, with those who have African and European features routinely dismissed as "racial charlatans," in ways that echo experiences both in the U.S. and the Caribbean.

Warren's chapter is critical to this volume's contention that race is a problem that needs to be studied in connection with indigeneity, not apart from it. His argument is critical not only for developing critical race studies, but also for political practice: the antiracist movement cannot be just a Black movement. It is not uncommon, otherwise, to still find volumes and encyclopedias of slavery being produced which remove the history of European enslavement of Indigenous peoples in the Americas, and reduce the phenomenon, largely or entirely, to one of African slavery alone, which Warren also notes in the case of Brazil. In addition, Warren's case reminds us of the history that makes a hemispheric framework necessary, by noting that the category "Indian" emerged from the colonial encounters within which the discourse of race emerged, and remains marked as a category that retains elements of this prior history.

The debates that Warren encounters seem to suggest that "race studies" is about Africans, and "ethnic studies" is about Indigenous peoples. Yet some scholars would disagree with either paradigm as being appropriate. Ward Churchill (1985) argued against what he saw as the misunderstanding of the contemporary situation of Indigenous peoples in the U.S. as that of ethnic or racial minorities – there are "at least 400 distinctly identifiable ethnicities comprising what is lumped into the catchall category of 'Native American'" (p. 30). Instead of ethnic groups, or race, Churchill prefers national identity: "indigenous peoples of the North have constituted, and continue to constitute nations in the strictest definition of this term" (Churchill, 1985, p. 30). One of the primary components of his argument is centred on treaty-making: under U.S. law, only nations can enter into treaties – none of the ethnic groups in the U.S. have any kind of treaty with the federal government, nor do they claim sovereignty. The unit of analysis here is thus the *colonized nation*.

The "Real Indian" as a Biological Body: DNA and Blood

"Do genetics make you Indian or does culture? Or can either one?" asked *The New York Times'* Jack Hitt (2005; similarly, see Harmon, 2006). The reason this question is even being raised is due both to the new project of recouping some form of Indigenous identity through scientific analysis, and to older determinations that stressed race as a putatively verifiable and objective identity. Rather than departing from racialization, the industry around "ancestral markers" involves "classifying DNA 'ethnoracially.'" Where phenotype dominated before as a marker of race, now there is "reading race in the DNA" (Abu El-Haj, 2007, pp. 287, 288). Race, science, and government oversight are never far from the picture of how indigeneity is (re)constructed in the U.S.

The dilemmas of the new biologization and racialization of U.S. indigeneity appear at the crossroads of different modes and logics of (dis) proving identities. These include (1) modes of proving Indigenous identity that respond to state surveillance and audit-like approaches to identity; (2) the instrumental uses of Indigenous identity in the quest for rights, rewards, and resources; (3) the incursions of capitalist commodification of identity, by industrializing it in the form of DNA-testing services; and (4) the role of "scientific expertise" and the formulation of gene-based identities whch are then made commercially applicable – "the commodification of race" (Abu El-Haj, 2007, p. 293). On the other hand, there are (1) pressures to reduce the numbers of claimants to membership in specific Indigenous nations, in order to preserve those nations' ability to survive on a limited resource base; (2) the impetus to eliminate an entire people by restricting the numbers of those who can "legitimately" claim an Indigenous identity – that is, "statistical extermination" (Weaver, 2001, p. 248); and (3) the pressures to expand beyond current forms of recognition, appropriate for a situation of Indigenous political resurgence and the demographic explosion that it has inspired.

Using the limited conceptual tools made available within a rigid cultural system, it is not surprising that even when challenging race, claimants to tribal nation membership utilize tools from the armory of the new race science of DNA testing. Timely when this volume was first conceived, and still timely now, is the debate over the inclusion or exclusion of the Cherokee Freedmen, ostensibly descendants of African slaves, but many also having ties of marriage and ancestry to the Cherokee. It is a debate that surfaces prominently in this volume with Julia

Coates's chapter (more below). As Harmon (2006) found, some Freedmen argued that DNA test results revealing the presence of "Indian ancestry" (there are no tribal genes, since tribes are political constructions) underscored their arguments that the Cherokee Nation of Oklahoma excluded them for racist reasons, because they look Black. An additional step was added to the Freedmen's argument: that the DNA test results establish "some degree of Indian blood" (Harmon, 2006), thereby transforming Cherokee identity into a question of genetics – paradoxically, in the name of anti-racism. Cherokee political authorities have rejected this position, stressing that their notion of "blood" is not a genetic or racial one, but one of kinship and cultural affinity. The Cherokee Nation insists that membership, as defined in their constitution, requires showing documented blood ties to a specific tribal member – DNA tests cannot do that, since they cannot point to which tribe an ancestor belonged.

As one of the current battle lines over inclusion-exclusion is being drawn between DNA and blood quantum, we can note that both are arguably rooted in racial ideologies. In the case of DNA, genetic markers are effectively being equated with cultural continuity, emphasizing the primacy of the biological as the ultimate determinant and arbiter of who is or can be a member of a given nation, and thus as a way to *measure* "who is truly Indian" (TallBear, 2003, pp. 82, 83). Like Julia Coates, whose chapter is discussed below, TallBear (2003) tends to agree that "blood quantum" (documented ties to a recognized citizen of a nation), as flawed as it can be, is still a more reliable indicator of cultural affiliation than genes. In emphasizing that "tribal ideas of kinship and community belonging are not synonymous with biology," TallBear warns that "if tribal political practice is not meaningfully informed by cultural practice and philosophy, it seems that tribes are abdicating self-determination" (2003, p. 84).

However, relatedness through blood quantum is still a biological measure – in this vein, TallBear argued that "the racial ideology that is the foundation of certain applications of DNA analysis is integral to (if not totally representative of) blood quantum" (2003, p. 82). Moreover, this "measuring of blood" was born from the U.S. federal government's colonization of American Indians, which established blood quantum policies "to determine who is really an Indian in an official capacity" (TallBear, 2003, p. 82). All three areas of law, biology, and culture overlap in having ties to "blood quantum standards associated with nineteenth- and early-twentieth-century theories of race" (Archuleta,

2005, p. 1; see also Churchill, 2004, p. 66). Some argue that the effect is to divide and alienate American Indian communities by enlisting them in perpetuating the colonial discourse of blood quantum, effectively "relocating inside Indian bodies the legal, physical, and politics wars between Indians and the federal government" (Archuleta, 2005, pp. 1, 4). While meant to ultimately reduce the number of bodies that can be classed as "Indian," blood quantum policies can also have the effect of culturally reducing indigeneity to a mere surface – as Cherokee legal scholar G. William Rice points out: "Most [people] would recognize the full-blood Indian who was enrolled in a federally recognized tribe as an Indian, even if the individual was adopted at birth by a non-Indian family and had never set foot in Indian country nor met another Indian" (quoted in Garroutte, 2001, p. 230). We must keep in mind that this system is regulated by the U.S. federal government, which is responsible for issuing to individuals the Certificate of Degree of Indian Blood (CDIB) – as Matthew Snipp noted, the relationship between Native Americans and the agency that issues the CDIB is "not too different than the relationship that exists for championship collies and the American Kennel Club" (quoted in Hitt, 2005).

Garroutte and Snipp in this volume note some of the additional, problematic conceptual issues raised by the quantification of identity, both as genetic testing and blood quantum. Quantification establishes distance as a prerequisite for measurement, "with the corollary that, at some point, individuals' connection to American Indian forebears becomes exhausted" (Garroutte & Snipp, this volume). Quantification of identity presupposes distance, and tends towards disappearance. It sets physical standards for ideational and subjective identities, even as it creates new subjectivities around the use of scientific resources. The right to measure involves a power to erase, just as the power to speak for Indigenous peoples, and to assign their identities, is the power to silence them, permanently.

Yet, with all of the quantification and fixity of indigeneity as if it were a substance, the U.S. federal government lacks correspondingly precise legal definitions of what constitutes an "Indian," which further fuels conflict and uncertainty. In the U.S. Constitution there is no legal definition of the term "Indian," and indeed the word is only used twice, with the issue generally left to various federal Departments and the courts to debate (Hagan, 1985, p. 310). The courts, however, did find two considerations to be most significant in determining Indian identity and status, as laid out in *United States v. Rogers* in 1846: "First, the individual must have some Indian blood; and, second, those Indians with whom he/she claimed affiliation must accept him/her as a fellow tribesman" (Hagan, 1985, p. 310).

Even if the debate between genetics and culture were to be resolved, the range of debates on identity would be far from exhausted. As Weaver observed, there is a tremendous degree of infighting among American Indians around issues of legitimate identities; Weaver argues that this possibly stems from a material calculation: "sometimes Native people, as well as the federal government, find a financial incentive to prevent others from declaring themselves to be indigenous" (2001, p. 249). What Weaver calls "internalized oppression," a by-product of colonization, is witnessed in how American Indians fight among themselves and accuse each other of "not being 'Indian enough' based on differences in politics, religion, or phenotype … In some regions of the country it is common to see the bumper sticker 'FBI: Full Blooded Indian.' What message does this communicate to people of mixed heritage?" (2001, p. 250; see Fonseca, 2012). As Garroutte and Snipp explain in this volume, there is a wide diversity of reasons and strategies for persons to assert (or deny) their indigeneity. In the U.S., where "blood quantum" is the rule for determining tribal membership status in at least two-thirds of tribal nations, demonstrating genealogical ties is one method. Another has been to find traces of Indigenous ancestry through DNA testing. Other means of demonstrating indigeneity are more broadly cultural and affective: practicing a language, getting actively involved in the performance of various rituals and public ceremonies, teaching, and so forth. Garroutte and Snipp pose some of the many questions that emerge: Why should anyone have to *prove* their identity? If identity can be proven by any number of ways, with varying demands and standards set by agencies that regulate identity, then what does that say about the very "provability" of Indigenous identity? *Who is an Indian?* Clearly it depends on who is asking, and why they are asking. It also depends on who is answering, and why they are answering.

Lastly, there is the question of the degree to which blood quantum appears in other parts of the Americas as a means of defining who is Indigenous. Despite the historical impact of colonization, racism, science, and principles of inclusion/exclusion and superiority/inferiority on the confinement and control of indigeneity across the Americas, blood quantum as such is not to be generally found across the hemipshere. To some degree, it appeared in Canada with the Gradual Enfranchisement Act of 1869, which was the first to mention blood quantum and which would remain law until 1927: "no person with 'less than one-fourth Indian blood' would be 'entitled to share in any annuity, interest or rents' of the band to which they belonged" (from Patrick, this volume). Moreover, the *Indian Act* of 1876 decreed that a woman was deprived of her status as "Indian" if she "'married a non-Indian ... and her children – and her children's children forever – would not be 'Indians'" – a measure that remained in place until the passage of Bill C-31 in 1985 (Patrick, this volume). Another measure designed to reduce Indian numbers in Canada was contained in section 12(1)(a)(iv) of the 1951 revision of the *Indian Act*: known as the "double mother clause," this removed Indian status from children when they turned twenty-one if their mother and paternal grandmother did not have status before marriage. Patrick (this volume), in agreement with Lawrence, argues that this was a "covert regulation of blood quantum" or a "de facto blood quantum" necessary to establish entitlement to Indian status under the *Indian Act*. As Patrick further notes in this volume, "blood quantum is now used by some bands to define membership," and even for the Inuit, despite the emphases on territory and language noted before, ancestry still matters – that is, being *a descendant of a recognized Inuit*. In the Caribbean, from my own research in Trinidad and the historical work produced by Hulme and Whitehead (1992), we see racial purity translated directly into concepts of blood purity, with the common refrain being that a "real Carib" is one of "pure blood"; this is usually ascertained by reference to stereotyped phenotypical traits, and silently reinforced by observation of the difference between a person's physical appearance and that of his/her African-descended neighbours.

In Latin America, however, neither blood quantum nor blood as such are deployed as the determinants of Indigenous identity. As José Antonio Lucero explains in this volume, "blood" is already incorporated in national ideologies of race-mixture, and is not specific and particular enough to be used as part of the regimes of identifying the Indigenous. As Lucero adds, "in a region where 'everyone' has native blood, but not everyone is 'Indian,' the social category and social fact of Indianness rely, necessarily, less on biology or blood than on the intersecting socio-cultural workings of politics, language, place, class, and gender" (Lucero, this volume).

Blood Quantum beyond Race? Nationality, Indigenous Sovereignty, and the Cherokee Freedmen

In the U.S., American Indian sovereignty means that each federally recognized nation has the right to establish and enforce its own legal criteria for citizenship. The most common criterion is that of blood quantum: "About two-thirds of all federally recognized tribes of the coterminous United States specify a minimum blood quantum in their legal citizenship criteria, with one-quarter blood degree being the most frequent minimum requirement" (Garroutte, 2001, p. 224; see also Hagan, 1985, p. 315). How this degree of blood is determined – that is, the biological relationship one has with an "unmixed" or "full-blooded" (i.e., "really real") Indian ancestor – is by reference to a "base roll" of tribal membership that was compiled by the U.S. federal government, often using spurious racial criteria for ascertaining full-bloodedness (Garroutte, 2001, p. 225). The ultimate intention, as Garroutte notes, was to eventually liquidate tribal lands and eliminate government trust responsibility, treaty rights, and reservations, as more and more tribal members married outside of their communities. While tribes maintain formal, legal authority over enrolment, the fact remains that there is federal review of tribal law, certification of due process in enrolment by the Bureau of Indian Affairs, and federal guidance on how to calculate blood quantum, among other measures (TallBear, 2003, p. 89).

Nonetheless, it is this system that some advocates of tribal sovereignty are upholding. Some argue that "blood" is understood differently by some American Indians, who see positive sides to blood imagery that stress connection and integration rather than calculation and differentiation (Strong & Van Winkle, 1996, p. 562). This is an argument which Melissa Meyer (2005) has developed at length, noting that American Indians' metaphorical notions of blood accord with ideas of family lineage, descent, ancestry, and group membership; she credits American Indian tribes with having their own agency, their own goals and understandings, in using the terminology of blood quantum. However, she too concedes that in their purest form, blood quantum requirements amount to a celebration of race, and while blood quantum might have found some support from alternative, Indigenous understandings, this would not spare tribes from the destructive consequences of basing their policies on racial criteria (Meyer, 2005). Whether a "tragically necessary" tool for resisting encroachment, as Strong and Van Winkle argue, or a "tragically strategic" adaptation (TallBear, 2003, p. 91), blood quantum continues to be actively upheld.

Indeed, the historical tendency has been towards *increased* and more widespread use of blood quantum among U.S. tribal nations. A study of 322 current and historic tribal constitutions, representing 245 federally recognized tribes in the lower forty-eight states of the U.S., revealed "striking changes in the types of membership rules chosen by tribes since modern constitution-writing began in the mid-1930s," with tribes increasingly using lineal descent and blood-quantum rules after 1970, "in place of the parental-enrollment or residency rules that were dominant in constitutions adopted in the 1930s" (Gover, 2008/2009, pp. 246–7). The tendency is thus for tribes to become more genealogical about tribe-specific descent, eschewing pan-tribal considerations. In total, "80.18% of tribes whose constitutions were first adopted after 1970 use either lineal descent or tribal blood in their membership regimes, compared with only 27.71% of tribal constitutions first adopted before 1950" (Gover, 2008/2009, p. 247n13). Gover believes that the effort to repair disruptions to historical continuity in communities, caused by federal termination and relocation policies, is the reason for this growing adoption of tribal descent rules (2008/2009, p. 248).

After a lawsuit was brought against the federal government and the Cherokee Nation of Oklahoma by the Eastern Cherokees (who had not been removed to Oklahoma, and wanted to be included on Cherokee rolls), the U.S. Supreme Court in 1885 offered "a signal victory for the right of the Cherokee Nation to determine its own criteria for citizenship, and the decision would be used as a precedent to ensure the same authority for other tribes" (Hagan, 1985, pp. 311–12). This recognition of Cherokee national sovereignty has come into even sharper focus with the currently ongoing dispute about the membership claims of the Cherokee Freedmen. Circe Sturm (1998, 2002) launched a relentless critique of the racism embedded in the "blood politics" of the Cherokee Nation's decision to exclude the Freedmen; that decision, and the ensuing public debate, were in fact among the original inspirations for this volume. Sturm argued, "Cherokee identity is socially and politically constructed around hegemonic notions of blood, colour, race, and culture that permeate discourses of social belonging in the United States" (1998, p. 231). Indeed, she specifically argues that it is Cherokee racism that is the basis for the exclusion of Cherokees with African ancestry (such as the Freedmen), while Cherokees who have White ancestry are retained – manifesting a long-term bias against African ancestry, and a Cherokee conflations of ideas of blood, colour, culture, and race (1998, p. 231). She roots this in the fact that some Cherokees owned African slaves in the early 1800s, and that they were loyal to the Confederacy during the Civil War (Sturm, 1998, p. 232). Ultimately, Sturm argues, this principle of exclusion is also structured by the Cherokee adopting the racial criteria of the Bureau of Indian Affairs (Sturm, 1998, p. 240), a somewhat empty and mimetic form of self-government.

The work by Julia Coates in this volume presents a much more complicated picture, however, one that rebuts Sturm on every major point, and is especially timely given recent news of heightened and expanded conflict around the Freedmen (see Harris, 2011; and Olafson, 2011). The Cherokee Nation of Oklahoma has come under fire for its exclusionary practices, in the face of a massive upsurge of people claiming Cherokee identity over the past years. Coates, along with Garroutte, is one of two Cherokee scholars contributing to this volume, and as a representative of the Cherokee Tribal Nation Council, she brings a unique perspective to this debate. She has direct, personal experience with the subject matter she presents, having also worked with citizen and non-citizen Cherokees in various states of the U.S., and having spent time teaching Cherokee history "on the road" to thousands of Cherokees.

In her chapter, "'This Sovereignty Thing': Nationality, Blood, and the Cherokee Resurgence," Coates strongly and productively challenges a number of prominent, published perspectives that have been critical of definitions of Cherokee identity set by the Tribal Nation's government. Coates argues that legal definitions are often overlooked in discussions of indigeneity, while race and culture gain greater attention. Yet, as she explains, many tribal governments in the U.S. regard legal definitions not as artificially imposed from external colonizing institutions, but as internally achieved definitions of *nationality* and their *sovereign* statuses. While the Cherokee Nation's lack of cultural requirements is frequently misunderstood by non-Indians and derided by other tribal nations, the Cherokee Nation has continued to assert that nationality derived from their specific history of tribal citizenship is a more inclusive category for contemporary times than race or cultural markers. This is almost a reversal of arguments criticizing the Tribal Nation's exclusion of certain persons. Based on interviews with what Coates calls "a particularly challenging group of Cherokee nationals," the 60 per cent of the citizenry living outside the tribal core in northeastern Oklahoma, her chapter examines the potential of *nationality* as a basis for self-identification for those in the Cherokee diaspora, and the role the concept of *citizen* plays in the contemporary Cherokee resurgence.

Coates points to problems with a debate that "focuses on identity construction as located in race, heritage, DNA, and cultural attributes and expressions" and that leaves out law and sovereignty. She says that one reason why the cultural, racial, and ethnic aspects of identity are primary sites for investigation and discussion for many Indigenous peoples may be the fact that many of them are not formally organized into nominally sovereign political entities with an internal jurisdiction.

Most academics seem to differ from tribal governments' rigid determinations of citizenship, and Coates suggests that this may be because academics tend to be more inclusive in their view of who is an American Indian – not wanting to serve as identity police, or impose definitions of Indigenous identity on Natives. Her emphasis is on nationality as a potential means for retention and resurgence (or what some call resilience), rather than simply as a colonialist mechanism of control and exclusion.

Contra Circe Sturm (1998), Coates makes the following points. First, race did not matter to the Cherokees as much as some might think, as evidenced by the fact that the Cherokees have been the most inclusive tribe in the U.S. (many members are 1/4096 degree of Indian blood). Second, *sovereignty is what is resurgent*, something regained as a result of a hard-fought struggle for treaty rights and self-determination, whereas the membership of the Cherokee Freedmen, currently disputed, was always something imposed on the Cherokees by an interventionist federal government. Third, the problem here is that the wider society understands Indigenous identity to be ethnic or racial, not national. Fourth, well before race categorizations were institutionalized in the U.S., and going back to the Cherokee Constitution of 1827, *not all descendants of a Cherokee parent were accepted, only those who were born of a Cherokee mother*, so that principles of exclusion were the norm, but were not race based, and had to do with Cherokee kinship rules. Fifth, with regard to the Confederacy and slavery, Coates argues that the Cherokees only reluctantly joined, and the Cherokees emancipated their slaves before the U.S. did – moreover, laws making mixing with Blacks illegal were imposed on them by successive U.S. and Confederate governments, and were not freely chosen. Sixth, the Cherokee Nation has not targeted the Freedmen alone for exclusion, but also the children of White fathers, as well as Shawnees and Delawares that the federal government had forced into the Cherokee Nation. Seventh, for the Cherokee Nation, the key criteria for citizenship are neither colour nor genes, but rather residency and proof of family ties. Lastly, Coates argues that the Cherokee notion of "full blood" is not racial, but instead describes individuals who speak the Cherokee language, were raised in traditional cultural practices, and hold an Indigenous thought process and worldview, and that this concept is "typically far more inclusive of individuals who were racially mixed than the Euroamerican definition," as today it is likely that the majority of individuals who are described or self-described as "full bloods" in the Cherokee Nation are of mixed ancestry. Coates's counter-critique is quite thorough, and it will be interesting to read the responses of scholars of Cherokee politics.

What Julia Coates provides us with, then, is the Cherokee Nation's answer to a variation of the question of who is an Indian – specifically, who is a citizen of the Nation. The answer is seemingly straightforward: those who are related to an already recognized Cherokee citizen, determined by matrilineal descent and a residency requirement. As she says in her chapter, "I always thought the question was, 'Am I Indian?' And I could never find a comfortable response. But that's not the question, is it? The question is, am I a citizen of the Cherokee Nation? And the answer is, yes, I am!"

Coates is, of course, not alone in making these arguments. Gover argues that "tribal blood quantum does not rest on an Indian/non-Indian dichotomy, but rather serves as a device for counting the number of a person's tribal ancestors" – ancestors who, in a racial model, may have themselves been very mixed (2008/2009, p. 252). It is also clear that the federal government could terminate a tribe if it is "over-inclusive," or it could self-determine its sovereignty away (Gover, 2008/2009, p. 264).

The fear expressed by some is that the alternative to enforcing blood quantum – *self-identification* – indulges "the preferences of individuals over the formally expressed will of the tribe that has declined to recognize them as citizens," as Garroutte puts it; she notes that "American Indian tribes have tended to place the authority of the group over the rights of the individual" (Garroutte, 2003, p. 88). The additional perceived "threat to sovereignty" posed by self-identification is the potential "cavalcade of self-identified people and groups who improperly present themselves as representing the views, values, commitments, or authority of entire Indian tribes" (Garroutte, 2003, p. 89). With this in mind, we turn to issues of self-identification, and then to the varieties of seemingly bizarre ways of making "Indians" out of "non-Indians," and making "non-Indians" out of "Indians," that can ultimately work to undermine and delegitimize the advocacy of sovereignty principles.

I Am an Indian

Jack Forbes argued that "*one of the fundamental human rights of individuals and of groups includes the right to self-identification and self-definition,* so long as one does not adopt an identity which has the effect of denying the same rights to others" (quoted in Garroutte, 2003, p. 94). The chapter by Eva Marie Garroutte and Matthew Snipp in this volume presents the confrontation between ascription and self-identification – or what the authors refer to as "processes of both 'assertion,' or self-perception, and 'assignment,' or the legitimation of those perceptions by others" – by describing and examining how these processes unfold in everyday life.

There is one recurring "problem" with Indigenous self-identification – or rather, a phenomenon that has been turned into a problem by those who seek to impose standards and limitations on Indigenous identity by turning it into something that can be verified and substantiated, something permeated with legal discourse and cognizant of policies on the distribution of resources. This "problem" is that historically high rates of intermarriage between Indigenous persons and those of other ethnicities have resulted in many descendants who now choose to emphasize their ties to Indigenous ancestors. This "threatens" to re-expand the Indigenous population mass, and that raises "concerns" for various interests that have been vested in controlling and/or minimizing the number of claimants to Indigenous identity (Garroutte and Snipp, this volume).

As Garroutte has explained elsewhere, the expression "self-identified Indian" is sometimes used to refer to "anyone who does not satisfy the requirements specifically of legal definitions" (2003, p. 82). Self-identification, she explains, describes "systems of rules that systematically direct attention away from questions of law, blood, or culture" and that involve a "personal profession of identity" (Garroutte, 2003, p. 82). Self-identification, particularly in the U.S. context, can clash with principles of tribal sovereignty, especially when the latter are further motivated by a fear of "illegitimate claimants" to an Indigenous identity who act out of calculated self-interest for material gains. This is a problematic defence, as it both imbibes Euro-American concepts of governance and endorses instrumentalist, rational-choice theories of behaviour. If there was so much to be gained and nothing to be lost by a simple identity switch, then we need an answer as to why only a tiny fraction of the U.S. population chooses to "shop" for an American Indian identity. For its part, while tribal sovereignty can derive legitimacy as a vehicle for opposing the impositions of the federal state, it can also imply a requirement to acquire the bureaucratic organizational norms of the very same state, along with its hierarchies, authority over citizens, coercion, and the very idea of governance as a separate and distinct sphere of life (Garroutte, 2003, p. 95). As Garroutte argues, following Gerald Taiaiake Alfred, "the most important criterion of belonging" to an Indigenous community, if one upholds traditional organizational values, "is not the formal citizenship bestowed by the tribal bureaucracy; it is that one is known and accepted by others like oneself" (Garroutte, 2003, p. 96). Garroutte agrees with the principle that "to try to grant a priori equal recognition to all identity claims ... amounts to taking none seriously" – however, as she notes, "efforts at boundary maintenance easily become self-defeating" (Garroutte, 2003, p. 98).

Indian Non-Indians, and Non-Indian Indians

New Indians. Born-again Indians. Hobby Indians. Wannabe Indians. Ersatz Indians. Indians of convenience. Generic Indians. There seem to be an awful lot of negative labels used in demarcating the zone of "fake indigeneity," that is, of ways of answering the question of who is *not* an "Indian." Here I want to highlight two related yet quite distinct processes, one being that of making "non-Indians" out of those people who could on many levels rightfully claim to be Indigenous, and that of making "Indians" out of people who sport none of the usual attributes of being an "Indian" when compared to fellow "Indians." Again, we are still at the crossroads between self-identification and government-regulated definitions; from this intersection, at which are revealed some of the contradictions of the existing system of regulation, and some of the obstacles placed in the way of demographic expansion, we may be able to see some ways forward.

This is a very productive area for research, given the many surprising discoveries that reveal the political arbitrariness of many institutionalized answers to the question of who is an "Indian." As Garroutte noted, "the 'Indians' and 'non-Indians' who emerge from the rigors of the definitional process do not always resemble what one might expect" (2001, p. 224). In addition, as Archuleta pointed out, "what it means to 'be Indian' often differs from what 'counts as Indian' for the federal government and even for many Indians themselves" (2005, p. 19). As David Treuer relates in a recent Op-Ed in *The New York Times*, "I know full-blooded Indians who have lived their entire lives on reservations but can't be enrolled because they have blood from many different tribes, and I know of non-Indians who have been enrolled by accident or stealth just because they'll get something out of it" (Treuer, 2011).

Let us first address how established rules work to produce "non-Indians" out of persons who might otherwise be fully accepted as Indigenous, what I am calling the "Indian non-Indians." Here I focus on the U.S. As Garroutte and Snipp explain in this volume, some tribes have patrilineal and others matrilineal rules for reckoning descent. In some cases, an individual may even have 100 per cent Indigenous ancestry, but be excluded from any one tribe: he is descended from one tribe through his father, but that tribe only recognizes descent via the mother; he is also descended from another tribe via his mother, but that tribe only recognizes descent via the father. He is thus permitted no tribal membership, and is officially treated as if he were not Indigenous. Here we have a counterintuitive, official answer to our lead question: Who is an "Indian"? Not someone who is 100 per cent "Indian."

Another way that "Indian non-Indians" are created happens in those many cases where individuals who are recognized by their tribes as citizens are nevertheless considered non-Indian for some or all federal purposes. The converse can be true as well (see Garroutte, 2001, p. 227). Even though, in the U.S., tribes are said to possess the right to formulate legal definitions governing their own citizenship, the federal government also has its own ways of distinguishing "Indians" from "non-Indians" – in fact, it has up to thirty-three separate definitions, as found in different pieces of legislation, and some of these can conflict with tribal definitions (Garroutte, 2001, p. 227).

A third way of producing "Indian non-Indians" occurs in those cases which I label as "Indian here, but not Indian over there." A related principle would be "Indian today, but not tomorrow" (or vice versa). In both instances, I am focusing on the Canadian case. In her chapter, "Federally Unrecognized Indigenous Communities in Canadian Contexts," Bonita Lawrence points out the cases of First Nations that span the Canada–U.S. border, where, for example, "the Passamaquoddy Nation of New Brunswick, or the Sinixt Nation, in British Columbia, have federal recognition in the United States but not in Canada," which, she argues, underscores the arbitrary, shifting, and inconsistent standards used by states to "appraise" indigeneity. Donna Patrick, in her chapter, draws attention to how some Métis could "become Indian" by refusing to accept promissory notes in exchange for land or cash, or could "choose" to become "non-Indian" by accepting such notes. As for the Inuit, "once the Supreme Court of Canada ruled that Inuit were 'Indians' for the purposes of Section 91(24), they too became the responsibility of the Department of Indian Affairs," Patrick tells us. As a result, "who counted" as Inuit "suddenly became a federal concern" – and thus the Inuit were "registered," each assigned a number embossed on a hard leather disk to be worn on a necklace. Inuit of mixed ancestry, however, were originally not counted, literally (Patrick, this volume).

What sometimes seem to garner far more media attention are those cases involving the production or exposure of "non-Indian Indians," that is to say, individuals who under few or none of the established definitions can claim an Indigenous identity. There are many high-profile celebrity cases in Canada and the U.S., ranging from Grey Owl, to Iron Eyes Cody, Chief Buffalo Child Long Lance, Chief Red Thundercloud, Lightfoot Talking Eagle, and Jamake Highwater among others. There seem to be both an established fear and disdain for the "wannabe" or "ersatz Indians"; as the president of the American Indian Society of Pennsylvania declared in the 1970s: "It is apparent the $2.00 head band and the Hong Kong medallion, with a self declaration, is going to be a method … by which the Indian population is going to boom" (quoted in Hagan, 1985, p. 318).

Going further back in history, Garroutte has outlined the many *institutionalized* ways in which "non-Indians" could acquire status as "Indians." As she explains, "non-Indian people who [had] made their way onto the tribal census lists" could "'become' Indian, in the legal sense," but also, "*nonexistent* people sometimes did, as well" – as in the many cases of fraudulent registrations (Garroutte, 2001, p. 233). In some places and times, non-Indian spouses were allowed to become citizens of Indian nations. Even in instances where an adopted white spouse was subsequently widowed, then remarried and had children by a non-Indian, the children (who had no tribal ancestry at all) were sometimes recognized as tribal citizens.

What to make of those cases of "wannabe Indians"? Should they simply be denounced as frauds? It depends on whether definitions of indigeneity are ultimately grounded in some objectified essence, or in a cultural affectivity and affinity that emerges from a process of growth, of becoming rather than just being. As Hitt (2005) tells us, while "it is easy to find Native Americans who denounce many of these new Indians as members of the wannabe tribe … it is also easy to find Indians like Clem Iron Wing, an elder among the Sioux, who sees this flood of new ethnic claims as magnificent, a surge of Indians 'trying to come home.' Those Indians who ridicule Iron Wing's lax sense of tribal membership have retrofitted the old genocidal system of blood quantum – measuring racial purity by blood – into the new standard for real Indianness, a choice rich with paradox." Even when defending lineal heritage as an important element of American Indian identity, Treuer (2011) also makes the critical observation of what "we [American Indians], with our fixation on blood, have forgotten: bending to a common purpose is more important than arising from a common place."

(Non)Recognition as Domination and Reduction

In her chapter in this volume, Bonita Lawrence explores identity issues among two federally unrecognized groups – the Algonquins of Eastern Ontario and the Mi'kmaqs of Newfoundland – which have been the subject of her research for the last several years, providing a window into how the Canadian state produces unrecognized Aboriginals. The primary means for such communities to gain federal recognition, to legally become Aboriginal again, is to assert Aboriginal title through the courts (if there is a treaty governing particular territory), or, as Lawrence outlines in her chapter, "to take part in the comprehensive claims process if no treaty has been signed in the territory." Otherwise, federally unrecognized Indigenous peoples are "incorporated simply as 'citizens' within the wider nation-state dominated by settlers" (Lawrence, this volume).

As Lawrence argues, placing these problems within a broader theoretical frame, "the central problem relating to membership in federally-unrecognized communities is precisely the intensity of colonial contact that almost always assaults and fragments Indigenous identities." The problem here again is that of determining "who is an Indian":

> In the wake of this massive and deliberately created cultural disarray, where many people no longer speak the languages that would have imparted their cultural knowledge, there is no clear consensus about what makes a person Indigenous in many Indigenous communities. In these circumstances, it has been easy for hegemonic considerations of Indigenous identity to take priority – so that increasing numbers of Native people only know themselves as Indian through their status card. (Lawrence, this volume)

Lawrence also brings these issues of fragmentation and official authentication into sharp focus in the other section of her chapter, dealing with the federal recognition of a Mi'kmaq community in Newfoundland. As she explains, for the Canadian government, "allowing *one* reserve to be created (to become, almost by definition, the 'real' Mi'kmaq of Newfoundland), was a crucial means through which the identities of all other Newfoundland Mi'kmaq could be called into question." Identity legislation thus creates one set of recognized Aboriginals, while simultaneously "unrecognizing" others.

Here *place* matters as well, as in Newfoundland only those Mi'kmaq separated from non-Native population centres and remotely located were deemed "viable" (Lawrence, this volume). Karen Stocker's chapter on Costa Rica makes a similar argument about the role of place, and the "trap of visibility." As Stocker explains, this is a form of visibility "that would more deeply entrench stereotypical expectations and images of Indigenous peoples."

There is also a political economy of Indigenous recognition that Lawrence's chapter brings to the fore. For example, Algonquin land claim negotiators who dealt with federally unrecognized Algonquins sought to narrow the criteria of who would benefit. They avoided "paper Indians" who might potentially "manipulate an Algonquin identity for private gain and therefore jeopardize the land claim" – they only wanted "real" Algonquins (Lawrence, this volume). In adopting a notion of the "real Algonquin," status Algonquins failed to understand that federally unrecognized Algonquins were not seeking recognition merely for personal gain, "but because it was an identity that their families, isolated in racist environments for generations, had been unable to either wholly claim or entirely leave behind" (Lawrence, this volume). In order to deal with the unrecognized Algonquins, the Algonquin Enrollment Law was enacted in 1995. It initially sought to limit inclusion to those of "one-quarter blood descent," to be proven via a "historic schedule of known Algonquins." This descent was traced through the male line, because the original schedule was drawn up by Europeans, who failed to recognize – or dismissed – the fact that Algonquins trace descent through the female line (Lawrence, this volume). As noted by Lawrence, the process of rebuilding Algonquin nationhood "continuously involved developing criteria that recreated the Indian Act."

Another hallmark of the manner in which the Canadian state goes about fragmenting Indigenous identities is underlined by Patrick in this volume. As she argues, the question of "who counts" is decided with reference to a plethora of categories used by the Canadian state to define and distinguish, and thus divide, these groups. Those categories include "First Nations, Inuit, and Métis, the three basic groups of Aboriginal peoples in Canada; status and non-status; on-reserve and off-reserve; treaty and non-treaty; rural and urban; and various mixed categories derived from these" (Patrick, this volume). State-controlled definitions of indigeneity tell us far more about the government and the colonial ideologies governing state actions than about indigeneity itself (Patrick, this volume).

One of the most prominent of those colonial ideologies, as alluded to by Patrick above and highlighted in this volume, is that of race. As Coates points out in this volume, the de facto termination of the

Cherokee Nation in 1907 rendered the Cherokee notion of "citizen" irrelevant, as the state defined Cherokees solely by blood identity – thus "denationalizing" the Cherokees and concomitantly racializing them. Under the 1834 Wheeler-Howard Indian Reorganization Act, recognized Indians included "all other persons of one-half or more Indian blood" (Hagan, 1985, p. 317). Indeed, as Gover explains, "Federal Indianness is not a genealogical measure. It measures the number of a person's racially Indian ancestors relative to the number of their non-Indian ancestors" (2008/2009, p. 250).

The process of defining "who is an Indian in Brazil" and what kind of recognition that entails, in broadly ideological terms, is also discussed by Jonathan Warren in this volume. There, being "Indian" historically carried certain dominant connotations of being "racially inferior, immoral, uncivilized impediments to progress," as well as "child-like subordinates who do not know what is in their best interests" (Warren, this volume). The "Indian" was a null set in the face of "development": "a development project only makes sense if the communities and environment in question are considered of little value: something is being brought to nothing" (Warren, this volume).

Recognition of the Indian in Costa Rica might have been spurred on by tourist interest and the value that tourists placed on the Indigenous, as hypothesized by Stocker in this volume. What we see in this instance is a transformation of *campesino* culture into a culture that is now marked as "Indigenous" and that caters to tourist expectations. We thus move from *what makes an Indian* to *what makes an Indian valuable,* which in turn transforms the definition and presentation of traits of Indianness.

The Geopolitics of Recognition

While some argue that race-making projects are always local (Biolsi, 2007, p. 415), in spite of the fact that colonialism unites the local and the global into a single continuum, we see work presented in this volume that provides us with an understanding of how international non-governmental organizations construct the meanings of indigeneity in relationships with Indigenous actors. José Antonio Lucero, in his chapter "Encountering Indigeneity: The International Funding of Indigeneity in Peru," takes the work of Oxfam America as the focus of his case study, as it has been among "the earliest funders of Indigenous activism." His chapter examines two different moments in the interactive process of legitimation between organizations such as Oxfam

America and Indigenous political organizations in Peru, with "development" serving as the interface between local and global discourses of indigeneity.

The "geopolitics of recognition" is conceptualized by Lucero as regimes of indigeneity that span local, national, and global scales. Lucero discusses how Indigenous people throughout the Americas (and beyond) have found it often inevitable, and sometimes useful, to engage a variety of legal, economic, and political systems. "Since the first contacts with missionaries, the state, and agents of global capital," he writes, "Indigenous people have found that new systems of domination are not without points of entry within which they can contest the very terms of domination," and in the present context, "the rising importance of non-state actors in the wake of aggressive neoliberal economic reforms (which shrank already weak states) provided an additional set of opportunities that Indigenous people have been able to use" (Lucero, this volume). However, one of the problems for Indigenous actors bound in relationships with external agencies is that the reconstruction of indigeneity that results is often Janus-faced, where "some discourses are for external consumption and have little to do with the lived 'social fact' of indigeneity at the local level" (Lucero, this volume).

Of course it is precisely the "social fact of indigeneity at the local level" that is up for grabs across the Americas, framed as a question, implying uncertainty and the need for some determining force. The chapters that follow take us further into the various stages of discussion and analysis of the kinds of questions that have been posed regarding the right and ability of persons and groups to declare themselves as Indigenous.

NOTE

1 Constitución Política de los Estados Unidos Mexicanos, at: http://constitucion.gob.mx/index.php?idseccion=11&ruta=1

REFERENCES

Abu El-Haj, N. (2007). The Genetic Reinscription of Race. *Annual Review of Anthropology*, *36*(1), 283–300. http://dx.doi.org/10.1146/annurev.anthro.34.081804.120522

Archuleta, E. (2005). Refiguring Indian Blood through Poetry, Photography, and Performance. *Studies in American Indian Literatures*, *17*(4), 1–26. http://dx.doi.org/10.1353/ail.2006.0001

Biolsi, T. (2007). Race Technologies. In D. Nugent & J. Vincent (Eds.), *A Companion to the Anthropology of Politics* (pp. 400–17). Oxford: Blackwell. http://dx.doi.org/10.1002/9780470693681.ch25

Churchill, W. (1985). The Situation of Indigenous Populations in the United States: A Contemporary Perspective. *Wicazo Sa Review*, *1*(1), 30–5. http://dx.doi.org/10.2307/1409421

Churchill, W. (2004). A Question of Identity. In S. Greymorning (Ed.), *A Will to Survive: Indigenous Essays on the Politics of Culture, Language and Identity* (pp. 59–94). Boston, MA: McGraw-Hill.

Coates, R.D. (2008). Covert Racism in the USA and Globally. *Social Compass*, *2*(1), 208–31. http://dx.doi.org/10.1111/j.1751-9020.2007.00057.x

De La Cadena, M. (2000). *Indigenous Mestizos: The Politics of Race and Culture in Cuzco, Peru, 1919–1991*. Durham, NC: Duke University Press.

Deloria, V. (1969). *Custer Died for Your Sins: An Indian Manifesto*. London: Collier-Macmillan Ltd.

Diamond, N., Bainbridge, C., & Hayes, J. (Directors). (2009). *Reel Injun* [Documentary]. Toronto: National Film Board of Canada.

Feagin, J.R. (2001). Racial Relations. In N.J. Smelser & P.B. Baltes (Eds.), *International Encyclopedia of the Social and Behavioral Sciences* (pp. 12711–716). New York: Elsevier Science Ltd. http://dx.doi.org/10.1016/B0-08-043076-7/01948-3

Field, L. (1994). Who Are the Indians? *Latin American Research Review*, *29*(3), 227–38.

Fonseca, F. (2012). Census Releases Data on American Indian Population. *Associated Press*, January 25. http://news.yahoo.com/census-releases-data-american-indian-population-205256402.html

Fredrickson, G.M. (2005). Mulattoes and Métis: Attitudes toward Miscegenation in the United States and France since the Seventeenth Century. *UNESCO*, 103–12.

Garroutte, E.M. (2001). The Racial Formation of American Indians: Negotiating Legitimate Identities within Tribal and Federal Law. *American Indian Quarterly*, *25*(2), 224–39. http://dx.doi.org/10.1353/aiq.2001.0020

Garroutte, E.M. (2003). *Real Indians: Identity and the Survival of Native America*. Berkeley, CA: University of California Press.

Gover, K. (2008/2009). Genealogy as Continuity: Explaining the Growing Tribal Preference for Descent Rules in Membership Governance in the United States. *American Indian Law Review*, *33*(1), 243–309. http://dx.doi.org/10.2307/20455382

Guitar, L., Ferbel-Azcarate, P., & Estevez, J. (2006). Ocama-Daca Taíno (Hear Me, I Am Taíno): Taíno Survival on Hispaniola, Focusing on the Dominican

Republic. In M.C. Forte (Ed.), *Indigenous Resurgence in the Contemporary Caribbean* (pp. 41–67). New York: Peter Lang USA.

Hagan, W.T. (1985). Full Blood, Mixed Blood, Generic, and Ersatz: The Problem of Indian Identity. *Arizona and the West*, *27*(4), 309–26.

Harmon, A. (2006). Seeking Ancestry in DNA Ties Uncovered by Tests. *The New York Times*, April 12.

Harris, P. (2011). US Government Warns Cherokee Nation Not To Exclude Black Freedmen. *The Guardian*, September 13. http://www.guardian.co.uk/world/2011/sep/13/us-government-cherokee-nation-freedmen

Hitt, J. (2005). The Newest Indians. *The New York Times*, August 21.

Hooker, J. (2005). "Beloved Enemies": Race and Official Mestizo Nationalism in Nicaragua. *Latin American Research Review*, *40*(3), 14–39. http://dx.doi.org/10.1353/lar.2005.0051

Hulme, P., & Whitehead, N.L. (Eds.). (1992). *Wild Majesty: Encounters with Caribs from Columbus to the Present Day – An Anthology*. Oxford: Clarendon Press.

Ifekwunigwe, J.O. (2004). Introduction: Rethinking "Mixed Race" Studies. In J. Ifekwunigwe (Ed.), *"Mixed Race" Studies: A Reader* (pp. 1–29). London: Routledge.

Jaimes, M.A. (1992). Federal Indian Identification Policy: A Usurpation of Indigenous Sovereignty in North America. In M.A. Jaimes (Ed.), *The State of Native America: Genocide, Colonization, and Resistance* (pp. 123–38). Boston, MA: South End Press.

Kuper, A. (1988). *The Invention of Primitive Society: Transformations of an Illusion*. New York: Routledge.

Kuper, A. (2003). The Return of the Native. *Current Anthropology*, *44*(3), 389–402. http://dx.doi.org/10.1086/368120

Lawrence, B. (2004). *"Real" Indians and Others: Mixed-Blood Urban Native Peoples and Indigenous Nationhood*. Vancouver, BC: UBC Press.

Lie, J. (2004). *Modern Peoplehood*. Cambridge, MA: Harvard University Press.

Lomnitz, C. (2001). *Deep Mexico, Silent Mexico: An Anthropology of Nationalism*. Minneapolis, MN: University of Minnesota Press.

Martinez Cruzado, J.C. (2002). The Use of Mitochondrial DNA to Discover Pre-Columbian Migrations to the Caribbean: Results from Puerto Rico and Expectations from the Dominican Republic. *Kacike: Journal of Caribbean Amerindian History and Anthropology* (Special Issue: New Directions in Taíno Research). http://web.archive.org/web/20081217205822/http://www.kacike.org/MartinezEnglish.pdf

Maybury-Lewis, D. (1993). A New World Dilemma: The Indian Question in the Americas. *Bulletin – American Academy of Arts and Sciences*, *46*(7), 44–59. http://dx.doi.org/10.2307/3824642

Meyer, M.L. (2005). *Thicker than Water: The Origins of Blood as Symbol and Ritual*. New York: Routledge.

Nagel, J. (1996). *American Indian Ethnic Renewal: Red Power and the Resurgence of Identity and Culture*. New York: Oxford University Press.

Olafson, S. (2011). Second-Largest U.S. Indian Tribe Expels Slave Descendants. *Reuters*, August 23. http://www.reuters.com/article/2011/08/24/us-oklahoma-cherokee-idUSTRE77N08F20110824

Redfield, R. (1940). The Indian in Mexico. *Annals of the American Academy of Political and Social Science*, *208*(1), 132–43. http://dx.doi.org/10.1177/000271624020800114

Schnapper, D. (2001). Race: History of the Concept. In N.J. Smelser & P.B. Baltes (Eds.), *International Encyclopedia of the Social and Behavioral Sciences* (pp. 12700–703). New York: Elsevier Science Ltd. http://dx.doi.org/10.1016/B0-08-043076-7/00140-6

Scott, J.C. (1999). *Seeing Like a State: How Certain Schemes to Improve the Human Condition Have Failed*. New Haven. CT: Yale University Press.

Shoemaker, N. (1999). *American Indian Population Recovery in the Twentieth Century*. Albuquerque, NM: University of New Mexico Press.

Sissons, J. (2005). *First Peoples: Indigenous Cultures and their Cutures*. London: Reaktion Books.

Stephen, L. (2002). *Zapata Lives! Histories and Cultural Politics in Southern Mexico*. Berkeley, CA: University of California Press. http://dx.doi.org/10.1525/california/9780520222373.001.0001

Stocker, K. (2005). *"I Won't Stay Indian, I'll Keep Studying": Race, Place, and Discrimination in a Costa Rican High School*. Boulder, CO: University Press of Colorado.

Strong, P.T., & Van Winkle, B. (1996). "Indian Blood": Reflections on the Reckoning and Refiguring of Native North American Identity. *Cultural Anthropology*, *11*(4), 547–76. http://dx.doi.org/10.1525/can.1996.11.4.02a00050

Sturm, C. (1998). Blood Politics, Racial Classification, and Cherokee National Identity: The Trials and Tribulations of the Cherokee Freedmen. *American Indian Quarterly*, *22*(1/2), 230–58.

Sturm, C. (2002). *Blood Politics: Race, Culture, and Identity in the Cherokee Nation of Oklahoma*. Berkeley, CA: University of California Press.

TallBear, K. (2003). DNA, Blood, and Racializing the Tribe. *Wicazo Sa Review*, *18*(1), 81–107. http://dx.doi.org/10.1353/wic.2003.0008

Tilley, V.Q. (2002). New Help or New Hegemony? The Transnational Indigenous Peoples' Movement and "Being Indian" in El Salvador. *Journal of Latin American Studies*, *34*(03), 525–44. http://dx.doi.org/10.1017/S0022216X0200651X

Treuer, D. (2011). How Do You Prove You're an Indian? *The New York Times*, December 21, p. A39.

Warren, J.W. (2001). *Racial Revolutions: Antiracism and Indian Resurgence in Brazil*. Durham, NC: Duke University Press.

Weaver, H.N. (2001). Indigenous Identity: What Is It, and Who Really Has It? *American Indian Quarterly*, *25*(2), 240–55. http://dx.doi.org/10.1353/aiq.2001.0030

Yellow Bird, M. (1999). What We Want to Be Called: Indigenous Peoples' Perspectives on Racial and Ethnic Identity Labels. *American Indian Quarterly*, *23*(2), 1–21. http://dx.doi.org/10.2307/1185964

1 Inuitness and Territoriality in Canada

DONNA PATRICK

There are many ways to address the question of "who counts" as a member of an Aboriginal group in Canada. These include appealing to band lists, legal jurisdictions, and family histories that describe membership in Aboriginal collectivities. But the particular history of these Aboriginal groups means that the question of "who counts" must also include reference to the categories created to define and distinguish these groups. Such categories include those of First Nations,[1] Inuit, and Métis, the three basic groups of Aboriginal peoples in Canada;[2] status and non-status; on-reserve and off-reserve; treaty and non-treaty;[3] rural and urban; and various mixed categories derived from these. This chapter explores the question of categorizing indigeneity in Canada by examining the linguistic, political, and judicial processes associated with the notions of territory, ancestry, and belonging that shape indigeneity today. My focus will be the Inuit in Canada, although I shall be situating my examination of them within a broader analysis of Aboriginal identity in Canada. Notwithstanding this focus, it is worth emphasizing that this analysis does not speak to the question of what it means to be Inuit in Canada – a question, of course, best left to Inuit themselves. Its aim is, rather, to see how Inuit individuals and collectivities have resisted state categorizations of "who counts" as Inuit, including the institutions stemming from land claim agreements and assertions of autonomy.

Two key findings will emerge from my analysis. The first is that Canadian discourse about Aboriginal identities has quite generally resisted the biopolitics of Indigenous identities found elsewhere in the Americas, eschewing notions such as blood quantum, racial phenotypes, and DNA. In particular, the actual measurement of "how much"

Indigenous blood an individual has and DNA analyses reflecting this are not part of the definitions of "status" as set out in Canadian colonial policies. This does not mean, however, that a "covert" or de facto blood quantum has not been part of policies governing Aboriginal, and in particular First Nations, peoples. As we shall see, the *Indian Act* – a very broad piece of legislation originally enacted over 130 years ago, and governing many aspects of the daily lives of First Nations peoples – does impose a de facto blood quantum in its provisions regarding the acquisition and loss of "registered" Indian status (Lawrence, 2003; Morse, 2002). Yet, while blood quantum has played at least a covert role in policy and judicial distinctions, it has not been used explicitly to define Indian status, and is only marginally used in defining First Nation band membership.

The second key finding of the analysis is that the construction of Inuit identity has been a process substantially distinct from that of First Nations identity. One basic reason for this is that the Inuit were not governed by the colonial state policies exemplified by the *Indian Act*. As such, the construction of "Inuitness" has followed a very different trajectory, guided not only by state policy and Inuit political mobilization, but also by traditional attachments to land and language. What I shall be suggesting, in fact, is that the notion of "territoriality" operates together with the notion of ancestry in shaping the identities of Inuit living in urban centres of the Canadian South as much as it does for those living in the Arctic.

In order to situate my analysis of Aboriginal identities, I shall begin with a historical consideration of Aboriginal-state relations in Canada. I shall describe how state processes – in particular, those serving to categorize Aboriginal peoples and to assimilate them into Canadian settler society – have determined "who counts" as First Nations, Métis, and Inuit. My point here will be that state-controlled definitions of indigeneity tell us far more about the government and the colonial ideologies governing state actions than they do about indigeneity itself. It is no surprise, then, that differences in the state's treatment of First Nations and Inuit have had a direct impact on "who has counted" as belonging to First Nations and Inuit peoples, respectively.

This historical analysis will set the stage for the second section of this chapter, which will explore how Inuit identities are articulated in urban centres as well as in the Arctic. What I shall be suggesting is that in both cases these identities are related to "territoriality," a notion that encompasses a sense of belonging to a "place" or "homeland" and involves cultural and geographical attachments to the land and to the people who have inhabited that land for centuries. Significantly, this notion is reflected in the text of the *Nunavut Land Claims Agreement*,[4] where Inuit status is defined in terms of self-identification and "Inuit customs and usages," the idea being that "Inuit are best able to define who is an Inuk."

Land, Policy, and the Historical Basis of "Who Counts" as an "Indian" in Canada

A good place to begin the discussion of Aboriginal identities in Canada is with the historical relations between Indigenous peoples and European settlers. Basic to this over two-century-old relationship has been Indigenous peoples' struggle for recognition of their right to their traditional lands. This has given rise to certain basic claims by Aboriginal peoples about these lands, namely, "that they owned their lands before contact with Europeans, that they made treaties with the European newcomers to share the land, and that after contact they never gave up their claims of ownership" (Turner, 2006, p. 4). Canadian Aboriginal policy, set in motion over 150 years ago, aimed to reduce the "Indian" population and to appropriate their lands for European ownership. The Crown's assimilationist agenda was carried out largely through policy and laws – and is apparent even from the names of some of these laws. These laws included the *Gradual Civilization Act* (1857), the *Gradual Enfranchisement Act* (1869), the *Indian Act* (1876) and its various revisions, the Indian Register (1951), and the proposed White Paper (1969). Such an agenda can also be discerned in current Aboriginal policy, including the *First Nations Governance Act* (proposed in 2002 but never passed), and Conservative Party policy initiatives, which have emerged as neoliberal manifestations of the same assimilationist impulse.

Studying these early manifestations of "Indian" law and policy can be useful as a "tool for studying government" (Shore & Wright, 1997, cited in Mackey, 2002, p. 108), shedding light on broader issues related to Inuit and other Aboriginal groups in Canada. In particular, this historical examination can help us to understand the racism and sexism that informed colonial attitudes and practices and that have reflected and shaped Euro-Canadian views of Aboriginal peoples. But it can also help us to understand the resurgence of discourse about land, culture, and language that constructs indigeneity in Canada. This is because the question of who counts as Aboriginal has long been linked to the question of who owns traditional Aboriginal lands and thus to issues of social justice and the well-being of Aboriginal peoples in Canada.

Sovereignty, Treaties, and "Indian" Policy

We can begin our discussion of Aboriginal policy in Canada with the history of treaties between Europeans and the Aboriginal peoples whom they encountered. The first such treaties were negotiated as part of military and economic alliances between European and Aboriginal partners, and were arguably seen by both sides as nation-to-nation agreements – hence the use of the word "treaty." These included the Treaty of Albany (1664) and the Peace and Friendship treaties between the Crown and the Wabanaki confederacy (1670–1). After the American Revolution, the Crown's focus shifted from the maintenance of these Aboriginal partnerships to the search for lands for fleeing United Empire Loyalists and Aboriginal peoples (Morse, 2004). From this point on, the Crown directed treaty-making in Canada towards the extinguishment of Aboriginal title in order to open up lands for settlement of the country.

The rapid pace of European settlement coincided with the need for statutes and policies to define both "Indian land" and "Indian identity" (where the term "Indian" was and still is used in the law to refer to First Nations peoples). Prior to this period, Aboriginal groups themselves defined who was a member of their society and "exercised that power of definition in a highly inclusive manner" (Miller, 2004, p. 13). This notion of inclusivity has been supported by numerous accounts of Euro-American settlers and soldiers being accepted and adopted into First Nations groups. The definition of "Indian" in these cases had little to do with race, biology, or ethnicity (see Miller, 2004, p. 13–14).

However, statutes defining "Indian identity" served to restrict inclusion into Aboriginal collectivities. The first such statute in which the Canadian colonial state set out to define "who counted" as Aboriginal persons was *An Act for the Better Protection of the Lands and Property of Indians in Lower Canada*, passed in 1850 in what is now Quebec. Included in the category of "Indians" were "persons of Indian blood, reputed to belong to a particular Body or Tribe of Indians interested in such lands," "persons intermarried," "persons residing among such Indians, whose parents … are Indians … or entitled to be considered as such," and "persons adopted in infancy." Included in all these categories were descendents of any of these persons (Miller, 2004, p. 16).

Other statutes of this kind – whose assimilationist objective was clear from their names, as already noted – were the *Gradual Civilization Act* (1857), which included a definition about how an "Indian" could cease to be an "Indian"; and the *Gradual Enfranchisement Act* (1869), which was the first to mention blood quantum and which would remain law until 1927. According to this statute, no person with "less than one-fourth Indian blood" would be "entitled to share in any annuity, interest or rents" of the band to which they belonged (Miller, 2004, p. 32). In addition, the Canadian Indian policy of 1869, which would eventually become the *Indian Act* of 1876, deprived women of their status as "Indians" if they "married a non-Indian … and her children – and her children's children forever – would not be 'Indians'" (Miller, 2004, p. 32). This provision would remain law until 1985, when the Supreme Court declared it to be unconstitutional. The result was the passing of Bill C-31 in 1985, which amended the *Indian Act* and entitled women and their children to regain their lost status.[5] A further measure to reduce Indian numbers was contained in section 12(1)(a)(iv) of the 1951 revision of the Act. Known as the "double mother clause," this removed Indian status from children when they turned 21 if their mother and paternal grandmother did not have status before marriage (Lawrence, 2003, p. 13).[6] This has been described as the "covert regulation of blood quantum" (Lawrence, 2003, p. 20) or as a "de facto blood quantum" necessary to establish entitlement to Indian status under the *Indian Act* (Morse, 2002, p. 11). In sum, "Indian" policy for generations either encouraged or forced enfranchisement and assimilation, thereby reducing the number of persons recognized as Aboriginal. Although amendments to the *Indian Act* reversed certain discriminatory aspects – and certain amendments required by recent court decisions will reverse these further[7] – it remains the case that the Act continues to promote a diminution in First Nations numbers.

Admittedly, these categories, while unrelated to traditional First Nations customs or practices and intended to serve purposes at odds with the growth of First Nations collectivities, have also played a role in Aboriginal mobilization. More specifically, they have served in struggles for increased First Nations autonomy and self-determination and adequate on-reserve education, social services, and health care. In addition, blood quantum is now used by some bands to define membership. Yet, this still does not mean that settler law definitions of "Indianness" and "Aboriginality" have become part of the everyday discursive construction of Indigenous identities in Canada. One reason for this divergence in the construction of "official" and personal identities might be that state categorizations and definitions for policy purposes do not necessarily coincide with people's own ways of defining themselves. The lack of correspondence between these two modes of defining Aboriginal identities has been particularly stark in Canada, where state Aboriginal policy has defined "Indianness" in the *Indian Act*, yet failed to acknowledge (let alone define) Inuit or Métis status until recently. I consider some consequences of this in the next section.

Definitions of "Indianness" and the Borders between "Indian," Métis, and Inuit

In the previous section, I described how state definitions of indigeneity in Canada served largely to restrict the number of individuals recognized as Aboriginal; but I also observed that such definitions ignored distinct Métis and Inuit identities altogether. One consequence of these gaps in the state's definition of Aboriginal people is that the state has, at times, categorized these groups as "Indians."

One such categorization was associated with the signing of the Prairie treaties in the 1870s. At this time, the federal government offered some Métis the choice of becoming treaty Indians or taking scrip, a promissory note exchangeable for land or cash. Government officials encouraged Métis to accept scrip, consistent with the government's objective of reducing Indian numbers. By accepting scrip, many individuals culturally and ethnically similar to those who "chose" to become Indians were not recognized to have Indian status themselves.

Another such categorization involved the Inuit, as a result of a 1939 Supreme Court of Canada case that determined that the Inuit were a federal responsibility, just as Indians were. At issue in this case was whether section 91(24) of the *British North America Act*, which assigned the federal government responsibility for "Indians and Lands reserved for the Indians," also applied to Inuit; and in particular whether the Inuit in Quebec were the responsibility of the federal or the provincial government. As it happens, the source of this problem was the absence of Inuit from the original 1876 *Indian Act*, and thus the federal government's failure to accord them the same rights as "Indians" – rights involving collective land bases (known as "reserve lands"), exemptions from taxation, and post-secondary education, among others.[8] Arguably, this failure can be traced in turn to the fact that Inuit lands were not desired by settlers in the same way as the more settled lands to the south. This had meant that Inuit had been virtually ignored until the Second World War, when military and economic interests in the Arctic brought attention to the plight of the Inuit, many of whom were trying to survive after the collapse of the fur trade and were facing starvation and increased prevalence of European diseases. This led the federal government to address Inuit hardship, and it began providing assistance in the form of family allowance cheques, with the aim of eventually settling and assimilating Inuit so that they could receive other federal services as Canadians did. Although the late arrival of government intervention has led to tremendous hardship for Inuit, it has, in fact, also allowed Inuit to pursue traditional harvesting practices and maintain their cultural beliefs and language, all of which remain part of defining Inuitness today – a point I shall return to in the next section.

Once the Supreme Court of Canada ruled that Inuit were "Indians" for the purposes of section 91(24), they too became the responsibility of the Department of Indian Affairs. As a result, "who counted" as Inuit suddenly became a federal concern; and the federal government implemented the Eskimo Disk List system in 1941, in order literally to "count" Inuit (as part of a national census) by assigning each one a number, which was embossed on a hard leather circular "tag" on a chain to be worn around the neck. While this gave Inuit "proof" of their Inuit status, those of mixed ancestry were initially not given disks – and hence were not seen as "Inuit" by the federal government.

Inuit resisted this control over who was and who was not Inuit (Smith, 1993). Inuit mobilization in the 1960s and early 1970s led to the demise of the Disk system, which was replaced by "Project Surname." Each number was thereby replaced with an official name for government records; the head of each Inuit family chose a surname for the family.[9] With this process, Inuit themselves thereby defined who was and who was not Inuit. As it happens, this question of who "counts" as Inuit is a complex one. It must take into account not only Inuit ancestry itself but also attachments to traditional territories and the linguistic, cultural, and other practices that are integral to "traditional" Inuitness – practices that have been retained in Inuit communities to a sufficient degree that they are also part of being a "modern" Inuk. This question must also take into account new forms of Inuit identity arising from political mobilization and from such contemporary processes as urbanization. I shall be considering these themes in more detail in the next section.

Inuitness, Ancestry, and Territoriality

Since Inuit have never been subjected to Canadian "Indian" policies that determined their status by "measuring" their ancestry in terms of blood quantum, the notion of blood quantum per se has never been part of Inuit discourse about "who counts" as Inuit. It is clear, however, that "counting" as Inuit does require at least being a descendant of Inuit. The question that this raises, then, is: what factors are involved both in being recognized and in recognizing oneself as Inuit?[10]

The importance of being recognized as Inuit is highlighted by the fact that, historically, Inuit have often welcomed outsiders into their communities who were nevertheless not accepted as Inuit. One example of such an outsider was Harold Udgarten, a Hudson's Bay Company employee and resident of Great Whale River in the early twentieth century. During fieldwork that I conducted in Great Whale River in the early 1990s, elders frequently spoke of Udgarten, who had been born at Moose Factory in 1875, spoke fluent Inuktitut, married into an Inuit family, and spent most of his life living among the Inuit (see Patrick, 2003a, p. 63). By all accounts, he had been well respected in the community and basically assimilated into the Inuit way of life around the trading post at the time. Nevertheless, he had not been considered "Inuit" and would always remain part Norwegian and part Métis. What is clear, though, is that if he had had children – as it happens, he did not – they and their descendents would have been Inuit without question. In other words, being born of an Inuk parent, with ancestral attachments to land and place, seems to have allowed for an identification as "Inuk."

The significance of ancestry is also highlighted by the life histories of such individuals as Kiviaq, the subject of the documentary *Kiviaq vs. Canada*. Kiviaq, a lawyer, politician, and former professional athlete, was born in 1936 around Chesterfield Inlet to an Inuk mother and a white father, but grew up in Edmonton and was known only by his English name, David Charles Ward. Despite growing up not speaking Inuktitut – his father forbade his mother from speaking to him in this language – and with a much diminished sense of Inuitness, Kiviaq was nevertheless recognized by his Inuit relatives as Inuk. Similar life histories can be found across the North, as explorers, whalers, traders, soldiers, and other colonial agents had children with Inuit women. Given the acceptance of these children as Inuit, there was likely resistance to the federal government's introduction of the Disk system in the 1940s and its determination of "who counted" as "Eskimo."

The Significance of Territory

While life histories like Kiviaq's reveal the importance of Inuit ancestry itself – of being descended from Inuit – they also reveal the importance of an attachment to traditional lands. In *Kiviaq vs. Canada*, one of Kiviaq's relatives points out that he is an "Inuk born on Inuit land." She asserts: "When we are born on the land, that is our home. That's what we Inuit say." In other words, it is as much ancestral attachments to land as ancestry itself that have allowed Kiviaq's relatives to identify him as "Inuk." Put another way, the notion of territoriality – and its linguistic, cultural, and economic associations – has been key in defining Inuitness across time and space. This notion of "territoriality" as I understand it here encompasses both "traditional" land-based beliefs and practices and the transformation of these through colonial contact and local, regional, national, and global processes. In the case of the Inuit of Nunavut and Nunavik (Northern Quebec), this involves attachments to the land and a sense of belonging to a "place" or an Inuit "homeland."

Arguably, the current importance of territoriality to Inuit identity is related to the political movement to secure a homeland for Inuit. This movement had its formal beginnings in 1971, the year that the Quebec government announced the first phase of the James Bay Hydroelectric Development Project, sparking resistance by the Cree and Inuit of Northern Quebec, who mobilized to try to stop the project. Mobilization by both Aboriginal groups led to the ratification of the James Bay and Northern Quebec Agreement in 1975. More recent mobilization has led to further negotiations between the Quebec Inuit, the federal government, and the province of Quebec to put in place an Inuit government for Nunavik (known in French as the "*gouvernement régional du Nunavik*" and in Inuktitut as "*Nunaviup Kavamanga*") (George, 2007). Interestingly, 1971 was also the year that the pan-Inuit organization called the Inuit Tapirisat of Canada (ITC) was created. This organization was instrumental in the founding of the Tunngavik Federation of Nunavut (TFN), which negotiated the comprehensive land claims agreement culminating in the formation of Nunavut in 1999.

Inuit mobilization around land claims negotiations – which affected virtually all Inuit, who were involved as a collectivity – introduced new forms of defining Inuitness based on territoriality.[11] Significantly, this mobilization arose when Inuit language, culture, and economic harvesting practices were still part of everyday life. While many younger Inuit had learned English or French, virtually all Inuit in the North still spoke Inuktitut and lived their everyday lives according to Inuit social and cultural values. Relatively late colonization of Inuit lands via federal policy and the lack of a settler insurgence, as already mentioned, have meant that Inuit continue to have a distinctive "territorial" identity, including strong attachments to traditional lands, language, and culture.

Yet this "traditional" identity, closely tied to ancestral lands and practices, currently faces at least two challenges. One is the rapid process of "modernization" that the North has also been undergoing, which is allowing Inuit to gain services and infrastructure enjoyed in the South. The difficulty here is that this process and the institutional structures associated with it remain highly "Euro-Canadian" in form, despite attempts to "Inuise" them. The other is the rapid urbanization of the Inuit (and other Aboriginal peoples), which challenges their attachments to traditional lands, language, and culture.

This means that the relation of territoriality to modern Inuit identities is a highly complex one. In what follows, I describe some of this complexity in order to provide some insight into the basis of Inuitness and the often contradictory social realities that are faced by Inuit in Canada today. My examples draw on land and locality, language and pluralingualism, and deterritorialization and reterritorialization in urban centres.

Land, Locality, and Identity

The most basic form of territoriality is attachment to particular lands – although processes of modernization have altered even this form of territoriality, as we shall see. In general, we might think of Inuitness as including attachments to particular places associated with *nuna* – an Inuktitut word usually translated as "land," although "it can also mean 'total habitat' including the sea, the ice, the mountains, the air, the animals, fish, and even souls and memories of events and the people who live in the past" (Jessen Williamson, 2006, p. 19; see also Nuttall, 1992). These habitats involve the space, usually some distance beyond the settlement, where families have hunted, fished, and lived for generations. In Inuktitut, one can express one's attachment to particular places by means of certain suffixes. Jessen Williamson (2006) notes that "as an Inuk, one usually identifies oneself as 'of a certain area' using the suffix '*mioq*'[12] [which] ... implies a strong sense of affinity with the dialect-group-identified area of *nuna*; it is an acknowledgement of one's own relation to the land of birth."

With settlement, however, the idea of belonging to a particular area of *nuna* has been transformed. The use of place names as identifying markers links smaller groups, such as those of family or clan, to the larger groups that are related to settlements and to still larger regional "territories." In other words, one can see identity, including linguistic and "dialect-group" identity, coalescing around settlements and the regions in which settlements are grouped. Transformations of space have also included the mapping and naming of territories: Nunatsiavut (Labrador), Nunavik (Quebec), Inuvialuit (NWT), and Nunavut (NT). In addition, supranational organizations such as the Inuit Circumpolar Council (ICC)[13] offer supranational forms of Inuit identity. According to the ICC charter, the Inuit are "indigenous members of the Inuit homeland recognized by Inuit as being members of their people and shall include the Inupiat, Yupik (Alaska), Inuit, Inuvialuit (Canada), Kalaallit (Greenland) and Yupik (Russia)" (ICC, 2002). This pan-Inuit view of "who counts" as Inuit has arisen out of the necessity of politicization and mobilization, and now overlaps with local attachments and identifications to place.

Language and Plurilingualism

Another aspect of territoriality, as already suggested, is attachment to the various practices associated with the land, including linguistic practices. While linguistic practices associated with earlier periods in Inuit history would generally have involved only Inuktitut,[14] the relation of linguistic practices to modern Inuit identities has become far more complex.

According to the research that I conducted in Great Whale River in the early 1990s, Inuktitut was in daily use in all aspects of community life, despite high levels of Inuktitut-English bilingualism and some Inuktitut-French-English trilingualism (Patrick, 2001, 2003a, 2003b). However, in Nunavut, English has been found to be gaining prominence over Inuktitut in some contexts (Dorais & Sammons, 2000); and anecdotal evidence suggests that other communities in Nunavik are also witnessing increased English usage. In fact, English has played, and continues to play, a paradoxical role in Inuit and other Aboriginal communities in Canada. As a language of the residential schools that Aboriginal children were forced to attend and as the language now most commonly used in the wider society, English has represented a real threat to Aboriginal language use. At the same time, English has been seen as a necessary tool for engaging with the legal and political systems of the state to rectify past wrongs, to assert Aboriginal rights and local control over institutions, and even to promote and protect the smaller Aboriginal languages that English is displacing. As such, English appears to figure prominently in the construction of modern Inuit identity. This view is reflected in remarks like the following one, from an interview reported in Patrick (2003b, p. 133): "Since I'm Inuk, English is my second language. The English came here and they wanted us to learn how to speak English. I really want to understand very much English."

Deterritorialization and Reterritorialization

A third aspect of territoriality that figures in modern forms of Inuit identity is related to the increasing movement of Inuit to cities. Of course, the notion of an Inuit "community" itself does not rely on any direct geographical connection to traditional lands. This is because the notion of "community" is quite abstract and bounded neither by time nor by geographical space. Most basically, then, it is conceptualized by those who are engaged in culturally specific practices and are part of the social networks and institutional landscapes that form this community (Lobo, 2001).

Despite this interconnectedness among urban Inuit, linkages with the "territorial" North remain prevalent. This is because traditional forms of linguistic and cultural capital continue to play a role in the construction of urban Inuitness; and many urban Inuit still maintain ties to their home communities by Internet or telephone or by interacting with Inuit who are visiting urban centres, generally to receive medical attention.[15]

These conclusions emerged from the research reported in Patrick et al. (2006), which is part of a project investigating language practices in the Inuit community in Ottawa. What we have found from interviews with urban Inuit is that the desire to be linked to the territorial North is a common aspect of Inuit life in the South. Such a desire can be seen in the remarks of two Southern-raised Inuit women, as given below:

> I didn't know much about the Inuit culture, my childhood home was filled with artefacts that I took for granted and did not inquire about. I didn't know the first thing about igloos or sled dogs, hunting or sealing, carving or throat singing. So when people did find out about my Inuit heritage and asked questions, I just made things up ... As an adult, I am striving

> to learn the more tangible cultural traditions. A good friend of mine is teaching me to throat sing and as my children hear and absorb everything around them, they are learning too.
>
> Upon graduation [from university] I moved to Ottawa. I started working as an employment counsellor, helping Inuit find jobs. Soon I moved on to the Inuit Head Start [preschool program], where I stayed for several years. It was like regaining the childhood I should have had. We taught the children their language, their culture, everything to instil in them that they should be extremely proud to be Inuk.

Worth noting here is the role of Inuktitut in the construction of these urban Inuit identities. Particularly for those raised in the South, as these women have been, access to Inuktitut and Inuit place-based knowledge becomes an important cultural resource, not only for defining Inuitness in Southern environments but also for accessing valued Northern Inuit resources, including connections to family, heritage, and place.

These women's remarks about Inuktitut find support in other interviews that we have been conducting with Inuit parents in Ottawa – who have noted the need for Inuktitut language instruction in preschool and after-school classes for their children. This is at least in part because those raised in the South commonly fail to learn Inuktitut, even when they have parents who were fluent in Inuktitut upon arrival in the South. As it happens, neither of these women were able to acquire Inuktitut, and it was English that had more practical value to them. This finding is consistent with what we have already seen in the Northern context, where the sense of being Inuit is linked to English as well as to Inuktitut. In this urban context, Inuit identity seems linked to an aspiration to use Inuktitut, which can be seen as an aspect of membership in community networks and practices and of an ancestral attachment to the North. Such aspirations and attachments can thus be seen to reflect the "reterritorialization" of "deterritorialized" Inuit identities.

This process of "reterritorialization" is, however, not without its own problems. In particular, urban Inuit are often sidelined, not only with respect to national bodies dealing with Inuit who live in the North, but also in the public imagination. In addition, Northern-raised and Southern-raised Inuit are often at odds with each other, given their respective geographic, historical, and cultural positions. Arguably, these tensions arise from the forms of desired symbolic capital that Northern-raised Inuit possess: linguistic and cultural knowledge seen as defining "authentic Inuitness." This knowledge is distinct from the symbolic capital of Southern-raised Inuit, which includes competence in English or French and the social capital necessary for urban life. Finally, urban Inuit populations in Ottawa (and elsewhere) display highly differentiated linguistic abilities, cultural knowledge, and socio-economic status. Notwithstanding these difficulties, however, communal ties continue to be an important aspect of imagined geographies for urban Inuit, who coalesce around common activities, heritage, and a sense of connectedness to the territorial North – even if physical "connectedness" to this North is absent (see Lobo, 2001; Howard-Bobiwash, 2003; Proulx, 2003; Weibel-Orlando, 1999).[16] Seen in this light, territoriality and identity formation are as much issues for Inuit in the South as they are for those in the North. What is more, Inuktitut, English, and French (the last particularly in Quebec) are all important – in the city and in the North – not just as a means to communicate and to survive, but as tangible identity markers, reflecting Inuitness in the twenty-first century.

Conclusion

In this chapter, I have shown how definitions of Aboriginal identity that have invoked blood quantum, racial phenotypes, and DNA analyses have had little currency in the discourse relating to Inuit identity in Canada – or to Aboriginal identity in Canada more generally. This is in spite of Canadian state policies governing indigeneity from the nineteenth century onward, which have sought to use such definitions to assimilate and ultimately eliminate the "Indian." One basic reason why the construction of Inuit identity was not significantly affected by these definitions is that such definitions largely disregarded the Inuit until the mid-twentieth century. I have also suggested a basis of both traditional and modern Inuit identity in ancestry and territoriality, highlighting the complexity of contemporary Inuit identity and its relation to territoriality.

Admittedly, this essay has been tentative and exploratory in nature and has drawn heavily from my experience as a non-Inuk living and working with Inuit. This means that a more exhaustive and nuanced discussion of Inuitness is still required, which must be left to Inuit investigators. Notwithstanding these limitations, the analysis presented here has, I hope, succeeded in giving some content and historical context to the notion of Inuit identity and territoriality. In particular, the analysis has pointed to links between language, culture, and the land

and suggested that the construction of Inuitness is not divorced from the struggles over sovereignty, autonomy, and resource management that have characterized contemporary Inuit political and social life.

NOTES

1 The First Nations of Canada include over 50 groups, such as the Cree, Haida, and Mohawk. See the Assembly of First Nations, "First Nations Population," at http://web.archive.org/web/20070319135953/http://www.afn.ca/article.asp?id=2918
2 These are the categories as specified as "Aboriginal" in section 35(2) of the *Constitution Act*, 1982. I use the term "Aboriginal" when referring to Indigenous peoples in the Canadian context; otherwise, the term "Indigenous" is used.
3 "Treaty Indians are persons who are registered under the *Indian Act* and can prove descent from a band that signed a treaty." Statistics Canada, "Registered Indian Status," http://www12.statcan.gc.ca/census-recensement/2006/dp-pd/prof/sip/Rp-eng.cfm?TABID=6&LANG=E&APATH=3&DETAIL=0&DIM=5&FL=A&FREE=0&GC=01&GID=614135&GK=1&GRP=1&PID=97450&PRID=0&PTYPE=97154&S=0&SHOWALL=0&SUB=0&Temporal=2006&THEME=73&VID=17726&VNAMEE=&VNAMEF=&D1=0&D2=0&D3=0&D4=0&D5=0&D6=0
4 *Nunavut Land Claims Agreement*, s. 35.3.1, at http://www.tunngavik.com/documents/beneficiaryProgramForms/Enrolment%20Program%20Description%20ENG.pdf
5 Note, however, that while Bill C-31 entitled women and their children to regain their lost status, it did not guarantee status for the next generation (that is, the children of these children) unless such children married status Indians. As it happens, band councils' recognition that large numbers of "C-31s" – that is, people who regained their Indian status after 1985 – would put too much pressure on limited band resources for housing, education, and social services led the federal government to distinguish between "Indian status," which it granted to those women and their descendents who qualified, and "Band membership," which was granted on the basis of criteria set by band leaders. The latter could be broader or narrower than the former and involve parents' status or blood quantum (50 per cent or 25 per cent), depending on the leadership (see Miller, 2004, pp. 43–6; Lawrence, 2003, p. 9).
6 See Lawrence (2003) for further discussion of this clause.

7 Provisions in the *Indian Act* that continue to discriminate against women were recently challenged under section 15 of the *Charter* in a British Columbia Court of Appeal case, *McIvor v. Canada (Registrar of Indian and Northern Affairs)*, 2009 BCCA 153. Chuck Strahl, the Minister of Indian Affairs, has recently announced that the Government will not appeal the British Columbia Court of Appeal's ruling on this case, paving the way for a more equitable treatment of women in the *Indian Act*.

8 This difference in the treatment of First Nations and Inuit by the federal government is the basis of ongoing legal action by Kiviaq, Canada's first Inuk lawyer – a matter described in the documentary *Kiviaq vs. Canada* (2006, Igloolik Isuma Productions Inc.).

9 On this, see, for example, Ann Meekitjuk Hanson, "What's in a Name? Names, as well as events, mark the road to Nunavut," at http://www.nunavut.com/nunavut99/english/name.html

10 It is important to note that while blood quantum does not define Inuitness, being a descendent of an Inuk does (and thus, having a "blood relation" is important). It is also important to note that while a "mixed-race" Inuk (i.e., a person with a White, Black, or Asian biological parent) might still "officially" count as Inuit, there are different forms of inclusion and exclusion at play in interpersonal relations at the community level. This raises questions regarding the legitimacy of one's "Inuit" status, or how "Inuit" one really is, based on the way one is perceived by other Inuit or the state. This point is taken up in more detail in the next section.

11 Mobilization for greater territorial control also coincided with mobilization for greater Inuit control over education, health care, law, environmental management, and social services. This movement for increased autonomy in the North has thus encompassed Inuit cultural, linguistic, and social practices as part of restructuring institutional arrangements and governance structures. This process has been conceived of as "Inuisation" (Quiñonez, 2003, p. 22), or the remaking of non-Inuit institutions into ones that are sensitive to Inuit needs, values, and futures (see, for example, Quiñonez, 2003; Berger, 2006; Simon, 2007; Inuit Tapiriit Kanatami and Inuit Circumpolar Council, 2007).

12 Although Jessen Williamson writes about Greenland and Greenlandic, the same naming practices apply to Inuktitut, which is closely related to Greenlandic.

13 Originally known as the Inuit Circumpolar Conference, this organization was founded in 1977.

14 However, Inuktitut-Cree bilingualism has been documented among Inuit who lived near Cree communities and were assisted by them in times of difficulty. On this, see Patrick (2003b).

15 It is worth noting that the maintenance of such territorial identities is greatly influenced by financial considerations related to the high cost of travel to and from the Arctic. For example, many Inuit in Ottawa can rarely if ever afford to visit their home communities.

16 Similar findings have been reported for other urban Aboriginal settings. According to Lobo (2001), for instance, new conceptions of Aboriginal space and place are being formed in urban centres. Urban Aboriginal communities emphasize participation, shared community activities, and networks of cooperation. While these communities are linked to rural spaces and traditions – links which can often be conceptualized as extensions of rural territories – the particular nature of these linkages varies among people and communities.

REFERENCES

Berger, T.R. (2006). Nunavut Land Claims Agreement Implementation Contract Negotiations for the Second Planning Period 2003–2013. Conciliator's Final Report, 1 March. http://www.aadnc-aandc.gc.ca/eng/1100100030982/1100100030985

Dorais, L.-J., & Sammons, S. (2000). Discourse and Identity in the Baffin Region. *Arctic Anthropology*, *37*(2), 92–110.

George, J. (2007). Nunavik Self-Rule Accord Looms. *Nunatsiaq News*. 20 July. http://www.nunatsiaqonline.ca/archives/2007/707/70720/news/nunavik/70720_328.html

Howard-Bobiwash, H. (2003). Women's Class Strategies as Activism in Native Community Building in Toronto 1950–1975. *American Indian Quarterly*, *27*(3/4), 566–82. http://dx.doi.org/10.1353/aiq.2004.0076

ICC. (2002). ICC-Alaska 2002 9th General Assembly of the Inuit Circumpolar Conference. http://inuitcircumpolar.com/index.php?ID=40&Lang=En

Inuit Tapiriit Kanatami and Inuit Circumpolar Council—Canada. (2007). Submission to the Parliamentary Review of the Canadian Environmental Protection Act (CEPA 1999), January. https://www.itk.ca/media/media-release/inuit-recommend-changes-canadian-environmental-protection-act

Jessen Williamson, K. (2006). *Inuit Post-Colonial Gender Relations in Greenland*. PhD Dissertation, Department of Anthropology, University of Aberdeen.

Lawrence, B. (2003). Gender, Race, and the Regulation of Native Identity in Canada and the United States: An Overview. *Hypatia, 18*(2), 3–31. http://dx.doi.org/10.1111/j.1527-2001.2003.tb00799.x

Lobo, S. (2001). Is Urban a Person or a Place? Characteristics of Urban Indian Country. In Susan Lobo & Kurt Peters (Eds.), *American Indians and the Urban Experience* (pp. 73–85). New York: Altamira Press.

Mackey, E. (2002). *The House of Difference: Cultural Politics and National Identity in Canada*. Toronto, ON: University of Toronto Press.

Miller, J.R. (2004). *Lethal Legacy: Current Native Controversies in Canada*. Toronto, ON: McClelland and Stewart.

Morse, B. (2002). *Comparative Assessments of the Position of Indigenous Peoples in Quebec, Canada, and Abroad*. Quebec City, QC: Bureau de coordination des études; Commission d'étude des questions afférents à l'accession du Québec à la souveraineté, Gouvernement du Québec. http://www.saic.gouv.qc.ca/publications/documents_inst_const/10-BradfordMorse.pdf

Morse, B. (2004). Presentation given at the Indigenous Law Conference, University of Ottawa, December.

Nuttall, M. (1992). *Arctic Homeland: Kinship, Community and Development in Northwest Greenland*. London: Belhaven Press.

Patrick, D. (2001). Languages of State and Social Categorization in an Arctic Quebec Community. In M. Heller and M. Martin-Jones (Eds.), *Voices of Authority: Education and Linguistic Difference* (pp. 297–314). Westport, CT: Ablex.

Patrick, D. (2003a). *Language, Politics, and Social Interaction in an Inuit Community*. New York: Mouton de Gruyter.

Patrick, D. (2003b). Language Socialization and Second Language Acquisition in a Multilingual Arctic Québec Community. In R. Bayley & S. Schecter (Eds.), *Language Socialization in Bi-and Multilingual Societies* (pp. 165–81). Clevedon, UK: Multilingual Matters.

Patrick, D., Tomiak, J., Brown, L., Langille, H., & Vieru, M. (2006). "Regaining The Childhood I Should Have Had": The Transformation of Inuit Identities, Institutions and Community in Ottawa. Paper presented to the Canadian Anthropology Society, Montreal, May.

Proulx, C. (2003). *Reclaiming Aboriginal Justice, Community and Identity*. Saskatoon, SK: Purich Publishing Ltd.

Quiñonez, C. (2003). Dentistry in Nunavut: Inuit Self-determination and the Politics of Health. In Jill E. Oakes et al. (Eds.), *Native Voices in Research* (pp. 21–33). Winnipeg: Aboriginal Issues Press.

Shore, C., & Wright, S. (1997). Policy: A New Field of Anthropology. In C. Shore & S. Wright (Eds.), *Anthropology of Policy* (pp. 3–39). London: Routledge.

Simon, M. (2007). Inuit: The Bedrock of Arctic Sovereignty. *Globe and Mail*, July 26, p. A15.

Smith, D. (1993). The Emergence of "Eskimo Status": An Examination of the Eskimo Disk List System and Its Social Consequences, 1925–1970. In N. Dyck & J. Waldram (Eds.), *Anthropology, Public Policy, and Native Peoples in Canada* (pp. 41–74). Montreal, QC: McGill-Queen's University Press.

Turner, D. (2006). *This Is Not a Peace Pipe: Towards a Critical Indigenous Philosophy*. Toronto, ON: University of Toronto Press.

Weibel-Orlando, J.A. (1999). *Indian Country, L.A.: Maintaining Ethnic Community in Complex Society* (Revised Edition). Chicago, IL: University of Illinois Press.

2 Federally Unrecognized Indigenous Communities in Canadian Contexts

BONITA LAWRENCE

Federally unrecognized Indigenous peoples are peoples that are not recognized as Indigenous by the state in which they are situated. Bruce Miller (2003) has addressed the fact that there are Indigenous peoples around the world who are unrecognized by states for a wide variety of reasons and face extremely diverse circumstances. For example, in some cases across the Americas, non-recognition relates to the policies of settler states which deny the existence of any Indigenous peoples within their boundaries at all, simply by declaring them as citizens incorporated into the nation – for example, in Peru, Uruguay, Guatemala (Miller, 2003), or French Guiana (Collomb, 2006). In other instances, where policies of *mestizaje* have suppressed language use and broken up communities, the most remote and culturally distinct peoples continue to be recognized as Indigenous; all others are said to have been incorporated into a culturally homogeneous nation, such as in Honduras (Euraque, 2007), or in certain regions of Nicaragua (Gould, 1998). In other places, particularly where African slavery was present for significant lengths of time, perceptions of Indigenous people are formulated through colonialist assumptions equating cultural purity with notions of racial purity. In these regions, Indigenous peoples have been assumed to be extinct, particularly throughout the Caribbean (Forte, 2006) or in parts of Brazil (Warren, 2001).

In Canada and the U.S., federal recognition is imbricated within bodies of law defining Indigenous identity. It is this context, where federal recognition is intimately tied to legal definitions of "who is an Indian," that concerns this chapter. While most of the existing writing concerns federally unrecognized tribes in the U.S., it is the Canadian context that will be the primary focus of this essay. In the process, the complexities of Indigenous identity and the divisions that can arise among federally unrecognized Indigenous communities will also be explored.

Federally Unrecognized Communities in Canada

Control of Indigenous people in Canada is maintained through a body of legislation known as the *Indian Act*. Through this legislation, the only level of Indigenous governance recognized by Canada has been the elected governments imposed at the local reserve or band level. Definitions of Indianness from the start have controlled who is recognized as an Indian band, who could get any land under the treaties, and who could live on this land. Under the *Indian Act*, both individuals and whole communities can lose (or be denied) Indian status for a variety of reasons (Lawrence, 2004). However, in Canada, unlike in the U.S., there is no explicit legal text or formal means whereby a federally unrecognized nation can gain federal recognition (Miller, 2003, p. 138). Existing bands can be amalgamated or divided, and new bands declared into existence by government action; however, to form a new band, all of the membership must be capable of acquiring Indian status. Many federally unrecognized bands have some members who have Indian status from relatives or ancestors; however, most members of federally unrecognized bands or nations, by definition, are composed of peoples who do not have, and cannot get, Indian status (W. Wabie, Beaverhouse First Nation, personal communication, August 2004).

There are a number of ways in which Indigenous groups in Canada can become federally unrecognized. Some small nations, such as the Passamaquoddy Nation of New Brunswick, or the Sinixt Nation in British Columbia, have federal recognition in the U.S. but not in Canada. Both nations have had lands which traditionally spanned the Canadian/American border, but both were, at different times, driven from their lands in Canada by a combination of settler violence, the establishment of the international border, and *Indian Act* policies which effectively prevent those enumerated in the U.S. from "counting" as Indians in Canada.[1]

Other bands are federally unrecognized because Canada has refused to honour historic relationships or has disregarded the traditional boundaries of Indigenous nations. The Caldwell Band in southwestern Ontario, for example, had their traditional lands recognized by colonial authorities after the war of 1812; however, their lands were subsequently taken by settlers (N. Johnson, personal communication,

November 1998). After 212 years, they finally won an agreement in principle with Ottawa to settle their land claim; however, they have had to fight considerable local resistance in their efforts to purchase the land for a reserve for their community (Smoke, 2001).

Another group whose traditional lands were affected by the arbitrary division of Cree territory into the provinces of Quebec and Ontario is MoCreebec Council of the Cree Nation. Its membership are all status Indians living in Moosonee and Moose Factory but who have no "reserve" or "band status." MoCreebec's traditional territories are in Quebec, where they have been denied recognition as beneficiaries of the James Bay and Northern Quebec Agreement (Kapashesit, 2004).

However, most federally unrecognized bands or nations are created by the nature of the treaty process itself. After the 1850s, most treaties were generally not negotiated on a nation-to-nation basis, but with multiple Indigenous bands of different nations for large areas of land at a time. In this process, it was common for some bands to be left out of the treaty process altogether, either through being overlooked by treaty commissioners or being elsewhere in their territories when the commissioners arrived to negotiate.

For example, the Teme-Augama Anishnabai in central Ontario were left out of the Robinson Huron Treaty in 1850, while the Lubicon Cree of northern Alberta were not included in Treaty Eight in 1899. Because of this, both groups were administratively eliminated as recognized groups, despite the fact that both had asserted their rights over their traditional territories for generations and at times had been acknowledged to have those rights by representatives of the federal governments. Both groups, faced with the destruction of their traditional territories, have used extensive means to protect their lands, and both have had to deal with the Canadian government's determination to stop them by attempting to stir up dissident factions within their communities or creating new bands and granting them rights to parts of the territory.[2]

The primary means by which federally unrecognized communities in Canada can gain federal recognition are either to assert Aboriginal title through the courts (if a treaty already exists for the territory), or to take part in the comprehensive claims process if no treaty has been signed in the territory. However, it is precisely through the process of seeking federal recognition that the informal boundaries maintaining "insider" and "outsider" status in federally unrecognized communities become formalized into definitions of "who is an Indian." It is therefore important to take into consideration the very real problems that Bruce Miller highlights: how is the membership within federally unrecognized communities to be understood?

Miller suggests that the central problem relating to membership in federally unrecognized communities is precisely the intensity of colonial contact that almost always assaults and fragments Indigenous identities (2003, p. 20). In Canada, legislation and policies aimed precisely at destroying the cultural identities of Native peoples were in place for over a century. From outlawing the spiritual and ceremonial practices that held people together, to taking Native children away to residential schools or the foster care system, these policies have had a shattering effect on Native communities (Fournier & Crey, 1997).

In the wake of this massive and deliberately created cultural disarray, where many people no longer speak the languages that would have imparted their cultural knowledge, there is no clear consensus about what makes a person Indigenous in many Indigenous communities. In these circumstances, it has been easy for hegemonic considerations of Indigenous identity to take priority – so that increasing numbers of Native people only know themselves as Indian through their status cards (Lawrence, 2004).

Moreover, federally unrecognized Indigenous communities have had to withstand the assimilative effects of having to blend in to the settler culture in order to survive on its fringes. For many of these communities, facing a continual risk of settler violence (Lovelace, 2006) has meant that speaking Indigenous languages was deliberately discouraged; it also has involved individuals doing their best to integrate themselves into the settler culture through adapting to its institutions (Huitema, 2000, p. 170). In some cases, individuals have adopted the identity of the dominant culture and severed their ties to Indigenous communities altogether, while many others have simply made efforts to hide their identities in order to protect themselves and their families from the effects of racism.

With this history, the elders from federally unrecognized communities may still carry a strong sense of cultural identity inside; however, as more and more of a suppressed culture becomes inaccessible to subsequent generations and phenotypic markers of "Indianness" are lost, many feel that they are "not really Indian" or "not Indian enough" (A. Cota III, personal communication, 4 November 2007). While some communities are focusing precisely on cultural revival in order to address this phenomenon, it is far more common for Indigenous identities in federally unrecognized communities to be in flux, rather than cohesive and intact.

Colonial policies have therefore created profound confusion in many communities about the boundaries between what is Indigenous and what is not. Because of this, disputes about identity claims frequently arise that are capable of fragmenting families and communities (Miller, 2003, p. 24). However, Miller also notes that Indigenous identities cannot be clarified by accepting external definitions, with their brutalizing, instrumental, and frequently politically motivated analyses of identity. He proposes, therefore, that federally unrecognized Indigenous identities can best be examined by taking both history and self-ascription into account, and relying on loose definitions rather than those that emphasize tightness, arbitrariness, and exclusion (2003, pp. 41–2). It is instructive to examine these processes in detail by exploring identity issues among two federally unrecognized groups – the Algonquins of eastern Ontario and the Mi'kmaqs of Newfoundland – that I have conducted research with for much of the past ten years.

Fractured Homeland: Federally Unrecognized Algonquins in Eastern Ontario

In 1992, land claim negotiations began between the Algonquins of Pikwakanagan, the only federally recognized Algonquin reserve in Ontario, and the governments of Ontario and Canada. From the moment that the land claim was launched, the existence of large numbers of Algonquins who had never been federally recognized as Indians rose to the forefront. With an estimated 1,900 Algonquins with Indian status (K. Whiteduck, personal communication, July 2005), and over 5,000 Algonquins who are non-status,[3] by far the majority of Algonquins in Ontario are non-status. To understand how this came about, the history is important.

The traditional home of Algonquin people has always been the Ottawa River watershed; however, the four centuries since Europeans first entered their territories have brought profound change. While the epidemics and warfare that marked the Algonquin experience of the French presence were traumatic (Trigger & Day, 1994, p. 70), the British victory over the French in 1763 was disastrous. A territorial marker was driven through the heart of the Algonquin homeland, as the *Constitution Act* of 1791 divided Algonquin territory into the Provinces of Upper and Lower Canada, with the Ottawa River as the dividing line (Holmes, 1993, vol. 1, p. 5). From the 1770s until the 1850s, as squatters, loggers, and settlers poured into the Ottawa Valley, the Algonquin leadership submitted at least twenty-eight petitions requesting a treaty to representatives of the Crown (Holmes, 1993, vol. 2). By the 1840s, however, petitions had also begun to come from individual groups of Algonquins whose traditional territories had been entirely overrun by settlers, seeking title to some part of their traditional lands to enable them to take up farming.

While land was promised in a number of locations, ultimately only the Golden Lake settlement was recognized as a reserve in 1873. Subsequently, all other Algonquins seeking settlements were ordered to either go there or to Maniwaki, one of the reserves set aside for Algonquins in Quebec (Holmes, 1993, vol. 2, pp. 139, 160). Many stayed in their family territories and refused to move. However, once an Algonquin reserve had been established in Ontario, Canada washed its hands of the off-reserve Algonquin presence in the Ottawa Valley. Subsequently, the only federally acknowledged Algonquins in Ontario were those at Golden Lake. While settler histories attest to a continued Algonquin presence throughout eastern Ontario, the presence of Algonquins who did not move to Golden Lake was ignored in official records.

Meanwhile, Algonquins in Ontario and Quebec faced diverging colonial experiences of "Algonquinness." In Ontario, by the turn of the century, survival for most Algonquins meant eking out a precarious existence, hunting and trapping "illegally," doing odd jobs for settlers, and barely surviving on marginal lands in areas too poor for farming. In such a context, language was suppressed and cultural practices diminished through alienation from the land.

In Quebec, however, logging, hydroelectic development, and mining did not begin to take place until much later in the nineteenth century, allowing the fur trade to remain central to peoples' livelihoods until the late 1940s (Holmes, 1993, vol. 2, pp. 210, 231, 252). Because of this, Algonquin language and land-based cultural practices have been maintained in Quebec, and over the years Algonquin identity in Quebec and Ontario has begun to reflect different experiences and histories.

In 1973, the Calder decision ruled that Canada has a legal obligation to address Aboriginal title (Monture-Angus, 1999, p. 66). In response, Canada developed the comprehensive claims policy to address areas where no treaties have been signed. With this policy, Canada defines the process and maintains firm control of what outcomes are considered possible. For First Nations, this generally means being offered powers akin to that of a municipality, a cash settlement, and the demarcation of some areas of shared jurisdiction. The price is the permanent surrender of Aboriginal title to their entire land base (Comprehensive

Land Claims Policy, 1987, p. 12). Despite these onerous terms, because Native peoples currently control less than 1 per cent of their traditional lands (St. Germain, 2001), many cherish the hope that through a land claim they can at least win back access to some of their territory. Others are skeptical about the process.

When Pikawakanagan discovered, during the process of conducting other research, that title to the Ottawa River watershed had never been surrendered, it therefore became apparent that the possibility existed for Algonquins to finally negotiate a treaty – by asserting Aboriginal title to the entire Ottawa River watershed.

Initially, it was envisioned that Quebec and Ontario would proceed together. However, the different circumstances facing Quebec and Ontario Algonquins – including the different provincial regimes that each group faced – did not easily allow for common priorities. While both sides initially planned to conduct research for the land claim, ultimately a decision was reached whereby Golden Lake would claim the Algonquin territory south of the Ottawa River while Quebec communities would eventually make a claim for Algonquin land north of the river (Sarazin, 1989, p. 191).

The result has been two land claims – one involving Quebec Algonquins, and one in Ontario for just under one-third of the territory that is south of the Ottawa River. The Canadian government thus negotiates separately with different parts of the Algonquin Nation, which profoundly weakens both sides.

In 1990, in an effort to ensure that as many Ontario Algonquins as possible were part of the land claim, Pikwakanagan began calling meetings in areas where federally unrecognized communities had historically existed. At those meetings, they encouraged those non-status Algonquins who attended to set up area committees to broadly represent each region where they were situated (Sarazin, 1998, p. 2). However, this process left out a handful of already-existing federally unrecognized communities that had formally organized themselves to protect their lands and revitalize their traditions before the land claim began (AAFNA, 1996).

It is almost certain that Pikwakanagan wanted groups of non-status Algonquins who were malleable, who would be grateful to be recognized by Pikwakanagan, and therefore would bolster the numbers of Algonquins in the land claim without disturbing a status quo managed by Pikwakanagan. By comparison, each of the three federally unrecognized communities that had already formally organized themselves had an expectation of self-representation, and had a strong leadership who might potentially represent a challenge to Pikwakanagan's control over the land claim (B. Lovelace, personal communication, July 2003).

However, in avoiding those communities whose leaders were strong, Pikwakanagan excluded the very people who had extensive experience of nation-building among federally unrecognized communities. By comparison, the Pikwakanagan leadership had little awareness or experience in working across the very real differences in recent histories, in the structures of their communities, and in the different legal regimes governing the status and non-status Algonquins.

Within the negotiations, these differences were manifested almost immediately around questions of enrolment and representation. The basic question – of how issues of eligibility could be sorted out without proper representation, and yet how representation could be determined without first addressing eligibility, that is, *who* is being represented – became highly charged.

Pikwakanagan chose to address the question of eligibility before an agreed-upon process for working together between Pikwakanagan and the area committees (formed to represent non-status Algonquins) had been worked out. This haste on the part of Pikwakanagan was deliberate. With potentially thousands of people of Algonquin descent situated throughout the Ottawa River watershed, the leadership wanted to narrow the criteria to allow in only those that they considered to be "real" Algonquins. From their perspective, failure to narrow the criteria would risk creating "paper Indians" who might potentially manipulate an Algonquin identity for private gain and therefore jeopardize the land claim.

The leadership of Pikwakanagan showed little comprehension of the identity issues that many non-status Algonquins were struggling with (Gehl, 2003). For those who were federally unrecognized, the land claim was forcing them, almost overnight, to address the complexities of Native identity and the rewriting of their immediate sense of self as "Indian." Status Algonquins had no means of understanding that many Algonquins were doing this not for personal gain, but because it was an identity that their families, isolated in racist environments for generations, had been unable to either wholly claim or entirely leave behind.

The Algonquin Enrollment Law, created by Pikwakanagan in 1995, required non-status Algonquins to prove their descent from a historic schedule of known Algonquins (Kanatiio, 1998) in order to take part in the land claim negotiations. Pikwakanagan initially required that individuals be of one-quarter blood descent from this list; in the face of massive resistance from non-status Algonquins, this was dropped to one-eighth blood quantum (Sarazin, 1998, p. 2). For the non-status Algonquins, the lower blood quantum requirement was needed to offset the manner in which the schedule that they had to trace their identities from minimized their provable blood quantum by disregarding Algonquin descent along female lines. The list of known Algonquins, drawn from European sources that disregarded Native women, contained only the names of Algonquin men, so that the non-status people had no means of proving any lineage derived from female Algonquin ancestors (Gehl, 2003, p. 66).

Finally, particularly for the older communities that had a cohesive sense of who the Algonquin people within them were, the Algonquin Enrollment Law allowed for no community recognition of membership. Pikwakanagan therefore denied the non-status communities the very right that most status Indian bands currently insist upon – the right to define their own membership.

Although nominally an attempt to move beyond the *Indian Act* to include Algonquins without Indian status, Pikwakanagan's version of rebuilding Algonquin nationhood continuously involved developing criteria that recreated the *Indian Act*. In the process, Pikwakanagan effectively forestalled any real organic process of identity-building or nation-rebuilding, both for the non-status Algonquins *and* for those with Indian status. Indeed, Pikwakanagan's leadership saw no apparent need or reason for those with Indian status to broaden their own vision of what an Algonquin was, but continued to maintain a vision of Algonquinness shaped by over a century of living under the *Indian Act*.

By 2000, the divisions between Pikwakanagan and the non-status representatives were nearing a crisis. The breaking point came over the issue of hunting when non-status representatives in the land claim were granted the right to maintain their own hunting regimes, distinct from Pikwakanagan's, and were granted an equal number of tags to shoot moose as Pikwakanagan was (Tennescoe, 2002). When this transpired, the tensions exploded into a generalized backlash from the leadership and general membership of Pikwakanagan against the non-status Algonquins (Majaury, 2005).

However, from the leaflets circulating through Pikwakanagan at the time (Algonquins of Greater Golden Lake First Nation, 2000), it was obvious that what was really fuelling the backlash was anger and fear that the rights and privileges attached to an Indian status card were being eroded and subsumed by the community membership cards issued by each of the non-status communities to enable their members to hunt. There was also a generalized feeling that far too many non-status people were being enrolled as Algonquins. The result was a call to stop the process by repealing the Enrollment Law, and to resume the land claim negotiations with only Pikwakanagan at the table, representing all status Algonquins (Ozawanimke, 2002).

After a two-year halt in the process, a fundamentally changed land claim process resumed. The status and non-status Algonquins were now separately represented, with the primary negotiations carried on by non-Native lawyers taking instruction from both groups. Under the new regime, there was to be no further talk of "nation-building" or "citizenship"; instead, there would be "electors" and "beneficiaries." In place of an organized Algonquin political representation on the land claim, speaking with one voice, there was to be a team of Algonquin negotiation representatives speaking without having any common voice to represent them (Potts, 2005).

Pikwakanagan was granted seven representatives, consisting of their chief and council, who could be deposed through normal band elections. For the non-status communities, however, who had almost no band structures outside of the leaders who spoke for them at the land claim table, each were granted one community representative, and these representatives were given inordinate levels of power in their communities. The representatives could not be deposed if the community wished it; while they could be voted out, the fact that as leaders they also controlled the lists of names for canvassing votes meant that every election that has taken place to the present has only confirmed their ongoing places at the negotiating table.

Nor could communities choose to opt out of the land claim if their representative did not wish to. Furthermore, the new regime enabled new communities to be formed by anybody with 125 supporters. As "communities" have multiplied, it has created tremendous fragmentation among the non-status Algonquins. It has also created tremendous factionalism within communities, as grassroots members continuously express their sense of outrage at the power vested in negotiators, the abuses and arbitrariness of that power, the potential for corruption, and the absolute disinterest in community building from representatives who focus on the land claim and little else. In general, the voices of dissidents, ignored by most of their own representatives, also tend to be ignored by the land claims administration.

The situation of the Newfoundland Mi'kmaq provides an interesting contrast. Although both the Algonquins and the Mi'kmaq are facing a federal government that utilizes identity legislation to divide people, the Mi'kmaq, with a different set of circumstances, have struggled not for a land claim, but for the option to be recognized under the *Indian Act*.

Reclaiming Ktaqamkuk: The Struggle for Recognition by Newfoundland Mi'kmaq

Like the Algonquins, most Newfoundland Mi'kmaq communities have not been federally recognized under the *Indian Act*. However, Indigenous people in Newfoundland are in a unique position in that Canada did not bring them under the *Indian Act* when Newfoundland joined Confederation in 1949, as had been normative whenever a province joined Confederation prior to that time. Newfoundland joined Canada at a time when Canada was already exploring possible ways of divesting federal responsibility for Indians (Hanrahan, 2003, p. 219). Jerry Wetzel (1999) has suggested that federal officials at the time were of the opinion that denying Indian status to Newfoundland's Mi'kmaq would allow forces of assimilation to work on the Mi'kmaq unobstructed by possible beneficial effects of federal services and benefits (p. 10). Given that substantial modernization and development policies were expected to be implemented in Newfoundland after Confederation, it would appear that denying Indian status to Newfoundland Mi'kmaq would have offered the federal government the perfect opportunity to observe just how long Native people could hang on to their identities without either access to their traditional lands *or* legal status as Indians.

Newfoundland Mi'kmaq are unique in another way, in that historically they have been subjected to a different colonial order than that of Native people in the rest of Canada. As a direct colony of Britain, no formal system of regulating Native identity, such as the *Indian Act*, was developed for Newfoundland. Furthermore, although considerable attempts had been made in the nineteenth century to effectively colonize and develop the interior of Newfoundland, the island remained fundamentally a fishing colony, with the greater part of its White population established along the shorelines, and only a few areas of resource development in specific locations within the interior. Because of this, Mi'kmaq people in Newfoundland enjoyed a relative freedom and access to land within the interior and along the west coast long after Mi'kmaq people in the Maritimes had had the bulk of their land and livelihood taken away.

For example, in 1822, at a time when land loss, starvation, and epidemics were decimating the Maritime Mi'kmaq, explorers into the interior of Newfoundland spoke with Mi'kmaq who had never seen a White man before (Hanrahan, 2003, p. 207). This is not to suggest that the interior of Newfoundland was entirely free of a White presence. But it was only in the late nineteenth century that hydroelectric development, large-scale logging, and the promotion of sport hunting for tourism began to make life on the land more precarious for Mi'kmaq people (Hanrahan, 2003, p. 209).

Prior to Confederation in 1949, there were sixty-five areas where Mi'kmaq people congregated (Agreement in Principle for the Recognition of the Qalipu Mi'kmaq First Nation, Appendix B, November 2007), while at the time of Confederation at least thirty-six distinct Mi'kmaq communities existed (ibid., 6). The more geographically isolated communities still relied on the land for the most of their food, and they were able to maintain cultural cohesion through their distance from white people. However, the communities that were located closer to areas of industrial development faced pressures to suppress language and to become silent about cultural affiliation. With Confederation, a program of road-building, centralization, and urbanization was begun. It was Mi'kmaq people who bore the brunt of this expansion, as it was primarily their lands which were used for development; moreover, with road-building, even the more remote communities were increasingly facing an influx of settlers who had been relocated from outport communities by Canadian government policies. With increased roads also came increased surveillance from game wardens and police, and the last subsistence economies began to unravel (C. White, Chief of Flat Bay, personal communication, July 2004). But it was not until drastic and unprecedented fines were introduced to prevent local people from hunting and fishing that the ability of Mi'kmaq communities to rely on the land at all was effectively curtailed. While sports hunting was being encouraged, local people faced massive fines, jail terms, and confiscation of their vehicles for violating game rules that made it difficult to get their food from the land (McGrath, 1996, p. 89). By the 1970s, as removal from the land forced Mi'kmaq people to disperse, less than a dozen communities existed.

Throughout the 1970s, Newfoundland Mi'kmaq began organizing to address their desire for federal recognition, submitting a comprehensive land claim to the southern third of the island, which encompassed the traditional territory that Mi'kmaq people had always used (Bartels, 1987, p. 32). While the federal government has alternately negotiated and forced the matter back into the courts, the Newfoundland government has consistently denied that the Mi'kmaq are Indigenous to Newfoundland (Hanrahan, 2003, p. 228).

Indeed, in Newfoundland, the relationship between Mi'kmaq peoples and the land has been continuously obscured and denied through what has been called the "Mi'kmaq mercenary myth" – the notion that the Mi'kmaq were imported from the Maritimes as mercenaries by the French to hunt down and destroy the Beothuk. Newfoundland Mi'kmaq, then, have been represented in the eyes of the public as just another settler group who are not Indigenous to Newfoundland, and who, moreover, are historically tainted for having murdered the Beothuk (Bartels & Bartels, 2005). While many contemporary Newfoundland writers appear to have finally rejected the Mi'kmaq mercenary myth, at all levels of Newfoundland society, there is still a silence about Mi'kmaq presence.

The registration of the people of Conne River under the *Indian Act* took place in 1984, after an extensive struggle by Mi'kmaq people across the province, including occupations of government offices and a hunger strike (Hanrahan, 2003, p. 221). However, registration for Conne River was easily justified in that the community was relatively isolated along the south coast; moreover, a reserve had once been surveyed there in the late nineteenth century (Jackson, 1993, p. 116).

For the Canadian government, allowing *one* reserve to be created (to become, almost by definition, the "real" Mi'kmaq of Newfoundland) was a crucial means through which the identities of all other Newfoundland Mi'kmaq could be called into question. To successfully maintain a system of identity legislation, with its grammar of racial difference, the presence of *some* "authentic Indians" is the tool through which other Native people can be dismissed as "inauthentic." In Newfoundland, remoteness from White settlements became the single criterion separating so-called real Mi'kmaqs from those who live among Whites. This distinction has been reproduced by bureaucrats and "experts" alike. For example, Noel Lyon of the Canadian Human Rights Commission, who is deeply sympathetic to Mi'kmaq concerns, nevertheless concluded that registration under the *Indian Act* was "unviable" for communities that share territory with non-Natives; from this perspective, only remote and so-called untouched Mi'kmaq are connected to the land and can *really* be Indians (Lyon, 1993, pp. 21–4).

However, non-status Mi'kmaq have often been reluctant to drive a wedge between themselves and their non-Mi'kmaq neighbours by speaking about Mi'kmaq land rights. For some bands, their traditional lands have already been appropriated by local Whites or destroyed for local industrial development. Others would like to assert jurisdiction over their land simply to protect it. The few people who have tried to assert their Aboriginal rights to hunt and fish have faced tremendous threats from local Whites (T. John, Glenwood First Nation, personal communication, July 2004). Furthermore, the notion of land rights has been confused with having a reserve, something that many Newfoundland Mi'kmaq are equivocal about, believing that they would be forced to give up their homes and move to a reserve if one was created for them (G. Mai Muise, personal communication, November 2007). At present, few Newfoundland grassroots people know anything about the concept of having urban reserves for economic development, which some Native communities in Western Canada have acquired. With a handful of urban reserves in different regions, Mi'kmaq people could provide local economies with a much-needed stimulus – not only for themselves, but for all Newfoundlanders.

Instead, in late 2007, an agreement in principle was reached between the Federation of Newfoundland Indians and the federal government to create a landless band known as Qalipu Mi'kmaq First Nations Band (Sheppard, 2008). The 10,500 Mi'kmaq who at the time were affiliated with nine federally unrecognized bands became part of one huge band. While the agreement in principle has suggested that the membership will be eligible for all benefits due to status Indians, Indian Affairs legislation currently stipulates that most benefits accrue only to status Indians who have a reserve.

Enrolment in the Qalipu Mi'kmaq First Nation is due to close by December 2012. By March 2012, almost 23,000 individuals were registered (according to Aboriginal Affairs and Northern Development Canada). While the Qalipu band governance is centralized to a chief and band council structure, it is further divided into nine wards, corresponding to the former nine unrecognized bands – thus enabling people to still deal at the local level with the structures that they are familiar with. Indeed, some communities, such as the Benoit Lnu'k/Mi'kmaq Community, while recognizing the leadership of the Qalipu Mi'kmaq First Nation and referring to themselves as status Indians under the Qalipu band, still consider their own community to be an independent First Nation (Benoit Lnu'k/Mi'kmaq Community, 2012).

It's important to note that those registered under the Qalipu Mi'kmaq First Nation as of December 2012 will be considered "Founding Members," with full Indian status. From this point onward, under the terms of the 1985 *Indian Act*, the descendents of these founding members will have full Indian status only if both of their parents are status Indians. Under current *Indian Act* rules, intermarriage is a ticking time bomb for status Indians, making it easy for successive generations of Newfoundland Mi'kmaq to lose the Indian status that they struggled for over thirty years to obtain.

Conclusions

For federally unrecognized Algonquins, the land claim was begun by Pikwakanagan but quickly became the venue whereby federal recognition became possible. Ultimately, however, Algonquins have been stymied by the divisions created through the colonial process, both between Quebec and Ontario and between status and non-status Algonquins. The land claim, ultimately, has only deepened the fissures and fractures among different parts of the Algonquin nation created initially by the colonization process. At this point, it is detrimental to the process of reunifying and rebuilding Algonquin nationhood, particularly for the federally unrecognized communities.

In Newfoundland, the drive to be recognized under the *Indian Act* was fragmented in 1984 by the recognition of one band, and the denial of recognition to nine others. The fault line of divisions that the federal government created was the notion that true "Indianness" vanishes with too much contact with Whites – and that reserves cannot be created in areas where Native peoples do not live apart from White societies. Ultimately, while the government has been successful in creating a permanent difference between Miawpukek (Conne River) as a First Nation with a reserve and Qalipu Mi'kmaq First Nation as a landless band, they have at least been unsuccessful in permanently dividing Newfoundland Mi'kmaq into status and non-status people.

It appears that to be truly effective, divisions between those with status and those who are non-status must take place over the long term. In the case of the Algonquins, Pikwakanagan was established in 1873; for over 130 years, they were treated as the only Algonquin community in Ontario. It is almost inevitable that gradually the people of Pikwakanagan would believe themselves to be "more Indian" than the non-status Algonquins, and therefore uniquely entitled not only to control what happens to Algonquin territory but to define who would be recognized as a non-status Algonquin for the purposes of the land claim.

By comparison, in the Newfoundland context, all individuals with a claim to Mi'kmaq ancestry were initially in the same boat – they all had to prove their ancestry through having their genealogies traced to ancestors who were known Mi'kmaqs. During the process, there were no pre-existing status Indians demanding that a certain level of blood quantum must be maintained, or otherwise attempting to control the means through which a non-status person was allowed to "count" as Mi'kmaq.

When the membership rolls for Qalipu Mi'kmaq First Nation are closed in December 2012, Indian status will be normative for all Newfoundland Mi'kmaq. In this context, the strong beliefs existing at present and frequently expressed – that all Mi'kmaq are one people, regardless of Indian status – may become eroded and corrupted by the process of coming under the *Indian Act*, particularly if individuals begin to lose their status through the myriad ways in which this can currently happen under the *Indian Act*. In a context where the only recognized Mi'kmaq are those who have Indian status, those who lose their Indian status will be marginalized, isolated, and considered non-Indian.

In the case of the Algonquins, a number of communities have turned their backs on the land claim, choosing to focus on rebuilding traditional governance, cultural renewal, and protecting their traditional lands. Some communities, such as Ardoch Algonquin First Nation, exemplify an ethic whereby Algonquin identity is believed to come from the land, rather than the land claim. Ardoch came into existence as a modern community through their struggles to protect their wild rice crop from provincial jurisdiction in 1979 (Delisle, 2001), and for over twenty years have fought to maintain Algonquin jurisdiction over the land. They have done so in the courts, where they have successfully asserted non-status Algonquin hunting rights through the *Perry* decision (Darwell, 1998); at an Environmental Review Tribunal, to protect water rights within the Rideau River watershed (Koschade, 2003); and through a blockade, to protect the land from uranium mining (AAFNA, 2007), despite fines and prison sentences. Indeed, some of the youth in the community have stated that every struggle that Ardoch engages with gives them a powerful sense of identity as an Algonquin in the twenty-first century. And while a number of other communities also have a history of independent organizing outside of the land claim, all of these communities are ultimately marginalized and rendered voiceless through a comprehensive claim process which has, in a sense, become hegemonic – through a negotiating committee that names itself the Algonquins of Ontario and claims to speak for all Algonquins. In 2012, as the possibility of an agreement looms, increasing numbers of non-status Algonquins are having their ancestry challenged by the Algonquins of Ontario (H. Majaury, personal communication, June 2011). There is no question that these individuals are of Native heritage – the question is whether their ancestors were Algonquin or whether they were from other Indigenous nations who historically had relations with Algonquins and therefore lived in the Algonquin homeland under Algonquin law.

It may be important to consider whether these kinds of divisions are an inevitable consequence of becoming federally recognized at all. It might be instrumental to look briefly at the U.S., where a federal recognition process has been in place since 1978. Sara-Larus Tolley, in focusing on the struggle of the California-based Honey Lake Maidus, has described how the drive for federal recognition for many federally unrecognized tribes generally originates from a desire to right historical wrongs, and to assert their sovereignty as Indigenous peoples despite discourses of extinction, as well as a desire for economic benefits for impoverished communities. And yet, for the Honey Lake Maidus, there is also an awareness that federal recognition inevitably involves a postural submission to the state, a requirement to bureaucratize and implement the procedures and formal definitions of tribal citizenship needed from federally recognized tribes. They acknowledge that this signifies the loss of other freedoms, such as the right to revitalize traditional governments and redevelop themselves according to their own culturally unique vision of who they are (Tolley, 2006, pp. 149, 191).

It may well be that the process of federal recognition inevitably divides, corrupts, and bureaucratizes Indigenous nations, and that other, and more traditional means of survival should be considered as alternatives.

NOTES

1 For an understanding of the issues relating to the Passamaquoddies, who are recognized in Maine but not New Brunswick, see Taillon (2001); for

issues relating to the Sinixt, who are recognized as belonging to the Colville Confederated Tribes in Washington but not as Sinixt in Canada, see Miller (2004), pp. 140–6.

2 For the history and circumstances of the Teme-Augama Anishnabai, see Potts (1989) and McNab (1998); for the Lubicon Cree, see Richardson (1989) and Miller (2003).

3 As of January 2005, Joan Holmes, enrollment officer for the Algonquin land claim, listed 5,327 non-status Algonquins potentially eligible to be registered as beneficiaries under the land claim; the process at that point was still unfinished (Holmes, 2005).

REFERENCES

AAFNA (Ardoch Algonquin First Nation and Allies). (1996). To All Members of the Ardoch Algonquin First Nation and Allies. February 7.

AAFNA (Ardoch Algonquin First Nation and Allies). (2007). Statement on Uranium Mining, June 23. http://www.aafna.ca/Uranium_mining.html

Algonquins of Greater Golden Lake First Nation. (2000). 21st Century Algonquin Moose War. http://www.greatergoldenlake.com/21st.html

Bartels, D. (1987). Ktaqamkuk Ilnui Saqimawoutie: Aboriginal Rights and the Myth of the Micmac Mercenaries in Newfoundland. In B. Cox (Ed.), *Native People, Native Lands: Canadian Indians, Inuit and Metis* (pp. 32–6). Ottawa, ON: Carlton University Press.

Bartels, D., & Bartels, A. (2005). Mi'gmaq Lives: Aboriginal Identity in Newfoundland. In U. Lischke & D. Mnab (Eds.), *Walking a Tightrope: Aboriginal People and Their Representations* (pp. 249–80). Waterloo, ON: Wilfrid Laurier University Press.

Benoit Lnu'k/Mi'kmaq Community. (2012). Penwa' Mawi-Amskwesewey L'nue'kati. March. http://www.benoitfirstnation.ca/bfn_home.html

Collomb, G. (2006). Disputing Aboriginality: French Amerindians in European Guiana. In M. Forte (Ed.), *Indigenous Resurgence in the Contemporary Caribbean* (pp. 197–212). New York: Peter Lang.

Comprehensive Land Claims Policy. (1987). Ottawa: Minister of Supply and Services Canada.

Darwell, T. (1998). *Canada and the History without a People: Identity, Tradition and Struggle in a Non-Status Aboriginal Community.* Unpublished MA Thesis, History Department, Queen's University, Kingston, ON.

Delisle, S. (2001). *Coming Out of the Shadows: Asserting Identity and Authority in a Layered Homeland: The 1979–82 Mud Lake Wild Rice Confrontation.* Unpublished MA Thesis, Department of Geography, Queen's University, Kingston, ON.

Euraque, D. (2007). Free Pardos and Mulattos Vanquish Indians: Cultural Civility as Conquest and Modernity in Honduras. In D. Davis (Ed.), *Beyond Slavery: The Multilayered Legacy of Africans in Latin America and the Caribbean* (pp. 81–108). Baltimore, MD: Rowman and Littlefield Publishing.

Forte, M. (2006). The Dual Absences of Extinction and Marginality – What Difference Does An Indigenous Presence Make? In M. Forte (Ed.), *Indigenous Resurgence in the Contemporary Caribbean* (pp. 1–18). New York: Peter Lang.

Fournier, S., & Crey, E. (1997). *Stolen From Our Embrace: The Abduction of First Nations Children and the Restoration of Aboriginal Communities*. Toronto, ON: Douglas and McIntyre.

Gehl, L. (2003). The Rebuilding of a Nation: A Grassroots Analysis of the Aboriginal Nation-Building Process in Canada. *Canadian Journal of Native Studies, 23*(1), 57–82.

Gould, J. (1998). *"To Die in This Way": Nicaraguan Indians and the Myth of Mestizaje, 1880–1965*. Durham, NC: Duke University Press.

Hanrahan, M. (2003). The Lasting Breach: The Omission of Aboriginal People from the Terms of Union between Newfoundland and Canada and its Ongoing Impacts. In V. Young, E. Davis, & J. Igloliorte (Commissioners), *Royal Commission on Renewing and Strengthening Our Place in Canada, Collected Research Papers* (pp. 207–78). St. John's, NL: Office of the Queen's Printer, Newfoundland and Labrador.

Holmes, J. (1993). *Algonquins of Golden Lake Claim, Vols. 1–8*. Report prepared for Ontario Native Affairs Secretariat.

Holmes, J. (2005). Progress Report to January 12. http://www.greatergoldenlake.com/prog1.html

Huitema, M. (2000). *Land of Which the Savages Stood in No Particular Need: Dispossessing the Algonquins of South-Eastern Ontario of Their Lands, 1760–1930*. Unpublished MA Thesis, Department of Geography, Queen's University, Kingston, ON.

Jackson, D. (1993). *"On the Country": The Micmac of Newfoundland*. G. Penney (Ed.). St. John's, NL: Harry Cuff.

Kanatiio (Ed.). (1998). *Tanakiwin*, 1(2), February.

Kapashesit, R. (2004). Misiwa Chiwaacheyemitinwaa. *MoCreebec Council of the Cree Nation 25th Anniversary Commemorative Report*. Moose Factory, ON: MoCreebec Council of the Cree Nation.

Koschade, B. (2003). *"The Tay River Watershed Is Our Responsibility": The Ardoch Algonquins and the 2000–2002 Environmental Review Tribunal Hearings*. Unpublished MA Thesis, Department of Geography, Queen's University, Kingston, ON.

Lawrence, B. (2004). *"Real" Indians and Others: Mixed-Blood Urban Native People and Indigenous Nationhood*. Vancouver, BC: UBC Press.

Lovelace, B. (2006). An Algonquin History. http://www.aafna.ca/history.html

Lyon, N. (1993). *The Mikmaqs of Newfoundland*. Ottawa, ON: Human Rights Promotion Branch, Canadian Human Rights Commission.

Majaury, H. (2005). Living inside Layers of Colonial Division: A Part of the Algonquin Story. *Atlantis, 29*(2), 145–7.

McGrath, D. (1996). Poaching in Newfoundland and Labrador: The Creation of an Issue. *Newfoundland Studies, 12*(2), 79–104.

McNab, D. (1998). Who Is on Trial? Teme-Augama Anishnabai Land Rights and George Ironside, Junior: Re-Considering Oral Tradition. *Canadian Journal of Native Studies, 18*(1), 117–33.

Miller, B. (2003). *Invisible Indigenes: The Politics of Nonrecognition*. Lincoln, NB: University of Nebraska Press.

Monture-Angus, P. (1999). *Journeying Forward: Dreaming First Nations Independence*. Halifax, NS: Fernwood Publishing.

Ozawanimke, L. (2002). Letter to the President, Algonquin Nation Negotiations Directorate, February 20. http://www.greatergoldenlake.com/dec19.html

Potts, G. (1989). Teme-Augama Anishnabai: Last-Ditch Defence of a Priceless Homeland. In B. Richardson (Ed.), *Drumbeat: Anger and Renewal in Indian Country* (pp. 201–28). Toronto, ON: Summerhill Press and the Assembly of First Nations.

Potts, R. (2005). Algonquins Selecting Negotiation Representatives. *Anishinabek News*, April.

Richardson, B. (1989). Wrestling with the Canadian Legal System: A Decade of Lubicon Frustration. In B. Richardson (Ed.), *Drumbeat: Anger and Renewal in Indian Country* (pp. 229–64). Toronto, ON: Summerhill Press and the Assembly of First Nations.

Sarazin, G. (1989). 220 Years of Broken Promises. In B. Richardson (Ed.), *Drumbeat: Anger and Renewal in Indian Country* (pp. 169–200). Toronto, ON: Summerhill Press and the Assembly of First Nations.

Sarazin, G. (1998). Consultation, Enrolment and Representation. *Tanakiwin (Our Homeland) 1*(2), February, 1–2.

Sheppard, B. (2008). Message from the President of the FNI. http://web.archive.org/web/20090504053815/http://www.qalipu.com/message.html

Smoke, D. (2001). Caldwell War Underway. Turtle Island Native Network News, April. http://www.turtleisland.org/news/news-smokecaldwell.htm

St. Germain, J. (2001). *Indian Treaty-Making Policy in the United States and Canada, 1867–1877*. Toronto, ON: University of Toronto Press.

Taillon, J. (2001). Land Grab Angers Passamaquoddy People. *Windspeaker*, November 1.

Tennescoe, G. (2002). More Moose Details. Letter to the Editor. *Eganville Leader*, November 6.

Tolley, S.-L. (2006). *Quest for Tribal Acknowledgement: California's Honey Lake Maidus*. Norman, OK: University of Oklahoma Press.

Trigger, B., & Day, G. (1994). Southern Algonquian Middlemen: Algonquin, Nipissing and Ottawa, 1550–1780. In E. Rogers & D. Smith (Eds.), *Aboriginal Ontario: Historical Perspectives on the First Nations* (pp. 64–77). Toronto, ON: Dundurn Press.

Warren, J. (2001). *Racial Revolutions: Antiracism and Indian Resurgence in Brazil*. Durham, NC: Duke University Press.

Wetzel, J. (1999). The Hidden Terms of Union: The Federal Decision to Abandon Its Constitutional Responsibility for the Welfare of the Newfoundland Mi'kmaq in 1949. Report prepared for presentation to the Canadian Human Rights Commission.

3 The Canary in the Coal Mine: What Sociology Can Learn from Ethnic Identity Debates among American Indians

EVA MARIE GARROUTTE
AND C. MATTHEW SNIPP

In his seminal book, Fredrick Barth (1969) suggested mutual self-awareness as a critical feature that formed the substance of racial-ethnic identity. Such self-awareness, according to Barth, requires several elements. On a personal level, individuals must attach themselves to group identity by associating with characteristics that members of that group share. The legitimacy of personal identities is then validated by a collective recognition that the individual possesses the requisite qualifications to be considered a group member. Others have described these processes as "assignment and assertion" (Cornell & Hartmann, 1998). One can *assert* a racial-ethnic identity, but for it to have social meaning it must be *assigned* by others as well. In a similar vein, Harris & Sim (2002) argue that such an identity depends as much on the perceptions of others as on self-perception.

Although most sociologists would not seriously disagree with Barth and his kindred thinkers, few studies have examined in detail how processes of assignment and assertion play out in everyday life. This essay focuses on two controversies involving identity claims and counter-claims associated with American Indians. As a group, Indians present an instructive opportunity to examine this interplay, for several reasons. First, unlike any other group in America, and especially in contrast with African Americans, American Indians have experienced the federal government's extensive involvement in setting minimum standards for who may legally claim a minority identity. Further, many Indian communities have been struggling for years to set conditions for tribal membership – in turn, determining political enfranchisement and access to resources. In recent years, the latter has been a growing controversy among tribes with successful business enterprises, casino developments being the most visible. Finally, because of high rates of intermarriage, many people have some plausible attachment to an American Indian population. Most do not consider themselves American Indians (Snipp, 1989), but occasionally such individuals decide to declare themselves; their claims invariably invite disagreements (Garroutte, 2003).

Such debates illuminate issues that may well affect many groups beyond American Indians. These issues became especially evident with changes in the 2000 U.S. census. This census was the first to invite respondents to "mark one or more" when identifying their race. The new phrasing allowed for 63 unique combinations (both White and Black, both Black and Asian, etc.). When responses to the race question were combined with the separate Hispanic ethnicity question, 126 possible combinations emerged (Snipp, 2003). One arena in which census data have special importance is civil rights enforcement. Federal agencies examine census statistics to discover and address systematic discrimination in areas such as hiring, housing, health care, banking, voting practices and education (Ferrante & Brown, 2001; Harrison, 2002). Yet such legislation was written under the assumption that each citizen could be classified into a single race, such that protected classes were easily distinguishable. How were government agencies to consider census respondents who positioned themselves astride racial boundaries, associating themselves with *both* a minority classification *and* the White majority?

Cognizant of this challenge, the Office of Management and Budget released a policy memorandum in March 2000. It directed that, for the purpose of federal civil rights enforcement, any respondent who self-identified as a combination of White and any minority race should be classified as a minority. This solution addressed a bureaucratic challenge but also raised serious objections. For example, one vocal opponent denounced the governmental decision as playing to the machinations of a "minority rights establishment" bent on multiplying their political clout (Van Tassell, 2000).[1] Such accusations may explain the concerns of Roderick Harrison (2002), who, as a member of the Office of Management and Budget's Tabulation Group, became well acquainted with issues related to the census's racial estimates. Harrison has warned that the policy change "leaves the entire statistical mechanism for monitoring and enforcing civil rights vulnerable to successful challenge in the courts for systematically inflating counts of minorities" (p. 159). Subsequently observed instabilities in the racial self-descriptions among census respondents do little to alleviate such concerns. A project comparing people's answers on the 2000 census to their responses on a follow-up questionnaire revealed that 40 per cent of individuals who had originally described themselves as multiracial had changed their mind only one year later, settling on a single race instead. About the same percentage of people who had earlier selected only one race later decided to identify with *more* than one (Prewitt, 2005, p. 12).

Disputes involving race and the U.S. census turn on whether Americans will perceive individuals who define themselves as belonging simultaneously to the majority and a minority group as legitimate claimants to legal protections. Who will legitimately "count" as a member of a minority group, their subjective identity assertions being rewarded with objective attributions? Issues of racial-ethnic "authenticity" have been actively engaged, in the case of American Indians, over many years, and they continue to evoke intense controversy (Garroutte, 2003). We suggest that this group's experiences may thus function as the canary in America's coalmine – a predictor of debates that other Americans, particularly mixed-race individuals, will increasingly confront. We attempt here to illuminate the problem of boundary maintenance for claimants to racial-ethnic identity, using a somewhat novel approach. After briefly reviewing some elements fundamental to the construction of racial-ethnic boundaries in American Indian groups, we examine in detail two controversies involving claims for recognition as American Indian. Our goal is to highlight the critiques accompanying such claims and the strategies that groups and individuals may take when their assertions are disputed. We mine these examples for insights into the possible future of other claimants to membership in minority groups, and for guidance in sociological research.

Racial-Ethnic Bonds and Boundaries

For Barth, the reflexive attachments that transform individual identities into racial-ethnic assignments depend on two contingencies. One is the ability to construct notions about "otherness": what qualities are *not* characteristic of the group or its members. Second, groups must construct boundaries that include and exclude persons depending on their particular qualities. Indeed, Barth sees such boundaries as crucial for preserving and reproducing the ethnic-specific behaviours, values, attitudes, and beliefs that allow for group survival (Barth, 1969). To preserve the integrity of racial-ethnic boundaries, groups devise a multiplicity of strategies for assigning insider and outsider status (Cornell & Hartmann, 1998). For example, a set of screening traits may be devised to determine whether a person's appearance, behaviour or ancestry recommend inclusion. At the same time, marginal claimants may seek to circumvent the more stringent requirements. Such efforts may involve challenging exclusionary criteria or denying the legitimacy of efforts to verify affiliation (Garroutte, 2003; Nagel, 1996).

Cornell and Hartmann (1998) argue that shared interests, shared institutions, and shared culture are three overlapping yet distinct bonds that provide connections among co-ethnics and form grounds for including or excluding a claim to group affiliation. A comprehensive discussion of the ways that these three bonds are deployed for the purpose of maintaining and circumventing racial-ethnic boundaries for American Indians is beyond the scope of this essay. Nevertheless, we briefly discuss how each of these ties influences the assertion and assignment of "American Indian" as a racial-ethnic identity. It is useful to position the case studies that follow in the context of these considerations, with attention to factors that make our examples more or less useful as a predictor of experiences that other groups may confront.

Shared Interests

Cornell and Hartmann (1998, p. 86) define "interests" to encompass a Weberian collection of different types of capital, organized around political, economic, and status resources. Co-ethnics share a common resource base with respect to power, material assets, and social position. In the case of American Indians, this base includes a unique legal and political position defined by their exercise of a form of political sovereignty that makes them self-governing and subject only to the authority of the federal government. Shared material assets for tribal members may include proceeds from tribal enterprises, services from their tribal government, and communal ownership of reservation lands held in trust by the federal government. The status resources of American Indians are more difficult to chart because in recent years, a romanticism has developed around American Indians that, in some respects, offsets their stigmatized position as one of the poorest, least educated groups in America (Garroutte, 2003).

Shared Institutions

The existence of common interests within a group leads to the development of institutions to realize and preserve those interests. One important institution for American Indians is the tribal government. Since 1934, tribes have had the opportunity to create constitutional governments. When they were initially formed, these polities possessed few resources and ambiguous jurisdiction. However, they began exercising increasing authority in the early 1960s and are today more prominent and locally influential than ever before. To generate resources, many tribal governments undertake business enterprises. This has led to the formation of new institutional arrangements to oversee larger projects intended to restore economic vitality to reservation communities and deal with problems associated with growth and development (Gonzales, 2003).

Shared Culture

The cultural revitalization of American Indians in the twentieth century has attracted attention from numerous social scientists (e.g., Cornell, 1988; Garroutte, 2003; Nagel, 1996). Historically, American Indians have been a poly-ethnic people, and in many respects they continue as such. For example, Navajo culture bears little resemblance to Salish culture, and neither much resembles Ojibwe culture. Nevertheless, since the Second World War, American Indians have experienced rapid urbanization; in the early 1970s, this encouraged a distinctive pan-Indian identity, mainly in the urban settings into which Indian people had migrated. Pan-Indianism gave urban Indians from diverse tribes a common set of beliefs and values about Indian-ness that were not wedded to specific, local communities. The new, global ideology was enacted in distinctive forms of cultural practice, the quintessential expression of which is the urban pow-wow, typically advertised as "intertribal." Likewise, in the 1960s and 1970s, intertribal organizations such as the American Indian Movement and Women of All Red Nations sprang up, along with informal networks of Indian people living away from their home communities. Such collectivities grew from and advanced perceptions that American Indians shared common concerns and a common destiny.

Constructing Legitimate Claims

Specific bonds to a community are often invoked as evidence of a valid connection between individual and group. Previous work shows that persons with few demonstrable ties often adopt strategies for solidifying their connections. It may be useful, for example, to reference family members or ancestry or to demonstrate cultural knowledge. Alternatively, the importance of such bonds may be discounted or their absence explained, or debates may be entirely reframed. In other cases, the importance of these bonds may be exaggerated or even fabricated (Garroutte, 2003; Nagel, 1996).

We chose the specific case studies that follow for their ability to illustrate the intricate dance by which social actors assert an identity, even while others contest and resist its assignment. On the one hand, the cases are united in that both examine controversies involving claims to American Indian identity which were followed by counter-claims and disputes. On the other hand, they present stark differences. One involves a collective claimant whose enormous wealth has endowed it with an extraordinary opportunity to represent its point of view; the other involves an individual claimant with absolutely no such ability. Throughout this discussion, we are not interested in either confirming or discrediting identity claims. We seek rather to illuminate the emergence and development of claims, to investigate the degree to which they are settled or remain unresolved, to understand the stakes that underpin the debates, and to draw out lessons that may go beyond the American Indian population and help us understand the future of ethnic identification in other American groups.

Case Study 1: The Mashantucket Pequots

Prior to first recorded European contact in 1632, the Pequot tribe was a daunting military presence in southeastern New England, controlling thousands of square miles in the Connecticut valley. Their population of about 13,000 was reduced by an estimated 55–95 per cent by the European-introduced epidemic diseases that soon beset them. Their numbers were further reduced in military conflicts, notably the Pequot War, during which hundreds of people were killed in a pre-dawn raid on one of the tribe's two principal villages. Carried out under the leadership of British troops allied with volunteers from the colonies and other local tribes, the 1637 massacre at Mystic Fort took the lives mostly of women and children, many of whom were deliberately burned alive while they slept. Pequots absent from the fort during the attack were subsequently hunted down and executed, forcibly dispersed among neighbouring tribes, or enslaved – sometimes as far away as the Caribbean. The 1638 Treaty of Hartford that concluded the war forbade any Pequots who might have escaped from returning to their villages, and even required that they cease referring to themselves as Pequots (Hauptman, 1990). The remnant tribe declined to cooperate with these injunctions, and in the 1650s the colony of Connecticut capitulated to their persistence by creating four Indian towns for them, finally establishing a 3,000-acre reservation at Mashantucket, near Ledyard, in 1666. Records from 1674 showed 300 male Pequots. Over the following centuries, the reservation was reduced to about 200 acres, and the population dwindled under the pressures of poverty and other hardships. By 1972, the total reservation population consisted of two elderly ladies, Elizabeth George Plouffe and her half-sister, Martha George Langevin Ellal. Plouffe died the next year, and her grandson Richard Hayward moved back to the reservation.[2]

With the advice of lawyer Tom Tureen, who was helping tribal groups in New England organize to bring land claims suits against the U.S. government, Hayward recruited individuals with Pequot ancestry to repopulate the reservation. By 1974, they had implemented formal governmental structures and created a tribal roll consisting of fifty-five persons descended from the few dozen individuals listed on the Indian supplement to the 1900–10 U.S. Census. In 1983, the group received federal acknowledgement by an act of Congress as the Mashantucket Pequot Tribal Nation; they also received money to buy back tribal lands that Connecticut had sold, over the years, without the federal oversight required by the Indian Trade and Intercourse Act of 1790 (Clinton & Hotopp, 1979–1980).

Federal acknowledgement transformed the Pequot petitioners into a sovereign, "domestic dependent" nation. This designation implies a governmental status superior to that of U.S. states and exempts tribes from a great deal of state taxation and regulation (O'Brien, 1993). It also made it possible for the Pequots, under subsequent legislation, to open Foxwoods – a gaming enterprise destined to become the world's most profitable casino, with annual profits topping one billion dollars in some years (Bodinger de Uriarte, 2003). The flow of cash allowed the tribe to organize a small-scale, well-managed, planned society with cradle-to-grave benefits – not only huge shares of profits from tribal revenues, but also free housing and day care, lucrative employment, free private education for children and enormous stipends for advanced study, and free health care – available to all individuals with any Pequot ancestry (Chappell, 1995). Current membership in the tribe that some call "Connecticut's royal family" (*60 Minutes*, 1994) is about 800 (Anthes, 2008; Lawlor, 2006).

Criticism of the Mashantucket Pequot has been commensurate with their success. One visible detractor has been casino mogul Donald Trump, who offered testimony protesting the tribes' competitive advantages in the gaming industry in Congressional hearings. Referring to the fact that the Pequot are a highly intermarried tribe, with many members showing obvious relationship to other racial groups – primarily African Americans, but also Caucasians (Pasquaretta, 2003, p. 104) – Trump informed Congress that "they don't look like Indians to me. They don't look like Indians to Indians" (U.S. Congress, 1994, p. 242). Tribal members also allege that Trump has publicly referred to them as "Michael Jordan Indians" (Chappell, 1995, p. 46).[3]

An even more voluble critic of Pequot claims to an Indian identity has emerged in Connecticut lawyer Jeff Benedict (2000). His book (*Without Reservation: The Making of America's Most Powerful Indian Tribe and the World's Largest Casino*) is a novelized account of Pequot renascence that accuses the tribe of manipulating the process by which the federal government legally acknowledges claimant groups as American Indian tribal nations. It describes the Mashantucket Pequots as a band of White and Black Americans who audaciously reinvented themselves as Indians when it became economically profitable to do so. The original tribal chairman Richard Hayward, the author alleges, had previously identified himself on sworn legal documents as White, while some of the tribal members he gathered up for the "return" to the reservation required a map to find their "homeland." Benedict has repeatedly urged Congress to revoke the Pequots' acknowledgement status. "It's fraudulent," he asserted in a televised interview. "[T]o go to Congress and portray yourself as something that you're not and get … dollars as a result … is fraudulent" (*60 Minutes*, 2000). Despite factual inaccuracies (Hauptman, 2000–2005), *Without Reservation* has attracted considerable public attention. Notably, it has stimulated support for the Connecticut Alliance against Casino Expansion, a grassroots non-profit that Benedict founded, as well as for his (unsuccessful) run for Congress in 2002.

The Pequots have countered assaults on their tribal identity with a range of responses. Perhaps the most interesting is the $193,000,000 Mashantucket Pequot Museum and Research Center (MPMRC).[4] A stunningly state-of-the-art facility that opened in 1998, it is the largest Native American museum in the world (Anthes, 2008). Staffed by professional archaeologists and historians and undergirded by the scholarship of academic luminaries, the MPMRC functions as a powerful "authenticating industry" for Pequot identity claims (Bodinger de Uriarte, 2007, p. 3). It is an important venue in which to observe the boundary-marking processes to which Barth draws our attention: a "prime site for understanding the revitalized formation of a national community and how public spaces of representation … are mobilized to support the parameters of community as an inclusive and exclusive construct" (p. 214).

The museum testifies to the coexisting, sometimes competing definitions of American Indian identity that inform norms of racial attribution in the United States.[5] One of the most practically significant of these definitions is the definition of identity grounded in *law* (cf. Garroutte, 2003). The ability of petitioning groups to lay legal claim to American Indian tribal status depends upon the federal government's willingness to extend formal acknowledgment. In particular, it depends on claimants' ability to satisfy requirements of what is viewed, with considerable justification, as a "hegemonic discourse" of identity imposed by the dominant society (Bodinger de Uriarte, 2007). Nevertheless, it is a legal definition of Indian identity that the MPMRC most wholeheartedly embraces.

The museum dedicates its "Federal Recognition Theater" and accompanying exhibits to educating visitors about the process the tribe endured in order to receive the federal imprimatur. Here, in a video entitled *Bring the People Home*, the museum-goer learns that the federal acknowledgement process required "a gigantic burden of proof" and that many other petitioners have been denied; the film also discounts Benedict's criticism that the tribe short-circuited the acknowledgment process by going through Congress rather than seeking a full review by the Branch of Acknowledgment and Research.[6] Accompanying exhibits instruct visitors in the rudiments of tribal sovereignty and discuss evidence that the tribe produced in support of their petition. The museum's response to a legal definition of Indian identity is, in short, one of acceptance and celebration.

As important as legal definitions are for establishing the political privileges of Indian tribes, identity attributions do not hinge merely on questions of law, at least not in the minds of many Americans. Another powerful definition commonly encountered in less formal contexts revolves around questions of *race*. "Race," as understood by contemporary social scientists, is a *social* rather than a biological classification (Krieger, 2000). The general public nevertheless still commonly believes in the physical reality of race, often construing phenotype as a marker of supposed genetic similarities. Consequently, like Donald Trump, most Americans want their Indians to "look Indian." In this matter, the MPMRC is far less accommodating of the larger society's expectation.

This rejection is most clearly observable in the last exhibit hall, which Bodinger de Uriarte (2007) describes as the museum's "most compelling display of oppositional discourse" (p. 9). "A Tribal Portrait Gallery" consists of larger-than-life-size photographs from which tribal members – most with phenotypical features that would be popularly categorized as Black or White – gaze back at their viewers without apology. The photos are accompanied by a "sound wash" – an audio feature that allows visitors to hear snippets from interviews with tribal members in which they describe experiences before and after reservation relocation. A number of the voices explicitly problematize racial-ethnic classification on the basis of physical appearance. One explains that the Pequots "look beyond skin color" in determining who is Indian. Another declares that "with Native Americans, [people] expect 'em to look like the guy on the nickel ... *Some* of them look that way, but we don't all look the same." Still another comment offers an alternative basis for the classification of Pequot tribal members into a single category of relatedness: "We're all Indians and we're all family. That's it."[7]

While it directly confronts phenotype as a presumptive marker of biological race, the museum's willingness to rebut common assumptions about race is strikingly selective. That is, the MPMRC is silent about another very commonly invoked racial marker: blood quantum. Blood quantum is a fraction intended to express immediacy of an individual's biological relationship to ancestors whose bloodlines are (supposedly) unmixed.[8] The concept of blood quantum has been sharply critiqued by many – including American Indian people themselves (e.g., Cook-Lynn, 1995) – and characterized as a colonial imposition (Wilson, 1992). Nevertheless, the federal government makes extensive use of its elaborate records of American Indian blood quantum for many purposes (Garroutte, 2003), and some minimum degree of "blood" ancestry determines eligibility for citizenship in the majority of American Indian tribes in the lower forty-eight states (Thornton, 1997). In addition, popular romanticism around Indian-ness displays a clear preference for "the full-blood" as the quintessential "real Indian."

Given the extreme preoccupation of nearly everyone else with this classificatory standard, the MPMRC's neglect of blood quantum as a marker of race is notable. Of course, the modern-day Pequot tribe, descended from a very small number of nineteenth-century survivors, would inevitably have experienced a great deal of exogamy, and their

Constitution allows them to accept members with any ancestry, without regard to specific blood quantum. The museum's refusal even to engage with issues of blood quantum might suggest an unwillingness to dignify an identity standard the tribe deems illegitimate. Yet complete silence on an identity standard that is so intertwined with the American consciousness and experience in regard to American Indians appears contrived. It testifies to the continuing power of blood quantum as a social fact that continues to influence the evaluations of claims to racial-ethnic identity in the larger society.

In addition to the criteria of law and of race, a third powerful, American criterion of Indian-ness revolves around *culture*. Indians diminish in their value as a source of popular entertainment and as a source of raw material for the exercise of scholarly intellection precisely to the extent that they become culturally similar to non-Indians. By virtue of this reality, the MPMRC cannot afford to ignore identity definitions that draw the boundaries of Indian-ness with reference to distinctive cultural practice. However, its attempts to respond to this definition alternate between attempts to reaffirm and to subvert cultural definitions of identity.

First, with the help of elaborate technology and fabulously crafted installations, the museum transports visitors back to the Ice Age in order to portray the Indians that museum-goers crave. In the "Arrival of the People" gallery and theatre, visitors may view artistic interpretations and watch videos featuring origin stories from various tribes (none of them Pequot, since these have not survived the long history of invasion and assault).[9] They then pass through displays of ancient artefacts recovered from archaeological excavations in Pequot territory and finally arrive at one of the museum's most elaborate exhibits: a sixteenth-century village populated with full-sized, buckskin-clad mannequins. Here, one can see and hear the plastic Pequots captured in the midst of daily activities that easily identify them as busy, pre-modern indigenes – hunting, flint-knapping, making a canoe, relaxing in their wigwams, or moving about near a sweat lodge. Their visages were created from masks crafted from the faces of living Indian people from less-intermarried tribes – faces that display features popularly recognized as "Indian." The figures even seem to murmur in an Indian language – Passamaquoddy, not Pequot, because the Pequot language is largely extinct. Subsequent museum displays similarly attempt to satisfy, as much as possible, the public demand that "authentic" Indians should maintain cultural practices from the distant past. The very first display of the museum is a placard that welcomes visitors and proclaims, "Our ancestors have lived here [at Mashantucket] for thousands of years, and we strive to carry on many of their traditions and ideals." Unfortunately, although the tribe has invested considerably in scholarly efforts at cultural recovery,[10] very few elements of culture that can be considered specifically Pequot weathered the tribal diaspora. Nevertheless, the MPMRC devotes several displays to evidence of Pequot culture surviving at least into the relatively recent past. One such display notes that the last fluent speaker of the Pequot language died in 1908, but documents the survival of a single Pequot word ("cane") that a contemporary tribal member recalls hearing from an elderly relative. Another exhibit introduces a Pequot woman "whose knowledge of [traditional herbal] medicine was recorded in 1939 ... She knew dozens of treatments that could be made from the plants found at or near Mashantucket." The text concludes: "[H]er recognition of these plants and broad understanding of their uses reveals that this traditional knowledge survived among the Pequots into the 20th century."

Perhaps because efforts at cultural recovery have proven so limited, the museum directs an even more concerted effort towards creating an apologia for the absence of cultural elements that visitors will likely consider "traditional." In this vein, an event to which the museum repeatedly returns is the 1637 massacre at Mystic Fort. The theme is elaborated from the moment the visitors enter the museum, when they are received into an enormous atrium (the Gathering Space) that architecturally models a seventeenth-century engraving of the attack.[11] Later, museum guests will see the engraving itself reproduced and discussed in at least two different places, and they can attend a continuously playing attraction at "The Pequot War Theater." In the graphic video *The Witness*, an ostensible survivor of the massacre recounts historic events to his grandson.[12] By focusing on the 1637 massacre and subsequent attempts to eradicate the Pequot people, even down to the memory of their name, the film makes it difficult to hold the *tribe* responsible for the disintegration of their culture. Rather, it elucidates the extent to which this outcome was produced by deliberate efforts on the part of colonizers. As the "Prelude to War" placard outside the theatre reads, "It was a war the Pequots did not choose to fight. Instead, the Pequot War was forced upon them, and it created losses and sorrows that reverberated for centuries."

At the same time as it rationalizes cultural discontinuity, however, *The Witness* video accomplishes something even more important. It *creates* a new cultural object that is well suited to fill the void left by the destruction of earlier Pequot traditions. The elderly narrator begins his account of the Pequot massacre by counselling his young listener that "it is through the story that we survive," and closes with an urgent injunction: "You must keep the story. You must keep the land." In this way, the video establishes a *new* origin story – a narrative that explains where the Pequot people came from, why their current circumstances are as they are, and how they can move together into the future. It also contextualizes the story in sacred space – the modern-day reservation, located only a few miles from the site of the Fort Mystic massacre.

Of course, rather than being handed down within the tribe as part of an intact and unbroken oral tradition (as the video's storytelling device might suggest), this story was doubtless recovered and fleshed out, at least for the great majority (if not all) of today's Pequots, with the help of professional historians (Hauptman, 1990, p. 70). It nevertheless functions as a touchstone for modern tribal identity: Pequots are Pequots, according to the video, because they recite this narrative and occupy the land to which it is tied. This story, by configuring facts assembled with the help of expert knowledge, thus becomes an object that stands in for the much larger body of symbolic capital that other tribes may be able to mobilize in formulating definitions of identity grounded in culture.

Bodinger de Uriarte (2003, 2007) analyses the Pequot Museum (along with the tribe's adjacent Foxwoods Resort Casino) as a primary site for the "invention of tradition" – locations in which the Pequots "imagine themselves" as a nation. *The Witness* video, we would argue, is a key moment in this creative process. While some scholarship has used accusations about the invention of tradition to discredit tribal identity assertions, even characterizing recent claimants to tribal identity as perpetrators of "ethnic fraud" (e.g., Quinn, 1990; Clifton, 1990), recent work suggests more measured interpretations. As Bodinger de Uriarte astutely points out, the social scientific identification of sites at which the modern-day Pequots construct their identity does not distinguish them from many other tribes: "The more than three hundred federally recognized American Indian tribes and tribal nations are, in large part, the invention of eighteenth- and nineteenth-century federal American Indian laws and treaties … Rather than being a question of *yes* or *no*, [social] construction [of tribal entities] then becomes a question of *when, how,* and *to what extent*" (2007, pp. 55–6).

The same author goes on to extend his analogies beyond the example of tribal peoples. He construes Pequot activities in the MPMRC and other arenas as part of the process of nation-building – a process that is similar, for instance, to those that historian Benedict Anderson (1983) has described as integral to the emergence of a national consciousness in the United States following the Revolutionary War. Indeed, for Bodinger de Uriarte (2007) the Pequots' invention of tradition is not a marker of ethnic fraud but a marker of ethnic *persistence*: "one proof of [a community's] continuity, a means of merging dynamic forces of change with particular, and adaptive, cultural practice" (p. 53; similarly, Hauptman, 1990).

This understanding of tribal renascence sophisticatedly critiques cynical interpretations of events at Mashantucket and beyond. Recent events, however, raise question about whether the challenges to Pequot identity will persist into the future, and further, whether the Pequot will need to continue to stringently monitor the circumstances by which individuals may claim an affiliation with the tribe. Consistent with the downturn in the larger American economy, by the spring of 2012, the tribe found itself $2.3 billion in debt (Sokolove, 2012). It suspended payments to tribal members and established food pantries for those members who now found themselves penniless (Melia, 2012). In May of 2012, the Federal Bureau of Investigation opened an inquiry into possible financial improprieties involving three tribal members, one a former tribal chairman and another the council treasurer.

The rise and the recent troubles of the Pequot bear directly on the legitimacy of group claims. It remains to be seen whether these claims will be reframed in light of the tribe's recent financial difficulties. Will the claims against Pequot "authenticity" remain salient, or will the group's status simply become irrelevant in the view of those who have objected in the past? In any event, as the next case study shows, equally complex issues in the American Indian identity controversies can emerge when we focus on individual rather than collective claims.

Case Study 2: Kennewick Man

In July 1996, two college students attended the annual hydroplane races in a park near Kennewick, Washington, about 140 miles southwest of Spokane. Poking around the shoreline of the Columbia River, they pulled up a strange, brownish rock. When they turned it over to examine it, the "rock" looked back from empty eye sockets. Concluding that they might have discovered the skull of a murder victim, the young men summoned the police – and set off a firestorm of controversy. Subsequent events illustrate that racial-ethnic boundaries do not enclose only the living; they can even define the dead, with important consequences for the ability of social groups to satisfy important legal, social, and political goals.[13]

Upon investigation of the human remains, the police contacted James Chatters, a local archaeologist and forensic anthropologist with a small consulting business. After investigating the discovery site and finding additional bones, Chatters offered assurances that the remains were not those of a recently deceased individual. However, certain features of the bones caught his interest. They showed a puzzling constellation of characteristics, with some suggesting European heritage and others more consistent with Native American ancestry. Chatters could not decide if the skeleton he was looking at had belonged to a nineteenth-century White settler, or to a much older, American Indian inhabitant. He took the remains to his home laboratory. When subsequent examinations revealed a stone projectile point embedded in the skeleton's pelvis, Chatters became increasingly intrigued and sent a bone sample for radiocarbon dating. When the results returned, they revealed that "Kennewick Man," as the deceased would come to be called, was somewhere in the vicinity of a jaw-dropping 9,000 years old.[14]

By this time, the Confederated Tribes of the Umatilla Indian Reservation,[15] whose Aboriginal lands include the area around the Columbia River where the remains were discovered, had requested that the skeleton be returned to them for treatment in accordance with tribal religious values, which recommended immediate reburial, without scientific analyses.[16] Tribal representatives expressed particular concern for preventing DNA analysis, which destroys small parts of bone. Their request to receive the remains was guided by an important piece of legislation, the Native American Graves Protection and Repatriation Act of 1990 or NAGPRA (Public Law 101–601; 25 U.S.C. 3001 et seq.). NAGPRA was written to redress a long-standing situation in which Indian people had been unable to prevent either archeologists or amateur "pot hunters" from excavating the graves of relatives and ancestors.[17] To protect such burials, this statute stipulates that "the ownership or control" of Native American human remains and funerary objects that "are discovered on, or excavated from, federal or tribal land ... shall be in ... the lineal descendants" of the deceased or (when such descendants cannot be identified) "in the Indian tribe … on whose tribal land such objects or remains were discovered."[18]

The Army Corps of Engineers, which manages the federal land in the Columbia River area, found the Umatilla request for repatriation reasonable under NAGPRA. It seized the skeleton, halting in-progress DNA analyses, and announced that Kennewick Man would be turned over to the tribal claimants. In any other tribal repatriation request, things might have proceeded smoothly. Kennewick Man, however, was not any skeleton. His were one of the oldest sets of human remains ever unearthed in North America, and one of the most complete. These facts made him an object of special scholarly interest. Scientists who learned of the discovery declared that, if they were allowed access to the remains, they might learn much about this mysterious man and the ancient world he had inhabited. He might, for example, help them refine the Bering Strait theory, which proposes that the first humans arrived in America by crossing over a land bridge from Siberia about 12,000 years ago.[19]

Thus motivated, a group of eight prominent archaeologists and physical anthropologists organized to bring a lawsuit against the federal government to prevent the return of Kennewick Man to the tribe (*Bonnichsen v. United States*, 1997). A long and complicated series of legal proceedings followed, all focused on the question of the skeleton's identity: *was* Kennewick Man a Native American whose repatriation was demanded by NAGPRA? The scientists' legal challenge prompted the court to order the Army Corps to review its position, and the Department of the Interior agreed to assist by commissioning additional scientific studies (measurements of the skull, teeth, and bones; more radiocarbon dating; soil and lithic analyses; etc.).

On the basis of the findings, the Interior Department subsequently announced a ruling: "as defined in NAGPRA, 'Native American' refers to human remains … relating to tribes, peoples or cultures that resided within the area now encompassed by the United States prior to historically documented arrival of European explorers" (McManamon, 2000). Because Kennewick Man was clearly pre-Columbian, Interior was satisfied that he should be considered Native American under NAGPRA. They then proceeded to the question of the particular, contemporary tribe to which his remains should be returned. Interior contracted with social scientific experts in archaeology, linguistics, and ethnographic information to prepare "cultural affiliation studies" to address this issue. These reports showed that tribes currently living in the Columbia River

Plateau did have a history of occupation extending back thousands of years, just as they claimed. Thus, one report focused on linguistic evidence (such as place names derived from Sahaptin and its predecessor languages) to show the tribes' historical rootedness in the area (Hunn, 2000, p. 12). Another report argued for the accuracy of tribal traditions, offering confirmatory geological data for tribal stories mentioning features of the ancient landscape (Boxberger, 2000). Upon reviewing the reports, Interior declared itself satisfied that a preponderance of the evidence supported that Kennewick Man *was* culturally affiliated with the tribes of the Columbia River Plateau, and he would be returned to them for reburial.[20]

Upon this announcement, the scientific plaintiffs reopened their earlier suit against the federal government. In the related court proceedings, the government's lawyers continued to argue that Kennewick Man's age and discovery within the United States made him presumptively Native American. Mr Rob Roy Smith (2004), a Seattle lawyer representing the Colville Tribe, would argue a further point in service of the same conclusion. Even if an interpretive rule based on age and location risked misidentifying an occasional ancient skeleton, Congress's intention in passing NAGPRA was to *protect Indians* in light of a history of past abuses: "Back in 1990 … the Senate report notes that there were between 10,000 and 200,000 Indian remains interred in museums across the country. And Congress sought to reign [*sic*] in this practice, but it wanted to give NAGPRA broad strokes, and it wanted to make sure that more remains than not fell under the Native American definition" (pp. 8–9). Given this intention, Smith argued, Indians should receive any benefit of the doubt in identifying ancient remains. They should not have to shoulder the burden of proof to show that human remains were *unquestionably* Native American.

The plaintiff scientists made a very different argument about how identity should be attributed. They argued that completed observations of cranial and other measurements did not conclusively support that Kennewick Man was the ancestor of *any* contemporary Native American group. While they agreed that it was possible that Kennewick man was simply an Indian with unusual characteristics, they argued that no one presently could *know* his proper classification. Indeed, their studies suggested that he had the most traits in common with the Ainu, an Indigenous people of the Japanese archipelago, along with some similarities with Polynesians, and some with the medieval Norse. The scientists accordingly demanded the opportunity to conduct additional,

DNA analyses that could show with certainty whether Kennewick Man *was* a genetic ancestor of contemporary American Indians.

After a long series of agency rulings, court orders, judgments, and appeals, the plaintiff scientists won a favourable ruling from the Ninth Circuit in 2004. The court ruled that "no reasonable person could conclude … that Kennewick Man is 'Native American' under NAGPRA" and that "no cognizable link" existed between Kennewick Man and the modern tribes of the Columbia Plateau (*Bonnichsen v. United States*, 2004, p. 5073). Tribal claimants thus could *not* demand his repatriation under NAGPRA: "Congress's purposes would not be served by requiring the transfer to modern American Indians of human remains that bear no relationship to them" (p. 5067). The decision allowed scientists to study the coveted bones and make the final decision about the man's "true" identity, as defined by their own criteria. Their first analyses occurred in July 2005.[21]

Decisions regarding the evidence necessary to support an identity attribution in the context of NAGPRA were a striking part of the legal dispute that spanned nine years following the discovery on the Columbia River. These decisions went outside the law to require a specific *type* of evidence, namely, physiological measurements that were then construed as indicators of underlying, genetic ancestry. In this, the courts endorsed an unacknowledged essentialism grounded on the assumption that people who share genetic characteristics necessarily share a special, fundamental quality: that they are, in some inexpressible way, the same "kind" of people and thus unalterably linked.[22] The courts assumed that the ties of genetic ancestry belong to the category of the "really real" – that they could define Kennewick Man's identity even in the absence of any information about his cultural or social relationships.

Such an assumption deserves investigation. On the one hand, it is clear that Interior's claim that *age* and *location* alone should define Kennewick Man as a Native American is troubled by uncertainty. It is possible that he did not belong in any personally meaningful sense – in his own understanding, or that of his contemporaries – among any of the tribes in the Columbia River Plateau that wished later to claim him. He might, as lawyers for the plaintiff scientists argued, have migrated into the area from some distant place (Ninth Circuit Court of Appeals, 2003, p. 16). At the same time, it is *also* possible that he did not belong to any of the group(s) with which he shared the most physiological or biological traits. Perhaps he had married, during his lifetime, into another group than the one into which he had been born. Perhaps he had been captured by another group or ceremonially adopted. Perhaps for some other reason he had given up or been rejected by his family of birth and sought relationship among the peoples from whose territory his remains were later recovered. There is no way to eliminate such uncertainties by analysis of his physical characteristics, any more than if one relies on his age and location for his identification. Age, location, *and* biological characteristics are, alike, nothing more than proxy measures for questions about assertion and attribution. They all leave us ignorant regarding the personal, social, and cultural *meanings* that may be associated with the findings available to researchers with expertise in biology and genetics.[23]

Confronted on either side by uncertainties, the court resolved the problem by simply choosing to privilege *one* type of evidence – namely, inferences derived from the skeleton's physiological measurements (and perhaps from subsequent DNA analyses). This choice advantages one class of claimants – namely, scientists in specific disciplines – making them the *legitimated agents of assignment* in relation to ancient human remains. The same choice seriously damaged another class of claimants; in allowing testing, the Ninth Circuit exposed the tribes to the very outcome they sought to avoid, which was to preserve the dead from activities they viewed as offending cultural and religious ideals (Ninth Circuit Court of Appeals, 2003, p. 8). Such issues notwithstanding, Kennewick Man's ultimate classification as non-Native American meant that he no longer enjoyed the protections of NAGPRA, which covers only Native American remains. His bones were subsequently interred at the Burke Museum in Seattle, Washington. There they rest today: the earthly remains of a person once defined as Native American but finally judged otherwise by application of a specific, if necessarily limited, set of scientific criteria.[24]

Discussion

Strict boundaries may regulate who does and does not qualify as a member of a racial-ethnic group. What might we learn from our two case studies that illuminates issues of assertion and assignment? How do the particular configurations of resources that figure into issues of identity assertion and attribution for American Indians – especially elements of interests, institutions and culture – distinguish their case? In what ways does the American Indian example nevertheless suggest trends that may increasingly affect other American groups and point the way forward in the sociological study of American racial-ethnic groups more broadly?

Certainly, our case studies show that the distinctions separating one racial group from another can be ambiguous and that very different definitions of identity can play a role in claimants' assertion and assignment. Exhibits at the Pequot tribe's MPMRC not only reveal how some of these definitions can be deployed but also allow observers to reflect upon how they can be invoked, counterposed, or obscured in the creation of identity claims. Future students of race and ethnicity will do well to examine similar types of boundary work in all groups whose claims are challenged: to consider how the existence of multiple, even competing, definitions of in-group and out-group affect processes of assertion and assignment.

The Mashantucket Pequots' status as a sovereign government that can operate gaming operations provides them material and institutional (especially political) resources that make them unique among American racial-ethnic groups. Yet the Pequot case suggests lessons not strictly about the possibilities that attend material abundance; it also reveals the interplay of different *types* of resources and suggests that claimants can advance their interests when they take advantage of resource fungibility. For example, while economic resources have undeniably enabled Pequot cultural reinvigoration, other clearly cultural resources – from the stereotyped "Indian" motifs that decorate casinos, to the experiences of other-ness offered to visitors in the MPMRC exhibits – have been turned into money (Anthes, 2008). The back-and-forth conversion of material and cultural resources suggests that both can be important to establishing racial-ethnic identities. It will be useful, in analysing the contested claims of American racial-ethnic groups, to relate their success to both the quantity and nature of their resources, considering whether different types of resources are especially suited to particular intermediate goals that groups may pursue at different moments in their boundary construction work. Others might investigate how groups may strategically transmute plentiful resources of one type into scarcer resources of another type.

While material resources have helped the Pequots assert and defend identity claims, their example makes clear the difficulties that the same resources present for struggles over attribution. The enormity of the tribe's economic success has made them vulnerable to the accusation that their identity claims are opportunistic. This is the case even when they pursue goals – such as cultural reclamation – that would typically be viewed as noble. Indeed, we might justifiably anticipate a broad trend for criticism of claimants' legitimacy as "real minorities" to grow in direct proportion to the material *gain* that observers associate with their claims.

While many critics have reduced Pequot identity assertions to the crassest motivations, the controversies over Kennewick Man make it clear that scientists – commonly viewed as impartial wielders of unbiased decision tools – are no more disinterested observers of tribal identity claims than other citizens. In this case, even the combined material, institutional, and cultural resources of a confederation of tribes and the U.S. Department of the Interior (who were on the same side of the controversy) did not carry the day when defendants of the skeleton's Indian identity faced off against a group of scientific plaintiffs. In the decision of the Ninth Circuit, Kennewick Man's physiology became his destiny. This example highlights the importance of new scientific methods for identity determination.

Some sociological thinkers might suppose that the possibility that the skeleton may have ancestries that place him into *several* racial categories will support the move, modelled by the most recent U.S. Census, to abandon the widespread "check one box" approach to racial identification. This interpretation suggests an increasing sophistication in America's conceptualization of racial categorization that might finally overturn the arguably racist assumption that every person can be definitively sorted into a single, or at least dominant, racial category based on some mysterious quality that inheres in his or her body.

Yet other sociologists might propose that the reliance on skeletal measurements and hopes for DNA analyses to decisively resolve questions of Kennewick Man's "true" identity presage a societal return to concepts of race and ethnicity that are fundamentally biological. While older, essentialist ideas about race and ethnicity have been largely swept aside as "bad" science, the court's decision in favour of a method of identity determination grounded in biological data may actually *foster* some forms of racism. In particular, they may give rise to a twenty-first-century version of old assumptions that people are somehow definitively distinguished by their genetic inheritance and that the real "stuff" of racial identity is observable and even quantifiable – a new and improved version of the conviction that "blood (now DNA) will tell." In any case, the court's decision about Kennewick Man clearly positions scientists – especially physical anthropologists and geneticists – as the final arbiters of disputed identity claims. Such claims are virtually unassailable by anyone outside the scientific community connected with this research. It also raises questions of who must bear the burden of establishing claims to a Native American identity, how they must do so, and what type of claim counts as *knowledge*, as opposed to speculation or belief. With the growing importance of genomic research, such controversies seem almost certain to be replayed in groups beyond American Indians.

Finally, the court's consent to the argument that specific types of scientific evidence are indispensable to judgments about the identity of ancient remains raises still another question with widespread generalizability. What if, in future cases involving identity claims and human remains, scientific testing shows biological relationships not only to multiple groups, but to groups that have different ideas regarding disposition? This issue was explicitly raised in the Kennewick Man case by the Asatru Folk Assembly, which has revived the worship of Thor, Odin and other pre-Christian gods of northern Europe. Members argued that the skeleton's possible linkages to the medieval Norse made him *their* ancestor; they demanded he be returned to *them*, rather than to the tribes calling for reburial, so that the Asatru could arrange scientific analyses (Lee, 1997, 2000).

While the Asatru eventually withdrew from legal proceedings, citing financial constraints, it is not clear how the concerns of more persistent claimants might be resolved in future, or how the debates might spill over into disputes about racial-ethnic assertion and assignment in other groups. One might, however, hazard a speculation. As noted in our analysis of the Pequot case, there is already a crude quantitative standard, in common use at least since the mid-nineteenth century, for expressing degree of American Indian ancestry among *living* people – namely, blood quantum. New fields of scientific inquiry, such as molecular archaeology, offer much more precise and reliable measures of "genetic distance," or degree of common ancestry, than does blood quantum (Thomas, 2000, pp. 172–4).

Can we expect that these new measures will lead to new quantitative standards for classifying degrees of relationship between persons by reference to biological criteria? There are definite hints in the judicial opinion regarding Kennewick Man that American courts would be agreeable to such innovation. In the Bonnichsen (2004) opinion, Judge Gould acknowledged that NAGPRA "does not specify precisely what *kind* of relationship or precisely *how strong* a relationship ancient human remains must bear to modern Indian groups to qualify as Native American." Nevertheless, he argued that "human remains that … bear only *incidental genetic resemblance* to modern-day American Indians … cannot be said to be the Indians' 'ancestors' within Congress's meaning" (pp. 5071–2, our emphasis). Such a reference clearly invites an expressly quantitative construction of human relatedness, with the corollary that, at some point, individuals' connection to American Indian forebears becomes exhausted. It is an implication that, as the first author has argued elsewhere, may differ substantially from assumptions characterizing a range of American Indian cultural traditions (Garroutte, 2003, pp. 113–39). Nevertheless, now that the courts have chosen a standard of identity that admits quantification, we should not be surprised if new standards for making determinations of identity emerge – for ancient people, and perhaps even for contemporary ones.

Conclusion

Americans live in an exciting period for debates about racial-ethnic identity – one characterized by countervailing pressures. We have examined two case studies: one that focuses on a collective claimant with considerable resources to speak for itself, and one with none at all. On the one hand stand the Pequots, whose massive "authenticating institution," the MPMRC, presents a range of definitions of ethnic identity while excluding all mention of the historic convention of blood quantum as a determinant of Indian identity. This example dovetails with the last census's reinstitutionalization of hypodescent and the rise of notions of racial-ethnic identity as fluid, individual, freely chosen, and always escaping rational calculation. On the other hand, one encounters Kennewick Man. His example suggests the contrary possibility that Americans may be witnessing the rise of a new racial science, complete with refashioned ideas of quantifiable ancestral substance that obfuscate questions about the unmeasurable meanings that attach to identities.

We do not anticipate that the tensions we delineate here will resolve quietly. Rather, even while American Indians bring a special and sometimes unique constellation of resources into a context of increasingly blurred racial-ethnic boundaries, we believe that their experiences may well be the harbinger of events that will affect many Americans – especially multiracial persons and others who occupy the borderlands between long-established minority groups. They direct researchers, moreover, to important questions in the study of racial-ethnic boundary construction in many different groups.

NOTES

1 The quoted speaker is director of research for the American Civil Rights Institute, an organization "created to educate the public on the harms of racial and gender preferences," retrieved 27 March 2008 from http://www.acri.org/about.html

2 In *The Pequots in Southern New England: The Fall and Rise of an American Indian Nation*, edited by Laurence M. Hauptman and James D. Wherry (1990), contributors provide a scholarly history of the Pequots from prehistoric times through 1990. Our historical sketch draws on the essays in this volume. Other important literature includes Cave (1996) and Salisbury (1982).

3 This phrase, with its sly implication that it is impossible for individuals with Black ancestry to be simultaneously ("real") Indians, reveals a peculiar norm of racial attribution in America: a "rule of hypodescent" which assumes that even a small amount of Black ancestry must cause an individual to be socially classified as Black (even against his will), whereas small amounts of White or Indian ancestry often do not cause a person to be correspondingly classified.

4 The museum website appears at http://www.pequotmuseum.org/

5 These following remarks are based on the first author's observations at the MPMRC in July 2005, August 2007, and May 2012.

6 Tribes can receive federal recognition by executive order or by an act of Congress, but most petitioners pass through the Federal Acknowledgement Process, administered at the time of the Pequot decision by the Bureau of Indian Affairs' Branch of Acknowledgment and Research (BAR). The Pequots sought an act of Congress. The original legislation passed both houses but was vetoed by President Reagan. Eventually, compromise legislation was successfully proposed, requiring the tribe to submit paperwork to the BAR to receive a cursory review (see the Mashantucket Pequot Indian Claims Settlement Act, Public Law 134, Title 25 U.S.C.A., pp. 1751–60).

7 Many thanks to Nora Costello, Reference/Info Tech Librarian at the Mashantucket Pequot Museum and Research Center, for providing the text of the sound wash from the museum galleries. The longer documentaries from which these comments were excerpted may be examined at the MPMRC library.

8 For example, a blood quantum of 4/4 indicates a person of exclusively Indian ancestry, while a blood quantum of 1/2 can be interpreted to mean

that one parent had exclusively Indian ancestry while the other had none. A blood quantum of 1/4 may mean that one grandparent had exclusively Indian ancestry, and so on.

9 For what is known of Pequot traditions, see Simmons (1986).

10 For instance, the tribe has sponsored important academic conferences. One of these conferences, held in 1987, led to the publication of the Hauptman and Wherry (1990) volume cited above. Another important conference in 2002 took up issues of language reclamation and the challenges confronting tribes hoping to reconstruct languages no longer spoken. Pequots have recovered enough words to create a tribal "flag song," which is now sung at their annual pow-wow and taught at their child development center (Daly, 2002).

11 A photo of this architectural feature appears in Bodinger de Uriarte (2007, p. 109).

12 The 30-minute video was directed by Keith Merrill and George Burdeau.

13 Useful books on Kennewick Man include Burke (2008), Chatters (2001), and Thomas (2000). Our analysis draws on these texts, along with the large collection of legal documents, press releases and news articles explaining the position of scientific and American Indian contributors to the debate. Of central importance are the court records pertaining to *Bonnichsen et al. v. United States of America.* Many related documents are available on the continuously updated site http://www.friendsofpast.org

14 Testing suggested that Kennewick Man is probably between 8,340 and 9,200 calendar years old (*Bonnichsen v. USI*, 2004, p. 5053).

15 The Confederated Tribes of the Umatilla Indian Reservation (CTUIR) comprise the Cayuse, Umatilla, and Walla Walla people, three bands that were combined on the Umatilla Indian Reservation under an 1855 treaty with the United States government and subsequently united under a single tribal government in the mid-twentieth century; the CTUIR currently has about 2,500 tribal citizens. (See further Confederated Tribes of the Umatilla Reservation, No date.) The CTUIR is commonly referred to simply as the Umatilla. Other local tribes that became involved in the Kennewick Man dispute included the Confederated Tribes & Bands of the Yakama Indian Nation, the Nez Perce Tribe of Idaho, the Confederated Tribes of the Colville Reservation, and the Wanapum Band (a non-federally recognized group).

16 The tribal claimants described cultural beliefs regarding immediate reburial of disturbed human remains as follows: "When a body goes into the ground, it is meant to stay there until the end of time. When remains are disturbed and remain above ground, their spirits are at unrest … To put these spirits at ease, the remains must be returned to the ground as soon as

possible" (Joint Tribal Amici Memorandum 1997, pp. 4–5, quoted in *Bonnichsen v. United States* [2004], p. 5056). They also explained their particular resistance to scientific analyses that required destruction of bone material (such as radiocarbon and DNA analyses): "The only way that we can come to the Creator at the time of our passing ... is to come to him in the form in which we are created ... to come to him 'whole'" (Dick, Jr., Dkt. No. 391, quoted in Smith, 2004, p. 5).

17 For perspectives on NAGPRA, see Echo-hawk & Echo-hawk (1994); Fine-Dare (2002); and Lovis, Kintigh, Steponaitis, & Goldstein (2004).

18 Retrieved 17 July 2005 from http://www.cr.nps.gov/local-law/FHPL_NAGPRA.pdf

19 Claims for the scientific importance of the Kennewick skeleton were not universally shared within the discipline of archaeology, especially when weighed against the ethical considerations connected with collection of human remains. Indeed, one argument made against curating the Kennewick skeleton claimed that there was likely very little new knowledge that might be gleaned from these remains. When juxtaposed against the vast body of extant knowledge about North American archaeology, the new knowledge that might be derived from the Kennewick remains appeared marginal, at least to some commentators. Others objected that the claims being made in the name of scientific interest represented an outdated and largely obsolete approach to archaeology – one that largely rested on theories and methods dating back to the early twentieth century (Thomas, 2000; Wilcox, 2000).

20 The studies are available at http://www.nps.gov/archeology/kennewick/

21 Early results were released in 2006 and have stimulated new theorizing about human migration. Scientists anticipate that additional analyses may reveal information such as Kennewick Man's diet and travels. They also hope to repeat early, failed efforts at DNA extraction and analysis.

22 As anthropologist David Schneider (1984) has pointed out, a similar and unacknowledged essentialism has prevailed in anthropological studies of kinship since the nineteenth century. These studies have single-mindedly tracked biological relationships while ignoring the many others ways that people may consider and cause themselves to be related (such as marriage and adoption). Subsequent anthropological work recognizes the limitations of approaching human relationships from a perspective of strict biological essentialism and offers alternative ways for understanding kinship (e.g., DeMallie's [1994] "cultural approach" that attempts to reconstruct the meanings that underwrite Lakota ideas about relatedness).

23 They even leave us ignorant of the majority of his genetic ancestry. As Kimberley TallBear, assistant professor of Science, Technology, and Environmental Policy at the University of California at Berkeley, points out, "going back 10 generations, one has 2,048 ancestors. Genetic analyses can account for only 2 [ancestral lines]. The vast majority of ancestors cannot be detected" (personal communication, 2007).

24 The final classification of Kennewick Man as non-Native American rendered irrelevant the painstaking work by which experts in archaeological, linguistic, and ethnographic evidence had attempted to establish his likely ties to a specific tribe. While Kennewick Man would ultimately not enjoy the protections of NAGPRA, the Department of the Interior subsequently sought to avoid debates over how that legislation would be applied in future disputes about ancient remains by issuing additional guidance. After receiving comments from interested parties, including tribal representatives and archaeologists, the Interior Department published a *Federal Register* notice in March 2010 that detailed its "final rule" regulating the disposition under NAGPRA of "those human remains, in collections, determined by museums and Federal agencies to be Native American, but for whom no relationship of shared group identity can be reasonably traced, historically or prehistorically, between a present day Indian tribe or Native Hawaiian organization and an identifiable earlier group." These guidelines confirmed NAGPRA's intent to allow transfer of such remains to any tribe in whose lands or "aboriginal occupancy area" they have surfaced – whether or not specific cultural affiliation is determinable; they also specifically require no consultation under the Native American Graves Protection and Repatriation or approval by the Secretary of the Interior (U.S. Department of the Interior, 2010).

This policy will appear to some as consistent with the original intent of NAGPRA to observe the rights of tribes and their ancestors and to deal ethically with the ancestral heritage of tribal communities. Others will view the revision of the guidelines as a procedurally flawed process that invites court challenge (e.g., Hutt, 2010).

REFERENCES

60 Minutes. (1994). Wampum Wonderland. CBS News Transcripts, 8 September. Burrelle's Information Services.

60 Minutes. (2000). Wampum Wonderland. CBS News Transcripts, 23 May. Burrelle's Information Services.

Anderson, B. (1983). *Imagined Communities*. London: Verso Editions.

Anthes, B. (2008). Learning from Foxwoods: Visualizing the Mashantucket Pequot Tribal Nation. *American Indian Quarterly*, *32*(2), 204–18. http://dx.doi.org/10.1353/aiq.2008.0011

Barth, F. (1969). *Ethnic Groups and Boundaries: The Social Organization of Culture Difference*. Boston, MA: Little, Brown.

Benedict, J. (2000). *Without Reservation: The Making of America's Most Powerful Indian Tribe and the World's Largest Casino*. New York: HarperCollins.

Bodinger de Uriarte, J.J. (2003). Imagining the Nation with House Odds: Representing American Indian Identity at Mashantucket. *Ethnohistory (Columbus, Ohio)*, *50*(3), 549–65. http://dx.doi.org/10.1215/00141801-50-3-549

Bodinger de Uriarte, J.J. (2007). *Casino and Museum: Representing Mashantucket Pequot Tribal Identity*. Tucson, AZ: University of Arizona Press.

Bonnichsen v. United States (Bonnichsen I). (1997). 969 F. Supp 614, 618. (D. Or.)

Bonnichsen v. United States (Bonnichsen III). (2004). 357 F.3d. (9th Cir.)

Boxberger, D.L. (2000, Sept.). Review of Traditional Historical and Ethnographic Information. In F.P. McManamon (Ed.), *Kennewick Man: Cultural Affiliation Report* (Chapter 3). National Park Service. http://www.ccr.nps.gov/aad/kennewick/boxberger.htm

Burke, H. (2008). *Kennewick Man: Perspectives on the Ancient One*. Walnut Creek, CA: Left Coast Press.

Cave, A. (1996). *The Pequot War*. Hanover, NH: The University Press of New England.

Chappell, K. (1995, June). Black Indians Hit the Jackpot in Casino Bonanza. *Ebony*, *50*, 46–52.

Chatters, J.C. (2001). *Ancient Encounters: Kennewick Man and The First Americans*. New York: Simon and Schuster.

Clifton, J.A. (Ed.). (1990). *The Invented Indian: Cultural fictions and Government Policies*. New Brunswick, NJ: Transaction.

Clinton, R.N., & Hotopp, M.T. (1979–1980). Judicial Enforcements of the Federal Restraints on Alienation of Indian Land: The Origins of the Eastern Land Claims. *Maine Law Review*, *31*, 17–90.

Confederated Tribes of the Umatilla Reservation. (No date). Official home page. http://www.umatilla.nsn.us/

Cook-Lynn, E. (1995). Literary and Political Questions of Transformation: American Indian Fiction Writers. *Wicazo Sa Review*, *11*(1), 46–51. http://dx.doi.org/10.2307/1409042

Cornell, S.E. (1988). *The Return of the Native: American Indian Political Resurgence*. New York: Oxford University Press.

Cornell, S.E., & Hartmann, D. (1998). *Ethnicity and Race: Making Identities in a Changing World*. Thousand Oaks, CA: Pine Forge Press.

Daly, G.E. (2002, April 6). Dreaming a Language Back to Life. *Canku Ota* (*Many Paths*) Newsletter, 58. http://www.turtletrack.org/Issues02/Co04062002/CO_04062002_Dreaming_Language.htm

DeMallie, R.J. (1994). Kinship and Biology in Sioux culture. In R. DeMallie & A. Ortiz (Eds.), *North American Indian Anthropology: Essays on Society and Culture* (pp. 125–46). Norman, OK: University of Oklahoma Press.

Echo-hawk, R.C., & Echo-hawk, W.R. (1994). *Battlefields and Burial Grounds: The Indian Struggle to Protect Ancestral Graves in the United States*. Minneapolis, MN: Lemer Publications.

Ferrante, J., & Browne, P., Jr. (2001). Federal and Program Uses of the Data Derived From Race and Ethnicity Questions – The U.S. Bureau of the Census (1990). In J. Ferrante & P. Browne Jr. (Eds.), *The Social Construction of Race and Ethnicity in the United States* (2nd. ed.) (pp. 493–96). Upper Saddle River, NJ: Prentice Hall.

Fine-Dare, K.S. (2002). *Grave Injustice: The American Indian Repatriation Movement and NAGPRA*. Lincoln, NB: University of Nebraska Press.

Garroutte, E.M. (2003). *Real Indians: Identity and the Survival of Native America*. Berkeley, CA: University of California Press.

Gonzales, A.A. (2003). American Indians: Their Contemporary Reality and Future Trajectory. In D.L. Brown & L.E. Swenson (Eds.), *Challenges for Rural America in the Twenty-First Century* (pp. 43–56). University Park, PA: Pennsylvania State University Press.

Harris, D.R., & Sim, J.J. (2002). Who Is Multiracial? Assessing the Complexity of Lived Race. *American Sociological Review*, *67*(4), 614–27. http://dx.doi.org/10.2307/3088948

Harrison, R.J. (2002). Inadequacies of Multiple-Response Race Data in the Federal Statistical System. In J. Perlman & M.C. Waters (Eds.), *The New Race Question: How the Census Counts Multiracial Individuals* (pp. 137–60). New York: Russell Sage.

Hauptman, L.M. (1990). The Pequot War and its legacies. In L.M. Hauptman & J.D. Wherry (Eds.), *The Pequots in Southern New England: The Fall and Rise of an American Indian Nation* (pp. 69–80). Norman, OK: University of Oklahoma Press.

Hauptman, L.M. (2000–2005). A Review of Jeff Benedict's *Without Reservation: The Making of America's Most Powerful Indian Tribe and Foxwoods, the World's Largest Casino*. National Indian Gaming Association. http://www.indiangaming.org/library/articles/novel-attack.shtml

Hauptman, L.M., & Wherry, J.D. (Eds.). (1990). *The Pequots in Southern New England: The Fall and Rise of an American Indian Nation*. Norman, OK: University of Oklahoma Press.

Hunn, E.S. (2000). Review of Linguistic Evaluation. In F.P. McManamon (Ed.), *Kennewick Man: Cultural Affiliation Report* (Chapter 4). http://web.archive.org/web/20010128120700/http://www.cr.nps.gov/aad/kennewick/HUNN.HTM

Hutt, S. (2010, May 13). Letter from the American Association of Museums. http://www.friendsofpast.org/nagpra/news.html

Krieger, N. (2000). Refiguring "Race": Epidemiology, Racialized Biology, and Biological Expressions of Race Relations. *International Journal of Health Services, 30*(1), 211–16. http://dx.doi.org/10.2190/672J-1PPF-K6QT-9N7U Medline:10707306

Lawlor, M. (2006). *Public Native America: Tribal Self-Representation in Museums, Powwows, and Casinos*. New Brunswick, NJ: Rutgers University Press.

Lee, M. (1997). Ancient Ritual Pays Tribute to Kennewick Man. *Tri-City Herald*, August 28.

Lee, M. (2000). Asatru Give up Kennewick Man Battle. *Tri-City Herald*, January 14.

Lovis, W.A., Kintigh, K.W., Steponaitis, V.P., & Goldstein, L.G. (2004). Archaeological Perspectives on NAGPRA: Underlying Principles, Legislative History, and Current Issues. In J.R. Richman & M.P. Forsyth (Eds.), *Legal Perspectives On Cultural Resources* (pp. 81–96). Walnut Creek, CA: AltaMira Press.

McManamon, F.P. (2000). Determination That the Kennewick Human Remains Are "Native American" For the Purposes of the Native American Graves Protection and Repatriation Act (NAGPRA). Letter to Robert G. Stanton, 11 January 2000. Retrieved 25 July 2005 from http://web.archive.org/web/20000302174855/http://www.cr.nps.gov/aad/kennewick/c14memo.htm

Melia, M. (2012). Tribe $2 Billion in Debt after Casino Bonanza. *MSNBC*, March 28. http://www.msnbc.msn.com/id/46883766/ns/us_news-life/t/tribe-billion-debt-after-casino-bonanza/#.T_N6EytYvN0

Nagel, J. (1996). *American Indian Ethnic Renewal: Red Power and the Resurgence of Identity and Culture*. New York: Oxford University Press.

Ninth Circuit Court of Appeals (2003). Oral Arguments. Unofficial transcript, September 10. http://www.friendsofpast.org/kennewick-man/court/briefs/030927Oral.html

O'Brien, S. (1993). *American Indian Tribal Governments*. Norman, OK: University of Oklahoma Press.

Pasquaretta, P. (2003). *Gambling and Survival in Native North America*. Tucson, AZ: University of Arizona Press.

Prewitt, K. (2005). Racial Classification in America: Where Do We Go From Here? *Daedalus, 134*(1), 5–17. http://dx.doi.org/10.1162/0011526053124370

Quinn, W.W., Jr. (1990). The Southeast Syndrome: Notes on Indian Descendant Recruitment Organizations and Their Perceptions of Native American Culture. *American Indian Quarterly, 14*(2), 147–54. http://dx.doi.org/10.2307/1185054

Salisbury, N.E. (1982). *Manitou and Providence: Europeans and the Making of New England, 1500–1643.* New York: Oxford University Press.

Schneider, D. (1984). *A Critique of the Study of Kinship.* Ann Arbor, MI: University of Michigan.

Simmons, W.S. (1986). *Spirit of the New England Tribes: Indian History and Folklore, 1620–1984.* Hanover, NH: University Press of New England.

Smith, R.R. (2004, August 3). Tribes' Response in Opposition to Request to Dismiss Intervenors. Oral Argument Requested. Ninth Circuit Court of Appeals (Dist OR), 3 August. http://www.friendsofpast.org/pdf/040803Tribes.pdf

Snipp, C.M. (1989). *American Indians: The First of This Land.* New York: Russell Sage Foundation.

Snipp, C.M. (2003). Racial Measurement in the American Census: Past Practices and Implications for the Future. *American Sociological Review, 29*(1), 563–88. http://dx.doi.org/10.1146/annurev.soc.29.010202.100006

Sokolove, M. (2012) A Big Bet Gone Bad. *New York Times Sunday Magazine,* March 18, p. MM36.

Thomas, D.H. (2000). *Skull Wars: Kennewick Man, Archaeology, and the Battle for Native American Identity.* New York: Basic Books.

Thornton, R. (1997). Tribal Membership Requirements and the Demography of "Old" and "New" Native Americans. *Population Research and Policy Review, 16*(1/2), 33–42. http://dx.doi.org/10.1023/A:1005776628534

U.S. Congress. House. (1994.) Testimony of Donald Trump before the Subcommittee on Native American Affairs of the Committee on Natural Resources. Implementation of Indian Gaming Regulatory Act. 103rd Congress, 1st sess., 5 October 1993. Serial No. 103–17, Part V. Washington, DC: U.S. Government Printing Office.

U.S. Department of the Interior. (2010). Native American Graves Protection and Repatriation Act Regulations – Disposition of Culturally Unidentifiable Human Remains. *Federal Register,* 75(49). Washington, DC: U.S. Government Printing Office.

Van Tassell, M.R. (2000, August 1). The One Drop Rule: R.I.P. *The Multiracial Activist,* August 1. http://multiracial.com/site/content/view/208/39/

Wilcox, Michael V. (2000). "Dialogue or Diatribe? Indians and Archaeologists in the Post-NAGPRA Era." In Ronald Niezen (Ed.), *Spirit Wars: Native North*

American Religions in the Age of Nation Building (pp. 190–3). Berkeley, CA: University of California Press.

Wilson, T.P. (1992). Blood Quantum: Native American Mixed Bloods. In M.P. Root (Ed.), *Racially Mixed People in America* (pp. 108–25). Newberry Park, CA: Sage.

4 "This Sovereignty Thing": Nationality, Blood, and the Cherokee Resurgence

JULIA M. COATES

At the 2007 Native American and Indigenous Studies meeting at the University of Oklahoma in Norman, a phenotypically "Black" woman made a comment after a session entitled "What Is This 'Black' in Native American Studies?" Stating that she had been raised in Georgia with family knowledge imparted to her from the time she was small that she had Cherokee Indian blood, she had been somewhat unpleasantly surprised to come to Oklahoma – the state to which the majority of the Cherokee Nation had been forcibly removed in 1838–9. In this state, she had discovered that her claims to Indian heritage were regarded somewhat skeptically by others, perhaps especially so since this was shortly after a vote in the Cherokee Nation concerning the status of the descendants of the Cherokee Freedmen. But race is perhaps irrelevant in this example, since similar statements are often heard from people who are phenotypically white and who also assert a Cherokee "heritage." "Here," she stated with a wave of her hand, "I suddenly find there is this sovereignty thing."

As shocking as such cavalier phrasing may be about a tenet which is so fundamental to the legal and political existence of tribes in the U.S. today, the remark did not elicit any comment from members of the audience, at least not as to its dismissive treatment of governmental powers. Perhaps scholars at the session realized the speaker was inexperienced or unschooled in the political functions of tribes within the country, and that a quick informative lesson would be inappropriate at this public moment, or simply impossible to impart in a shorthanded way.

But academic theorizing about "sovereignty" and its meanings has expanded far beyond the typical political/legal/governmental definitions of the word as first elaborated in the U.S.-tribal context by Vine Deloria Jr. and Clifford Lytle (1983, 1984), Deloria and David Wilkins (1999), and Wilkins and K. Tsianina Lomawaima (2001). Other scholars have described "sovereignty" as also encompassing economic, linguistic, and cultural aspects and have pondered it relationships to "settler" states and law as well as its impacts on tribal lifeways and communities (Cattelino, 2008; Jorgensen, 2007; Warrior, 1994). Some have even questioned whether it is a useful term or have insisted that it is not in the Indigenous context (Alfred, 2009; Womack, 1999). The expansion of the concept beyond Western legal philosophies is an exciting endeavour in Native American Studies and correlates more smoothly with current theoretical trends in ethnic studies, American studies, and anthropology, which take comparative and global approaches. As the debate focuses on indigeneity as located in heritage, DNA, and cultural attributes and expressions, the panels at this and subsequent conferences have emphasized language, literature, culture, Indigenous experience from the southern hemisphere, the Pacific regions, race, and identity construction. As such, the particular legal bases of political sovereignty that tribes within the U.S. assert, as evidenced by treaties, judicial precedent, and Congressional dictate, is not an experience that lends itself well to the comparative endeavour, since it more often *contrasts* with the experiences of Indigenous communities elsewhere. For most Indigenous peoples, the cultural, racial, and ethnic aspects of identity may indeed be the primary sites for investigation and discussion.

Since these aspects are relevant also for Natives within the U.S., it is natural that they be a part of these discussions. The problem is that if these are the *only* aspects of the dialogue, or even the primary aspects of the dialogue as it relates to Indigenous peoples within the U.S., it leaves a sense that the cultural/ethnic/racial dimensions of identity carry the greatest weight in that country as well. But this perception presents a dilemma for many tribal governments, who are the arbiters of the *political* identity of their "members" (citizens) vis-à-vis the U.S., and who may hold very different standards than claims of race, culture, or ethnicity in making those determinations.

Encountering Cherokee Identity as a Nationality

In her work *Real Indians, Identity and the Survival of Native America* (2003), Cherokee scholar Eva Marie Garroutte teases out the strands of Native identity as popularly understood by Natives themselves within the

United States. Biological (racial), cultural, and legal identities are each addressed in separate chapters, even as it readily apparent that the categories are rarely, if ever, actually discrete. The discussion of legal identity is interesting and bears strong relationship to a fourth chapter on self-identification, although the connections are not immediately made and the chapters are not placed next to each other in the work. While detailing the myriad of historic tribal experiences in formulating base rolls from which legal identities are constructed by tribes in the U.S., the chapter reflects the perspective taken by many in academia that legal definitions are, in general, externally imposed by federal agencies and authorities, and thus impinge on tribal cultural definitions as well as individual claims. The questioning began decades ago and was put forth perhaps most notably by my former colleague at UC Davis, Jack Forbes, who saw legal determinations as not only undermining tribal cultural methods of determining members, but as exclusionary of those with legitimate tribal heritage and connections.

Academia has been reluctant to adopt requirements of legal identity in admission, hiring, publishing, and representation, viewing such practices as a "policing" of tribal identity. But as the recent case of former law professor Elizabeth Warren makes clear, even very sincerely held beliefs about ethnic heritage are often contested by tribal governments who increasingly insist that a privileging of legal Native identities upholds tribal political sovereignty, and that not doing so is undermining.

While it may appear that the emphasis on a legal or political identity is exclusionary to those making claims on cultural or racial bases, which many academics view as more valid locations of sovereignty than the "settler" legal realm, in the case of the Cherokee Nation the privileging of legal identities has become critical in deflecting the literally hundreds of thousands of spurious claims made by individuals with no perceived racial, cultural, or community affiliation. But rather than being exclusionary of those who have legitimate claims, the Cherokee Nation's own particular history ensures that the privileging of a legal Cherokee identity is, in fact, highly inclusive of hundreds of thousands of other Cherokees who might be marginalized by other definitions. Even as accounts of the Cherokee Nation's legal disputes with other tribes or the descendants of Freedmen dominate the public imagination, another group which is much more representative of demographic trends occurring throughout Native America more quietly finds a place for inclusion and continuing relationship with their people and government. These Cherokees are the majority of the tribal citizens who reside outside the Nation's jurisdiction, often in urban areas in the western and Pacific states. For them, the legal definition provides an umbrella of national continuity and presents interesting potentials for the retention and resurgence of culture, language, and community, rather than simply acting as colonialist mechanisms of control and exclusion.

This segment of the Cherokee Nation's citizenry is called the "At Large" Cherokee citizens. They constitute about 62 per cent of the Cherokee Nation's membership and are defined as those who reside outside the historic jurisdictional boundaries (also known as the "fourteen counties") of north-eastern Oklahoma.[1] They are the Cherokee Nation's expatriates, and they are found from coast to coast, although the greatest single concentration outside of Oklahoma is in California. In the late 1990s, as part of my dissertation research, I began an interviewing project among Cherokees outside the boundaries. Approaching several Cherokee organizations that had formed in the early part of the decade in Albuquerque, Houston, and northern California, I spoke with both citizen and non-citizen Cherokees in an attempt to understand the bases upon which they configured and manifested their identities as "Cherokees." These first interviews contained questions about family, place, cultural practices, civic and political activity, and blood quantum disputes. I collected some basic genealogical information as well as a short oral history of the family's emigration story from each participant.

In 1999, I also was recruited by the Cherokee Nation's newly elected principal chief, Chad Smith, whom I had met several years earlier through an organization of Cherokees in Albuquerque where I was a graduate student. He asked if I would consider returning to north-eastern Oklahoma to develop a project to teach tribal history to the employees and communities of the Cherokee Nation. My own dissertation challenged the constructions of race and class that American historians had applied in their analyses of the historic Cherokees, and I discovered that my ethnohistorical challenge paralleled Chief Smith's legal and political interpretations of Cherokee nationalistic identity. Ultimately, I was able to secure support to teach this class "on the road" to the expatriate Cherokees, and to date, this forty-hour course has been taught over thirty times to thousands of Cherokees in the diaspora.

In 2004–6, I continued the interviewing project of expatriate Cherokee citizens through a postdoctoral fellowship with the University of California. By this time, the emphasis had shifted as I was now working on behalf of the Cherokee Nation to develop models for retention of diasporic citizens in civic and cultural connections actively supported and fostered by the tribal government. The research focused almost entirely on Cherokee citizens and their manifestations of "Cherokee" identity in racial, cultural, social, and political senses. Thus, through these research efforts and employment with the Cherokee Nation, I have been both observer and participant in the resurgence of identity among expatriate Cherokees. A heightened understanding and privileging of the nationality of these expatriates (above quantum, phenotype, cultural knowledge, etc.) has strengthened their identities as Cherokees as well as their relationship and standing within the Cherokee Nation.

Recapturing Cherokee Governance

Without question, the Cherokees are the tribal group within the U.S. that has experienced the greatest surge in new claimants. As noted by an official of the Cherokee Nation in response to the participant at the OU conference, it seems it is almost impossible these days, especially in the south-eastern U.S., to walk into a gathering of more than three people without someone announcing that they have Cherokee blood.[2] The Cherokees have historically been a large tribe and have experienced great dispersion over three hundred years and so there may be some historical basis for the widespread claims, which are made almost entirely on the basis of alleged ethnic heritage. Most claimants have little or no connection to tribal government, nor historical knowledge of the distinct political existence of the Cherokee Nation. The presumption often seems to be that descent alone from a Cherokee/Indian ancestor affords one the right to assert claims of heritage, much as an Italian-American or an Irish-American would be proud to proclaim their ethnic background.

But the Cherokees established and functioned under a historical government that was relatively unique among Native Americans. Unlike almost any other tribe in the country (except for the others of the Five "Civilized" Tribes, a category into which the Cherokees have been placed by federal officials and historians), the Cherokee Nation has also implemented well-defined citizenship criteria along nationalistic lines for the past 200 years (McLoughlin, 1986, 1993). Therefore, while there has been tremendous dispersion, there has also long been a well-established basis for identifying those who were recognized as part of a tribal citizenry in relation to those who were not. This historical fact contributes to re-emergent identity within the Cherokee citizenry, both within north-eastern Oklahoma and particularly among the expatriate population.

Interestingly, in emphasizing nationality in the contemporary era the Cherokees are returning to their own nineteenth-century standards, rather than elaborating on twentieth-century understandings derived from federal models such as the *Indian Reorganization Act* (1934) or the *Oklahoma Indian Welfare Act* (1936), as is the case for many other tribes. For the majority of the twentieth century, the Cherokees had little but a nominal "national" government, and in the view of some, actually returned to organization more similar to eighteenth-century norms of decentralized autonomous community governing structures (Meredith, 1985). With their national government dismantled after Oklahoma statehood in 1907, Cherokee communities marginalized in the hills in the north-eastern part of the state endured conditions of racism, dire poverty, and cultural decline for decades throughout the early and mid-twentieth century. Without a national/tribal political entity to advocate on their behalf, some Cherokees formed loose consortiums of grassroots organizations for mutual support. Others ceased teaching language and cultural practices to the next generations, believing it would be better and safer for them to simply become "Americans." And many expatriated themselves from the region entirely, looking for employment elsewhere that would relieve them and their family members "back home" from the situation of unrelenting poverty. For at least six decades and three generations, Cherokees in north-eastern Oklahoma lost the strong presence of the tribal government that had enveloped their ancestors in highly supportive Indigenous republican systems throughout the 1800s. State and federal institutions began to privilege those of lower native blood degree, coercing them into such identities as "American" and "White" while discriminating against those of higher quantum. Throughout the twentieth century, social wedges were driven among the Cherokees along the lines of race as the social costs of being Cherokee were either minimized or maximized according to quantum, and internal resentments understandably emerged (Coates, 2002).

The beginning of a resurgence of Cherokee identity claims occurred not coincidentally with the reorganization of tribal government in the late 1960s, but having lacked that government for three generations, the new claims were strongly along the lines of popular conceptions of race and culture rather than being nationalistic, especially in the generation of young adults. The resurgence existed in an atmosphere of heightened awareness of blood quantum, and often emerged from those who had returned to north-eastern Oklahoma from urban areas after the implementation of Bureau of Indian Affairs relocation policies. In addition, the Carnegie Project, anthropological fieldwork funded by the University of Chicago and under the direction of Sol Tax, brought graduate students such as Albert Wahrhaftig and Robert K. Thomas into the mix alongside seasoned activists such as Clyde Warrior, who, although himself a Ponca, resided among the Cherokees (Cobb, 2007). The Doris Duke Project also employed fieldworkers such as Howard Tyner as interviewers collected oral histories from residents of traditional Cherokee communities and focused on recording "traditional" cultural beliefs and practices.[3] The emphasis on cultural survival and blood degree is clearly reflected in the analyses from these sources which assert a distinction between "real" Cherokees and "White" Indians – and bestow legitimacy exclusively on the former. Wahrhaftig's analysis also describes the re-emerging Cherokee government and its executive, Principal Chief W.W. Keeler, as an "establishment" (using Vietnam war-era rhetoric), largely on the basis of Keeler's perceived low blood degree and his status as President of Phillips Petroleum – damning attributes in the view of these researchers and activists (Wahrhaftig, 1975a, 1975b, 1978; Wahrhaftig & Lukens-Wahrhaftig, 1977). Keeler's long connections with rural Cherokee communities were ignored and the high regard in which he was held by most traditional Cherokees of older generations was regarded as a sort of false consciousness. The newly reorganized Cherokee government was challenged and skeptically viewed from the start. Expectations were high, and it did not meet them, nor could it possibly have met them.

This perspective was shared by many Cherokees of the time, and also exists today as a consistently oppositional counterpoint to Cherokee government, no matter the administration.[4] However, there has been another concurrent attitude exhibited more quietly, but just as persistently. Less impacted by popular social movements, and more attuned to behaviours derived from Cherokee cultural and spiritual beliefs, many Cherokees have found ways in the generations of the twentieth century to leave a space open for continuing interactions between Cherokees of diverse social and political strata, including those exhibiting a range of blood degrees and cultural expressions. Within these segments of the Cherokee citizenry, a resurgence of identity is also occurring. It is a resurgence that emphasizes the specific Cherokee history of national identity and cultural adaptation, while rejecting twentieth-century constructions of blood quantum and static cultural markers. This nationalistic interpretation began to be supported institutionally by the tribal government under the twelve years of the Chad Smith administration from 1999 to 2011. For the first time since the dismantling of the Cherokee republic in preparation for Oklahoma statehood more than a century ago, the rhetoric of political nationality is widely disseminated and increasingly in use both publicly (i.e., the tribal press) and privately. Discussions of *citizenship* in the tribal government (rather than "membership") and the expression and defence of Cherokee political sovereignty are becoming almost as commonplace as they seem to have been within the Cherokee citizenry of the nineteenth century.

Nationality versus Race

The Cherokees are derided today by many other tribal peoples in the U.S. for their lack of quantum requirements. Jokes abound about how many Cherokees one would need to cram into a teepee to comprise a "full-blood," as do comments about nosebleeds and finger pricks. At present, there are some infants and toddlers registered as citizens of the Cherokee Nation who carry a Certificate of Degree of Indian Blood (CDIB) card issued by the BIA with a fraction listed of 1/4,096.[5] While many Cherokees are also shocked and dismayed to discover this, officials of the Cherokee Nation have used this fact as a demonstration of the political rather than racially constructed nature of Cherokee identity. This assertion of racial inclusiveness in the national citizenry has been especially pronounced as recent media analyses have concluded that, as a result of the tribal vote concerning the status of descendants of Cherokee Freedmen in March 2007, the "racist" Cherokees are "kicking out" "Black" Cherokees while retaining "White" Cherokees as citizens. In a particularly interesting rebuttal, the Cherokee Nation produced a media response that included photos of twelve individuals under the heading "We Are Cherokee" who are variously defined as Cherokee-Mexican, Cherokee Full-Blood, Cherokee-Ecuadorian, Cherokee–African American, Cherokee-German, Cherokee-Vietnamese, Cherokee-Irish, and Cherokee-Kickapoo, but who all held citizenship in the Cherokee Nation. The hyphenated descriptions are a rhetorical device to smooth the understanding of an American public attuned to multiculturalism; one never actually hears such hyphenated identifiers used within the Cherokee Nation or by its citizenry. But the visual evidence of a citizenry not bounded by racial constructions or phenotype accompanied text which affirmed the Cherokee Nation's historic legacy of inclusion on the basis of "one drop" concepts – in this case, one drop of Cherokee blood and you're in, *as long as the historical political citizenship of one's immediate ancestors can also be demonstrated.*

Without digressing into the complexities of the legal arguments made on both sides of this issue, it can still be noted that the distinctions between blood degree and political nationality have long been regulated by the Cherokee Nation itself. In earliest times, a strictly social definition through matrilineal clans solely defined who was considered Cherokee, excluding those who had Cherokee fathers but non-Cherokee mothers (Perdue, 1998). However, cultural boundaries could be transcended by tribal outsiders through ceremonial adoption into Cherokee clans, resulting in full incorporation into Cherokee institutions and social systems. Later, after contact, racially constructed boundaries were also transcended as "non-Indian" individuals – usually the European spouses of Cherokees in the 1600s and 1700s – became members of clans and were incorporated into the society (along with their children) as "Cherokees." The practice of inclusion of outsiders was deeply established in Cherokee social custom by the time constructions of race based in phenotype were introduced by Europeans to the Cherokees. Even afterwards, Cherokees did not seem to grasp, or perhaps consciously rejected as irrelevant to their own social classifications, these Euro-American constructs of race and blood degree (Perdue, 2003).

Instead, the Cherokee response to colonization was the development of political nationalism. By 1800, after devastating military encounters of the 1700s in both the French and Indian Wars and especially the American Revolution, younger leadership within the Cherokees was advocating the development of political nationality as the strongest way to counter the adversarial power of the U.S. in non-military fashion. The process of substantial governmental reform, ultimately leading to the implementation of a constitutional system in 1827, spanned more than two decades. There were challenges throughout as more conservative Cherokees and those of older generations resisted political restructuring. Although clearly in response to colonial occupation, the development of a national, constitutional government was entirely the desire and effort of Cherokees themselves, and not externally foisted on them by the U.S.[6] Instead, the U.S. only unwittingly assisted the Cherokees' process of nation-building by continuing to exploit the inability of their decentralized Indigenous system to defend its land in the face of federal expansionism (Hatley, 1993; Hudson, 1976; McLoughlin, 1986).

The Cherokees used their new political structures to both adapt and retain aspects of Cherokee political and social values, which were codified by statutes developed and passed by the Cherokee National Council beginning in 1808. Although not fully institutionalized until the development of the 1827 Cherokee Constitution, significant governmental restructuring along nationalist lines had already been achieved by 1817 through legislation called the *Act of Reform*.[7] In that legislation, Cherokee identity began to be redefined as a political/national rather than a social category. "Citizen" was rhetorically employed and was initially defined not by quantum, but by residency. In a coercive move intended to discourage Cherokees considering federally sponsored emigration to Arkansas Territory, the Cherokee National Council established that citizenship would thereafter be held only by those residing within Cherokee territories in the south-eastern U.S., by that time reduced to portions of Georgia, Alabama, Tennessee, and North Carolina.[8]

Political definitions of citizenship were further refined in 1819 as additional legislation was passed incorporating the intermarried White spouses of Cherokees as citizens of the nation.[9] But their citizenship had certain limitations. It extended only so far as connection to Cherokees "by blood" was retained, either through marriage or parentage. Upon the dissolution of a marriage, a non-Cherokee spouse lost their citizenship. If widowed, citizenship was retained only if there were children of the marriage. Although citizenship was not dependent on having Cherokee blood oneself, it was dependent on close familial connection with those who did. Connections between blood and political citizenship began to be made, and were internally regulated by the Cherokees themselves, but it is likely the Cherokee understanding of "blood" had more to do with familial relationships than it did with Euro-American constructs of race.

Exclusions to political citizenship in the Cherokee Nation were also elaborated in the 1820s. Several anti-miscegenation laws prohibiting intermarriage between Cherokees and Blacks, or intermarried White citizens and Blacks, were passed, along with prohibitions from including the children of such liaisons as citizens of the nation.[10] In this era, most Cherokees may still have been at odds with Euro-American constructs of race as based in phenotypic characteristics conceptually linked to social categories and characteristics, as "race" is popularly understood in contemporary times. It is questioned by some as to whether Americans even constructed racial categories in the nineteenth century in just the same way they are presently constructed. But most theorists regard racial construction, in the past or the present, as ultimately rooted in power dynamics, with phenotype as but a physical representation of those dynamics (Omi & Winant, 1994). In an era when phenotype had little or no relationship to the social categories that *were* constructed by the Cherokees – each of the seven clans within their society and the eighth category they regarded internally as "other" – they nevertheless were affected by power dynamics within the American South and they undoubtedly noted differences of appearance.

Cherokee leadership was diverse. Some members of the governing body, the National Council, were businessmen who were the descendants of European traders and Cherokee women. Some were Cherokees who had been raised in hunter-warrior cultural traditions but who had developed plantations and were slaveholders themselves. Others were traditionalists and ceremonialists who came from a subsistence-based economic stratum. Still others were professed Christians, educated at mission schools, but practitioners of a syncretic faith. While those who were more acculturated to the Euro-American system undoubtedly grasped its racial constructs, the majority of Cherokees unquestionably did not. It would have been a difficult concept to translate, not only across words but worldviews. But social power was a familiar concept in both societies, and colonization was beginning to be overtly identified by Cherokees as well, even though it was not named such at the time.

Located in the American South as they were, Cherokees were familiar with the region's power dynamics and their place within them. Categorized along with free Blacks in the Southern states as second-class "free persons of color," the restrictive category meant that under the laws of Southern states, Cherokees could not vote (probably of negligible importance to them), but also that Cherokee land titles were denied, as free persons of colour were restricted from landholding. At a critical moment, when the pressures for removal were rising against them in a dramatic way, the need to defend themselves, their government, and their land base required that the Cherokees conceptually separate themselves in the eyes of Americans and southerners from any group regarded as holding a politically or socially disadvantaged position. Thus the need to conceptually separate themselves from Africans in the view of White southerners was strategically important and evidenced in the passage of the anti-miscegenation laws of the 1820s. These laws and the refusal to accept those of Cherokee-African ancestry as citizens were initially the result of ugly, pragmatic, nationalist considerations (Perdue, 2003; Yarbrough, 2008).

But they also corresponded with Cherokee social custom. As liaisons between Blacks and Cherokees most often involved a Cherokee man and a Black woman, the children of such relationships wouldn't have had clans under the Cherokees' matrilineal system, and thus wouldn't have been accepted under older social custom, either. That the Cherokees still held a residual conceptual coupling of clans with citizenship is indicated by the passage of additional legislation in 1825 which incorporated the children of Cherokee men and *White* women (emphasis mine) as citizens of the Cherokee Nation, consciously separating the social concept of clan from nationality, and again privileging the political/national definition over the social.[11] The specific inclusion of the children of White women (who would not have had Cherokee clans) may be evidence of Cherokee acceptance of Euro-American racial constructs, or it may instead be further awareness of Southern power dynamics which elevated the status of phenotypic "Whites" above that of phenotypic "Indians." Although some members of Cherokee society were phenotypically White, Southern society still regarded them as Indians and therefore inferior in their rights and social standing. Intermarriages with Whites – particularly White women in an era when relationships between White women and men of colour were not only scandalous, but often dangerous for all parties – challenged Southern power structures. The desire of Whites to marry Indians and to reside and raise their children in Indian society supported the Cherokee insistence at the time of the rights, even the superiority, of their society over that of southerners and Americans generally (Perdue, 2003).

As nationalistic definitions of identity rose in the first decades of the 1800s, racialized Cherokee identities also began to be implemented by the U.S. As justification of intensifying pressures to remove Cherokees to lands west of the Mississippi River, federal reports painted a picture of a Cherokee population in which "mixed-blood" leaders, exercising authority disproportionate to their overall numbers within the tribe, were manipulating ignorant "full-bloods" into blind resistance against their own best interests, which federal authorities posited as being removal to areas where they could have a longer period of time to adjust to "civilizing" policies.[12] However, the Cherokees reframed the racialized terminologies, especially that of "full-blood," applying sociocultural definitions instead which are in use to this day among the citizenry. Describing individuals who spoke the Cherokee language, were raised in traditional cultural practices, and held an Indigenous thought process and worldview, the Cherokee definition of "full-blood" was not only more substantial in its meaning, it was typically far more inclusive of those individuals who met the above criteria but who were also racially mixed. And today, it is likely that the majority of individuals who are described or who self-describe as "full-bloods" in the Cherokee Nation are of mixed racial ancestry (Coates, 2002).

Unquestionable evidence of Cherokee rejection of racialized identities is found in the Cherokee selection of their principal chief throughout the middle decades of the nineteenth century. John Ross, always described by historians as a wealthy, elite, mixed-blood Cherokee of "only" one-eighth blood degree, was consistently re-elected for thirty-eight years by a citizenry that was comprised overwhelmingly of "full-bloods" – by both American racial and Cherokee sociocultural constructs.[13] However, Ross had the all the attributes that made him a Cherokee by anyone's reckoning in this transitional period between social definitions (clan) and political definitions (residency and descent) of citizenship. Himself an ardent nationalist, Ross's administration successfully promoted deep Cherokee investment in the national definition.

The restructuring as a national government allowed the Cherokees to defend their sovereignty and their territory in the south-east for longer than any other tribal group. But ultimately, the Cherokees, too, were forcibly removed from their homelands in the ethnic cleansing known as the Trail of Tears. In their new lands in the Indian Territory (present-day Oklahoma), a superseding constitution was developed by September 1839, demonstrating the priority the Cherokees gave to the re-establishment of a national government. The residency requirement for citizenship was continued, defined now as residency in the new lands. Those who had remained in the south-east or who had not completed the journey to the Indian Territory lost their citizenship by those actions. To address this reality, the 1839 Cherokee Constitution gave the National Council the authority to reinstate citizenship to Cherokees who moved into the national boundaries, and about 5,000 additional Cherokees received citizenship in this fashion, the majority during the pre-allotment period of the 1880s and 1890s (Burton, 1995; Sober, 1991).

Sovereignty and Indigeneity

In general, the treaties between the U.S. and the Cherokee Nation in the early 1800s acknowledge the national status and the jurisdictional and regulatory authority of the Cherokee Nation over its citizens of varying blood degrees and racial constructions, as well as the sovereign right of the Cherokee Nation to set its own citizenship criteria. Although the U.S. courts began to erode Cherokee jurisdictional sovereignty over its intermarried White citizens as early as 1846 in the case of *US v. Rogers*, the relatively low level of federal interference throughout the mid-nineteenth century into Cherokee national affairs, coupled with the fee simple ownership of their lands via federal patent, allowed the Cherokees to quickly re-establish and elaborate republican institutions, which were nonetheless adapted to Indigenous customs and tribal patterns of collective land usage. A "Golden Age" resulted, evidenced by high rates of literacy, public co-educational institutions funded by the Cherokee government, and general prosperity even within the subsistence class to which the vast majority of Cherokees belonged.

Federal imposition into determinations of Cherokee citizenship began after the American Civil War. Approximately 3 per cent of the Cherokees had been owners of Black chattel slaves. Drawn into a war in which the great majority did not perceive themselves as having an interest, and forced to make a strategic alliance with the Confederacy even though 70 per cent of the citizenry had no such sympathies, the Cherokees freed themselves from that alliance by early 1863 (McLoughlin, 1993). Rejecting those Cherokees still willingly allying with Confederate forces, the Cherokee national government, still under the leadership of John Ross, passed an emancipation proclamation as part of their repudiation of the Confederate treaty. However, that proclamation, while freeing the slaves, also explicitly stated that they were not to be incorporated as citizens of the Cherokee Nation (Denson, 2004, p. 75). Cherokee perceptions may have been that the majority of those slaves did not meet the "blood" criteria they had long been using for citizenship – not as people who were racially "Indian," but as people who had familial connections to Cherokees by marriage or parentage, even as they were not themselves Cherokee.

In the years afterwards, as one of many punitive measures in retaliation for the Cherokees' brief, strategic Southern alliance, the U.S. forced the Cherokees to reverse their own decision regarding citizenship criteria and incorporate their Freedmen, as well as Delawares and Shawnees being relocated from reservations in Kansas, into their citizenry. The Cherokees resisted the incorporation of all three groups, but held hostage by the U.S. government to their need to re-establish the federal treaty relationship which had been broken by their Confederate treaty, the Cherokees had little choice but to acquiesce to federal demands (McLoughlin, 1993). The coercive 1866 Treaty defines the Freedmen as having "rights," which may or may not indicate citizenship. The citizenship of Freedmen was perhaps more clearly defined by an amendment to the 1839 Cherokee Constitution. In article nine of the treaty itself, the Cherokees attempted to limit the numbers of Freedmen they would be compelled to incorporate by extending only a six-month window of opportunity from the date of the treaty's ratification as the time frame within which their claims could be made.[14] After that date, the offer closed. Knowing that many of the Freedmen had fled the Indian Territory during the Civil War (as had many Indians), the Cherokee Nation was betting that many of them would not hear of the extension of citizenship and would not return to the Nation in time to make a claim. It was a good bet on the Cherokees' part, but it also led to disputes with the Freedmen for decades afterwards until the time of Oklahoma statehood in 1907.

The resistance on the part of the Cherokees to the incorporation of not only the Freedmen but also the Delawares and Shawnees likely stemmed from a single source – the great majority of them were not of Cherokee descent, nor did they have close familial connections to those who were. This had long been the standard that Cherokees had applied in regulating their own citizenry. The era immediately following the Civil War represents the first serious imposition of the federal government into definitions of citizenship, and the beginning of an unrelenting federal erosion of Cherokee political sovereignty in general. Protested by not only the Cherokees, but also the Delawares and Shawnees, whose own tribal existences were being forcibly subsumed into Cherokee nationality, the disputes between the four groups – Cherokees, Freedmen, Delawares, and Shawnees – continued throughout the nineteenth century and extend into this day as evidence of the problematic results of an occupying nation's interference into the process of Indigenous self-definition.

These impositions only heightened the resistant sense of national identity among the Cherokees. Throughout the last decades of the 1800s, the Cherokee Nation kept a lobbying delegation in Washington that employed a sophisticated rhetoric of nationality as the basis for the nation's defence against movements for allotment, territorial organization, and Oklahoma statehood. At home, a lively discussion of the increasing threats to national sovereignty was carried out in the tribal newspapers and in written and verbal communications among the Cherokee citizens. In 1888 and 1892, the Cherokee National Council printed texts in both English and the Cherokee syllabary that contained the treaties, constitution, and laws of the Cherokee Nation. Many citizens purchased these texts and these little antique books are retained in Cherokee families today. By the late 1800s, it would have been difficult to identify Cherokees, even among the most conservative classes, who did not hold a deep, abiding belief in and love of their national government, and who were not cognizant of the political basis of the struggle to retain it.

Also by the late 1800s, a familiar phenomenon was already occurring. After the Civil War, many impoverished or dispossessed southerners, both White and Black – or those who had engaged in criminal activity – migrated to the Indian Territory seeking a place to start over or simply escape. Soon after, the Cherokee Nation again began to assert its jurisdictional authority over labour and citizenship, limiting the numbers of Americans that Cherokee employers could legally hire and tightening the requirements by which Whites could attain citizenship through intermarriage with Cherokees (there was no acknowledgment of intermarriage between Cherokees and Blacks). In the three decades afterwards, still more intruders were drawn to the Cherokee Nation seeking to take advantage of the free public educational system, the thriving economy, the sophisticated government, occasional per capita payments, and the perception that "free" land was available. Claims of Cherokee ancestry by many of these immigrants resulted in increasing demands to be recognized as citizens in order to share in the perceived bounty (Sober, 1991).

By 1887, the Cherokee Nation had established citizenship courts to examine the many claims. Almost immediately, 2,100 petitions for citizenship, perhaps representing as many as 6,000 individuals (sometimes an entire family would be on one petition), were filed with the commission. In the five years in which the courts operated, over 5,000 individuals, mainly family members of Cherokee citizens who had recently moved to the Cherokee Nation from other parts of the country, were incorporated as they satisfied the residency requirement and the proof of familial ties. But in the same years, the Cherokees also denied over

7,000 petitions, perhaps representing as many as 20,000 individuals, on the grounds that they had no Cherokee ancestry themselves and no family ties to those who did. The Cherokee attempt to once again regulate citizenship requirements had been undercut by the federal court, which ordered that if a citizenship petition was denied by the Cherokee court, an appeal could be filed with the federal court – and while the appeal was pending, the intruder could continue to reside in the Cherokee Nation, now with legal status. The petitions thus represented a win-win situation for the illegal intruders in the Cherokee Nation, who, by 1890, outnumbered the Cherokees themselves (Sober, 1991).

The allotment fiasco followed soon after. The clamour for "free" land led to 300,000 claims of citizenship throughout the Indian Territory, despite estimates that only about 100,000 people were regarded as eligible for allotments. At this point, the Cherokee Nation's insistence in the recent decades that citizenship requirements were within its own purview, and the continuous regulatory attempts, proved beneficial to the enrolment process. The Dawes Commission followed relatively closely the Cherokees' own determinations of its citizens in either accepting or denying potential enrollees. But the Dawes Commission also recorded blood degrees of enrollees, something the Cherokee Nation had never used as a determinant of rights or identity within the political nation (Carter, 1999). Most of those fractional determinations were made hastily, cavalierly, and on the flimsiest of bases, but they became useful in the twentieth century in dividing a national group. As the land was quickly occupied by Whites, all that remained was to occupy the collective sense of identity of the former Cherokee citizenry.

The de facto (although not actually legally enacted) termination of the Cherokee Nation occurred at the time of Oklahoma statehood in 1907, and with the ending of a strong tribal-national presence, "citizen" became irrelevant and state and federal institutions promoted the perception of Cherokees as a people defined solely by a blood identity, rather than a combined descent and political status. Cherokee became a "heritage" rather than a nationality. Some persons of Cherokee heritage were entirely acceptable to state and federal structures. Those who were more acculturated, who spoke English, who had Western-style educations, and who had experience with a cash economy became regional political figures and served as mayors, on school boards and town councils, and as local law enforcement. Some even became state or federal legislators. The hegemonic institutions were eager to uphold such individuals as examples of the progressive nature of "our" Cherokees as the Indian Territory origins of the new state were symbolically celebrated (Coates, 2002; Wahrhaftig & Lukens-Wahrhaftig, 1977).

But the larger reality of those origins was inconvenient, and the state turned its gaze away from another stratum of Cherokees. Those who lived a subsistence lifestyle were negatively stereotyped as ignorant, superstitious, uneducated, and drunken, and they faced the extreme social costs. Economically and politically marginalized after statehood, these communities withdrew into isolation and deep, endemic poverty, which persisted for decades and only began to truly be addressed once the Cherokee Nation re-established a governmental existence in the 1970s.

These strata were often identified in racial and phenotypic terms. The first group was described as having Cherokee "blood," while the other was described (even by those who had Cherokee blood themselves) as the "Indians." But between these two groups – one encouraged to be proud of their Cherokee heritage, the other unable to escape it – a third Cherokee population existed. Those Cherokees were from rural and working-class families, lacking the prominence required for their heritage to be strategically touted, but ambiguous enough in their appearance and behaviours for their Indianness to be denied, rejected, or ignored by the larger society. These persons had probably comprised the largest stratum of the Cherokee citizenry at the time of Oklahoma statehood, and they were the stratum for whom Cherokee identity probably rested most in their nationality, rather than racial or cultural markers. With the loss of that nation/nationality, they were left vulnerable to coercive measures that shifted them away from an identity as "Cherokee" and towards an identity as "White" and "American." In interviews in the Western History Collection at the University of Oklahoma, as well as interviews I have conducted with expatriate Cherokees today, numerous Cherokees who were children in the 1930s and 1940s, when Johnson-O'Malley (JOM) school programs for Indian children were introduced, recall their experiences of raising their hands when the Indian children were asked to identify themselves by the teacher for federal counting purposes, and then being told to put their hands down because they didn't appear to have enough blood quantum to qualify. That so many research subjects, independent of each other, recalled this moment indicates the power it held for them as small children in denying their nascent identity (Coates, 2005). Conversely, the same practice may have been the beginning of a sense on the part of those of higher quantum that they were the "real" Indians, the only real Indians.

But in adults of the 1920s, 1930s, and 1940s, the recollection of nation was still sharp. Renowned University of Oklahoma historian E.E. Dale recounted an interview with a Cherokee woman from the late 1940s in which she had begun to cry at the memory of the day Oklahoma became a state, for that was the day when she "lost her country and her people's country" (Gregory & Strickland, 1981). By the 1920s, in the midst of the endemic poverty of traditional communities, grassroots political activity emerged as an attempt to replace the supportive and protective functions the Cherokee Nation had previously exercised. A consortium of organizations existed which by the 1940s was being referred to as an "Executive Council," echoing the business model that had been promoted by federal legislations such as the *Indian Reorganization Act* and the *Oklahoma Indian Welfare Act*. The consortium's organizational members ranged from ceremonial groups such as the Nighthawk Keetoowah Society and the Four Mothers Society to the more acculturated Cherokees of the Seminary Students Alumni Association. These were the strata of Cherokee society that had been able to retain identity, either as a heritage to be celebrated or as a marginalized existence imposed by state and federal institutions. But all retained strong recollections of republic and nation, and of a Cherokee society that had been politically integrated, despite diversity and upheaval, under the umbrella of shared nationality (Meredith, 1985).

From this mid-century leadership of well-known individuals such as Jesse Bartley (J.B.) Milam, Levi Gritts, Gabriel Tarrepin, and Sam Smith, figures that exemplify the range of strata and quanta within which Cherokee nationalism still simmered, that nation began to be refashioned. Milam, appointed in 1941 by President Franklin Roosevelt as principal chief, was also one of the founders of the National Congress of American Indians (NCAI). He used the possibility of Cherokee participation in the NCAI as a tool to argue to the Bureau of Indian Affairs for the re-establishment of a Cherokee tribal council. The argument was accepted by the bureau, but unfortunately, the Cherokees were unable to agree on its composition. At the same time, Gritts and Tarrepin sought additional assistance for Cherokee communities through the federal establishment, under the terms of the *Oklahoma Indian Welfare Act*, of their community organization as a band within the Cherokee Nation called the United Keetoowah Band (UKB). With the establishment of this corporate group, additional programs and funding offered under the OIWA could be accessed. Smith and the ceremonial Nighthawk Keetoowahs (a different organization from the UKB) also demonstrated their continuing commitment to Cherokee nationality by urging the Gritts-Tarrepin organization to "stay with the Cherokee Nation" (Meredith, 1985).

The former citizenry that was less able to "stay with the Cherokee Nation" were the majority whose existence lay in the cracks somewhere between a renowned heritage and cultural conservatism. With their nationality erased, suffering the same loss of land and governmental support resulting from the allotment and tribal termination, and not as tied culturally to traditional systems of mutual support as those in the conservative communities, many began to leave the region throughout the 1930s and 1940s in search of work. Over four decades, the Cherokee diaspora emerged as, ultimately, about 60 per cent of the Cherokee population was drawn away from north-eastern Oklahoma on an "Economic Trail of Tears." Today, the largest concentration of those persons are in California (where tribal citizens of the Cherokee Nation comprise the largest tribal group in the state), with Texas, Oregon, Washington state, and Kansas also displaying significant Cherokee populations (Coates, 2002).

As efforts to re-establish nationality increased during the 1950s and 1960s, and were finally achieved in the early 1970s, lineages from the Executive Council of the 1940s are clearly observable. As oil-company executive W.W. Keeler and banker Ross Swimmer became principal chiefs in these decades, the confidence of heritage displayed by the renowned Cherokees combined with the grassroots efforts of the Original Cherokee Community Organizations (OCCO) to redevelop tribal legislative and constitutional structures in the 1970s. Although younger and more urban activists of the era challenged both Keeler and Swimmer, more traditional Cherokees had an abiding love for Keeler in particular (Mankiller & Wallis, 1993).[15] The devotion to a barely existent nationality that had endured more than sixty years of suppression in the twentieth century was reinvigorated in Cherokees of vastly different experience, who nevertheless committed themselves to a rocky relationship with each other in order to see the Cherokee Nation revitalized.

Together, the executive branch and community organizations developed a superseding constitution, which was ratified in 1975. This constitution, developed by the Cherokees themselves, references the Dawes Rolls as the base rolls for membership in the late twentieth century, but, following the historic Cherokee assertion of a political rather than racial identity, has no reference to a minimum required blood degree, only to descent.[16] It removed the residency requirement of the preceding 1839 constitution, since there was no longer any tribal land base to speak of. By the 1980s, an aggressive registration effort, spurred by the administration of Wilma Mankiller, was underway as the tens of thousands of Cherokees outside the boundary were sought and registered.[17] With the re-establishment of national structures, the door was opened for the majority of the Cherokees – those whose ancestors' primary identity had been located in citizenship – to be reclaimed.

The loss of political identity has been especially pronounced in the expatriate citizenry. Popular notions of blood and heritage abound, and the relationships to Cherokee identity among those individuals who are of relatively low blood degree are complex. Most participants state a real pride in their heritage and claim it openly, although this pride is often accompanied by a remark that they have "not very much" Cherokee blood. Some are aware of challenges to their claims by those of higher quantum, but many state that they have never been challenged nor had any problems related to their blood degree.[18] Overall, however, in both those who have had difficulties related to quantum and cultural attributes, there is some insecurity about their right to make such claims and defensiveness stemming from repeated rejection of their claims.

However, one thing that becomes immediately apparent from my collection of interviews is that the Cherokee Nation's historic emphasis on a political nation and citizenry has resulted in a greatly strengthened knowledge of one's Cherokee family in the present citizens as opposed to the descendants of non-citizens. Those who were citizens of the Cherokee Nation were able to tell me the family names of their ancestors and the communities they were from in Oklahoma. They knew where their allotment lands had been located and what had caused their family to leave. Most had continuing communications and interactions with Oklahoma, and many made a point of regularly visiting.

Those who were not citizens generally had only a story in the family about a distant ancestor who was Cherokee, but they had as yet been unable to verify it, or had even found documentation tending to discount the claim.[19] They had family stories that they willingly shared, mostly set in Texas, Arkansas, and Missouri, and many of them were at least plausible in that they could possibly be explained within the context of Cherokee historical dispersion of individuals. Others, however, were clearly without merit, even as the speaker genuinely believed and was deeply invested in their ancestor's alleged Cherokee identity.

However, a study of the history of nationalism and national identity among the Cherokees clarifies the confusions many people have about themselves, their claims, and their place both as part of the diaspora and in relation to the Cherokee Nation. In the U.S., the line defining Indigenous identity is fuzzy around the question of identity based in blood degree, cultural attributes, linguistic characteristics, and descent. But in the Cherokee Nation, a long history of defining "citizen" has been inclusive of great diversity under an overarching standard of descent and residency. There has been clarity, as long as the Cherokee Nation itself was making those determinations.[20]

Nationalism and Citizenship as Resurgence

For those confused as to why they are not accepted as citizens of the Cherokee Nation in the present day, an understanding of the political distinctions made not on the basis of blood degree, but on that of historic residency, clarifies the issue without calling their ethnic ancestry into question.[21] For those who are citizens of the Cherokee Nation but have insecurity about their status on the basis of low blood degree, an understanding of nationality reinforces the validity of their claims.[22] One expatriate, who had wrestled for many years with questions of identity, summed up his shifted conception after coming to a better understanding of the particular history of the Cherokee Nation. "I always thought the question was, 'Am I Indian?' And I could never find a comfortable response. But that's not the question, is it? The question is, 'Am I a citizen of the Cherokee Nation?' And the answer is, 'Yes, I am!'"[23]

The focus on nationality thus contributes to resurgent potentials for Cherokee Nation citizens both within the boundaries, where the possibility for interaction with cultural communities and the tribal government are readily available, and especially for diasporic citizens who have fewer opportunities to manifest their Cherokee identities through cultural expressions or racial identification. National identity as a "citizen" encourages a sense of inclusion and confidence to pursue greater cultural knowledge and civic interaction among their own people while standing up to the challenges to their identity from those who don't have the knowledge of the Cherokees' particular history. The privileging and support of the national aspect of identity by the tribal government tends to subdue the challenges from within, as well as give expatriates a tangible place to reconnect.

In addition, the Cherokee Nation is aware of its own history of dispersion and dispersed individuals, and today hopes to open a space for participation by non-citizens committed to developing civic and cultural connections with the Nation in respectful, responsible ways. "Satellite" organizations of the Cherokee Nation have been established in areas where there are concentrations of citizens, but non-citizen Cherokee claimants are also welcome to participate, as long as the direction of the group remains firmly under Cherokee citizens. This serves a dual purpose of keeping non-citizens aligned to Cherokee culture and communities in a more authentic way while at the same time marginalizing those individuals and organizations who act in a fashion that competes with and challenges the Cherokee Nation's rights of representation and jurisdiction.

Clearly the nationalistic definition is not as historically pronounced for most tribal groups in the U.S. as it has been for the Cherokees. But in the twentieth century and leading up to the present time, tribes in this country are enacting sovereignty in ways that clearly meld an asserted national existence with Indigenous customs and values. Academia, while it may focus on ethnic, racial, and cultural discussions in its global, comparative investigations of indigeneity, would best serve the tribal governments of the U.S. by bringing the component of Indigenous nationality to the forefront in order that it not undermine that which is so very crucial to tribes in the U.S. While recognizing that ethnic and cultural identities also exist in Indigenous peoples in the U.S., academia must be sensitive and supportive to the privileging of national/legal identities within the U.S., not necessarily and not always as federally imposed mechanisms of colonization, but in some instances as internally regulated standards exercised by the tribes themselves and based in their own particular histories. Tribal governments in the U.S. cannot afford to lose control of this process if they are to maintain this "sovereignty thing!"

NOTES

1 Approximately 180,000 of the Cherokee Nation's 305,000 citizens reside outside the Nation's jurisdictional boundaries, according to data from the Cherokee Nation's Registration and GIS departments.

2 Paraphrased from a statement by Dr. Richard Allen, Cherokee Nation policy analyst, 4 May 2007.

3 These interviews are part of the Doris Duke collection at the Western History Museum at the University of Oklahoma.

4 This oppositional counterpoint is very prominent in Circe Sturm's *Blood Politics, Race, Culture, and Identity in the Cherokee Nation of Oklahoma*, for instance, which relied heavily on an informant who has aggressively challenged every administration of the Cherokee Nation in the past three decades and the communities and individuals with whom he was affiliated that share the same oppositional stances. While this is certainly one segment of the Cherokee society, it is not the only segment, nor is it even the sole

perspective from the "core" traditionalist segment, though it was generally represented in Dr. Sturm's work as though it is. It is also a perspective that tends to be very fluid in individuals, depending upon the particular issue or circumstance.

5 As reported by the late Lela Ummerteskee, Cherokee Nation Registrar.

6 It is interesting to consider that even when internally instigated, dramatic governmental reforms and the resulting investment of a population in constitutional processes may nevertheless take decades or even generations to achieve. This certainly would not seem to bode well for reforms imposed from outside.

7 Laws of the Cherokee Nation (LCN) 4–5, passed 6 May 1817.

8 Two years later, in the 1819 treaty amendments, the residency requirement resulted in the loss of Cherokee Nation citizenship for hundreds of Cherokees in western North Carolina as Cherokee land in that region was ceded to the United States. This population politically evolved to become the Eastern Band of Cherokee Indians, and have been separate from the citizenry of the Cherokee Nation since 1819.

9 LCN 10, passed 2 November 1819.

10 LCN 38, passed 11 November 1824.

11 LCN 57, passed 10 November 1825.

12 These racialized constructions have been largely uncritically replicated (with some exceptions) by American historians of the Cherokees.

13 Ross's blood degree never goes without mention by historians and is apparently confounding to Americans.

14 Article 9 of the 1866 Treaty reads, "The Cherokee Nation, having voluntarily, in February, eighteen hundred and sixty-three, by an act of the national council, forever abolished slavery, hereby covenant and agree that never hereafter shall either slavery or involuntary servitude exist in their nation otherwise than in the punishment of crime, whereof the party shall have been duly convicted, in accordance with the laws applicable to all the members of said tribe alike. They further agree that all Freedmen who have been liberated by a voluntary act of their former owners or by law, as well as all free colored persons who were in the country at the commencement of the rebellion, and are now residents therein, or who may return within six months, and their descendants, shall have all the rights of native Cherokees: Provided, That owners of slaves so emancipated in the Cherokee Nation shall never receive any compensation or pay for the slaves so emancipated."

15 Keeler, whose mother displayed extrasensory abilities, was deeply interested in paranormal phenomena, and Swimmer frequently consulted Cherokee medicine people after being diagnosed with cancer in the 1980s.

These attributes alone, displayed by some of the wealthiest and most acculturated Cherokees of their time, indicate a complexity in their relationships to more traditional beliefs and values that endeared these men to many of their more conservative compatriots.

16 Interestingly, the language of "membership" is used throughout, and only once does a reference to "citizen" appear, as meaning someone who is listed as an original enrollee on the Dawes Commission Rolls.

17 "The boundary" refers to the jurisdictional service area of the Cherokee Nation today, which is within fourteen counties of north-eastern Oklahoma. It represents the former Cherokee land base ceded to the Nation by the U.S. in 1828.

18 It becomes somewhat apparent, however, that this is primarily because they don't interact very frequently with Indians of other tribes.

19 Many had, in fact, found record of the ancestor in question stating that the person was "White." The fact that a Black-White racial binary existed throughout the South in the late nineteenth and twentieth centuries may obscure other ancestries.

20 However, federal interference into the questions of citizenship criteria that began immediately after the Civil War has reverberated to this day, resulting in a distinct lack of clarity.

21 The Cherokee Nation has been active in the early twenty-first century in repudiating such claims when the claimant or group of claimants is asserting rights of representation, jurisdiction, or government that compete with the historic standing of the Cherokee Nation.

22 A friend of mine, when asked how much Cherokee he is, responds by posing a counter question: "Well, how much Baptist are you?" No one would think to ask a person how much American they are, and this becomes apparent when we think in nationalistic rather than racial/genetic terms.

23 From a conversation with a Cherokee Nation History Course participant, San Francisco, CA, 2003.

REFERENCES

Alfred, G.T. (1999). *Peace, Power, Righteousness: An Indigenous Manifesto*. Don Mills, ON: Oxford University Press.

Burton, J. (1995). *Indian Territory and the United States, 1866–1906*. Norman, OK: University of Oklahoma Press.

Carter, K. (1999). *The Dawes Commission and the Allotment of the Five Civilized Tribes, 1893–1914*. Orem, UT: Ancestry.com Incorporated.

Cattelino, J.R. (2008). *High Stakes, Florida Seminole Gaming and Sovereignty*. Durham, NC: Duke University Press.

Coates, J. (2002). *None of Us Are Supposed to Be Here: Ethnicity, Nationality, and the Production of Cherokee Histories*. Unpublished PhD Dissertation, American Studies, University of New Mexico.

Coates, J. (2005). The Expatriate Phenomenon, Cherokee Displacement in the 1900s. Presentation at the Oklahoma Historical Society's annual meeting, Muskogee, OK, unpublished.

Cobb, D. (2007). Devils in Disguise, the Carnegie Project, the Cherokee Nation and the 1960s. *American Indian Quarterly*, *31*(3), 465–90. http://dx.doi.org/10.1353/aiq.2007.0030

Deloria, V., & Clifford, M.L. (1983). *American Indians, American Justice*. Austin, TX: University of Texas Press.

Deloria, V., & Clifford, M.L. (1984). *The Nations Within: The Past, Present and Future of American Indian Sovereignty*. New York: Pantheon.

Deloria, V., & Wilkins, D.E. (1999). *Tribes, Treaties, and Constitutional Tribulations*. Austin, TX: University of Texas Press.

Denson, A. (2004). *Demanding the Cherokee Nation, Indian Autonomy and American Culture, 1830–1900*. Lincoln, NB: University of Nebraska Press.

Garroutte, E.M. (2003). *Real Indians, Identity and the Survival of Native America*. Berkeley, CA: University of California Press.

Gregory, J., & Strickland, R. (1981). *Indians in Oklahoma*. Norman, OK: University of Oklahoma Press.

Hatley, T. (1993). *The Dividing Paths: Cherokees and South Carolinians through the Era of the Revolution*. New York: Oxford University Press.

Hudson, C. (1976). *The Southeastern Indians*. Knoxville, TN: University of Tennessee Press.

Jorgensen, M. (Ed.). (2007). *Rebuilding Native Nations, Strategies for Governance and Development*. Tucson, AZ: University of Arizona Press.

Mankiller, W., & Wallis, M. (1993). *Mankiller, a Chief and Her People*. New York: St. Martin's Press.

McLoughlin, W. (1986). *Cherokee Renascence in the New Republic*. Princeton: Princeton University Press.

McLoughlin, W. (1993). *After the Trail of Tears, the Cherokees' Struggle for Sovereignty 1839–1880*. Chapel Hill, NC: University of North Carolina Press.

Meredith, H.L. (1985). *Bartley Milam, Principal Chief of the Cherokee Nation*. Muskogee, IN: Indian University Press.

Omi, M., & Winant, H. (1994). *Racial Formation in the United States* (2nd ed.). New York: Routledge.

Perdue, T. (1998). *Cherokee Women*. Lincoln, NB: University of Nebraska Press.

Perdue, T. (2003). *Mixed Blood Indians, Racial Construction in the Early South*. Athens, GA: University of Georgia Press.

Sober, N. (1991). *The Intruders, the Illegal Residents of the Cherokee Nation 1866–1907*. Ponca City, OK: Cherokee Books.

Wahrhaftig, A. (1975a). *In the Aftermath of Civilization*. Unpublished PhD dissertation, Anthropology, University of Chicago.

Wahrhaftig, A. (1975b). Institution Building among Oklahoma's Traditional Cherokees. In C. Hudson (Ed.), *Four Centuries of Southern Indians* (pp. 132–47). Athens, GA: University of Georgia Press.

Wahrhaftig, A. (1978). Making Do with the Dark Meat: A Report on the Cherokee Indians in Oklahoma. In S. Stanley (Ed.), *American Indian Economic Development* (pp. 409–510). The Hague: Moulton Publishers. http://dx.doi.org/10.1515/9783110800029.409

Wahrhaftig, A., & Lukens-Wahrhaftig, J. (1977). The Thrice Powerless: Cherokee Indians in Oklahoma. In R.D. Fogelson & R.N. Adams (Eds.), *The Anthropology of Power: Ethnographic Studies from Asia, Oceania, and the New World* (pp. 225–36). New York: Academic Press.

Warrior, R. (1994). *Tribal Secrets: Recovering American Indian Intellectual Traditions*. Minneapolis, MN: University of Minnesota Press.

Wilkins, D.E., & Lomawaima, K.T. (2001). *Uneven Ground: American Indian Sovereignty and Federal Law*. Norman, OK: University of Oklahoma Press.

Womack, C. (1999). *Red on Red: Native American Literary Separatism*. Minneapolis, MN: University of Minnesota Press.

Yarbrough, F.A. (2008). *Race and the Cherokee Nation, Sovereignty in the Nineteenth Century*. Philadelphia, PA: University of Pennsylvania Press.

5 Locating Identity: The Role of Place in Costa Rican Chorotega Identity

KAREN STOCKER

By performing customs for national and international tourist audiences, the Chorotega of Costa Rica are both asserting their authenticity as bearers of an Indigenous label and working within the global and national circumstances that have influenced the range of economic options available to them. While place of residence once constituted the basis of discrimination against them, inhabitants of the Chorotega reservation now rely on the designation of their land as a reservation to authenticate their practices as Indigenous. At the same time that local place takes on such great significance, global phenomena, too, have left their mark. Community members are now resorting to the written records of the conquistadors – the very people responsible for the legacy of marginalization still lived by the modern-day Chorotega – at the same time that they interpret and enact those writings through the lenses of popular global media and academic discourse for use towards self-definition and autonomy. Recurrent throughout discussions of identity and representation for the Chorotega of Costa Rica is the salience of place as constituting either the basis of stigma or value, as local, national, and global discourses shift the meaning of indigeneity and the perceptions of cultural practices stemming from it.

In 1999, the festival in honour of the Virgin of Guadalupe to be held in Guanacaste, Costa Rica, was advertised on posters that demonstrated the syncretic nature of this particular event. The elements of the celebration that bear European roots were evident in its underlying Catholicism. These were left implicit in the advertisement. The image that served, explicitly, to announce the impending festival bore symbols of Indianness that would be recognized as such by a wide audience. The image of a dark-skinned man with a wig of long, black, slightly tangled hair, bright war paint, and feathers reminiscent of stereotypical Indians sat astride a mare (in a subtle reference to local lore) draped in ancient textiles. In the parade that constituted a major part of the event itself, parishioners, townspeople, and clergy marched down the centre of town with the figure of the Virgin of Guadalupe, clad in her finest regalia. Leading this parade was a row of young boys dressed in the attire of Costa Rican traditional dancers performing the role of rural dweller or *campesino*. The drums they played, painted with tomahawks, established the practice, implicitly, as Indigenous, although tomahawks are not part of the local archaeological record, and face paint and feathers are classic Hollywood's signature way of homogenizing Indigenous peoples. Although most of the image bears no semblance to current or past Chorotega Indigenous[1] reality, foreign visitors (and locals, as well) would recognize it as smacking of an ostensibly (albeit erroneously so) homogenized Indianness. Tourists and others that might miss the subtle visual allusion to local oral history about the Virgin-turned-mare that saved belligerent drunkards from death would surely recognize the advertised Indianness on the poster and in the event itself. Nearly ten years later, a new performance has residents of the reservation dressed in ways reflecting conquistadors' descriptions and adorned with body paint more in keeping with the image of U.S. Western films than of ancient practice.

Such pageantry should be taken neither as indication of local ignorance nor as the willful manipulation of consumers of culture. It is a product of history in a place that denied Indigenous existence for centuries, followed by a legal system that recognized it, encapsulated it in reservations, and sought to assimilate it. The "success" of such assimilation projects is evident in the fact that in order to present Chorotega Indigenous imagery today, it must be done through artefacts left over from a past when Indigenous existence was undeniable, or it must follow stereotypes plain enough to be recognized as Indian in a nation whose appropriation of Indigenous traditions has rendered them ineffective at evoking recognition of their Chorotega origins. These stereotypical images, in turn, also filter back into local conceptions of indigeneity. In the absence of a legal definition of "Indigenous" in Costa Rica, the implicit definition in the north-western province of Guanacaste is marked by residence within a reservation. However, various interpretations of the label exist both within and outside of the Chorotega reservation. Social class and approximation to stereotypical views of what an Indigenous person looks like also play a role in individuals' working definitions of

Indigenous identity, as does the social location and relative power of the person providing the definition.

This chapter, based on ethnographic research carried out between 1993 and 2007, will address how various residents of the Chorotega reservation, those who live just outside the reservation, scholars, legal discourse, historical discourse, those who have resided or studied in other Costa Rican reservations, and, more recently, the tourism industry have defined Indigenous identity in contradictory ways, and in manners that have had varying consequences for those labelled as Chorotega in Costa Rica. I will address the history of these definitions, their effects on the present-day Chorotega, and their implications for the future. Specifically, I will trace the way in which one set of customs has gone from Indigenous to non-Indigenous national custom and back again, as a result of the shifting of discourses around it. A common thread through all of these definitions and interpretations of indigeneity is the role of place, and how the same concept that mired inhabitants of the Chorotega reservation in discrimination now serves to authenticate its practices. By performing customs for tourist audiences, the Chorotega of Costa Rica are marketing identity at once as an economic venture and also as a community-building exercise, in response to global forces that both led to this new economic endeavour and infuse its imagery.

Definitions from Historical, Legal, and Social Science Discourse[2]

While it is not uncommon for Indigenous peoples to be identified with past history as opposed to current existence, or to be spoken of as part of the past, history in Costa Rica puts that in writing. In history texts in Costa Rica, the Chorotega are often written about in the past tense (Gagini, 1917; Monge Alfaro, 1960).[3] An early historian, writing in 1893, described the "complete disappearance" of the Chorotega (de Peralta, 1893, pp. xvi–xvii). In part, this is a result of a frequently recounted, but drastically incorrect, national myth suggesting that Costa Rica lacked a sizeable Indigenous population at the time of Spanish contact. Purportedly, as slanted history would have it, this was because Indigenous peoples died of illness stemming from contact with unfamiliar pathogens that reached Costa Rica before their Spanish carriers did. The reported result is a written national history lacking reference to the directly exploitative era of contact (in spite of an actual history of forced labour) for which many other Latin American nations are known.

However incorrect this version of history might be, it is widespread. It was not uncommon for people throughout the country to respond to me, upon learning of my profession as an anthropologist (and assuming that that necessarily meant working with Indigenous peoples), by assuring me that there is little Indigenous presence in Costa Rica. Some pointed to Talamanca, in the south-eastern part of the country, where the better-known Bribrí live, as a place where Indigenous peoples reside. Most people with whom I spoke did not know that there was a reservation in the north-western part of the country. This is in spite of the fact that several practices deemed "national" – including food, dance, and narrative lore – have their roots in Chorotega culture (as shall be discussed shortly). This historical discourse commonly reflected in popular thought was first contradicted by the law, and was later mirrored in social science discourse.

Hundreds of years after the demise of Costa Rican Indigenous populations as reported by historiographers, in 1977 legal processes began that concluded in an assimilationist policy entailing the official recognition of eight Indigenous groups within the nation's borders and the creation of twenty-three reservations (Matamoros Carvajal, 1990, p. 69). These reservations were made either where peoples self-identified as Indigenous or where chronicles left by Spanish conquistadors attested to the existence of Indigenous peoples in the 1500s. The Chorotega reservation met the latter criterion. Given that the whole Nicoya Peninsula was populated by the Chorotega in pre-colonial times, officials had to select one community within that area to be designated as the Chorotega reservation. Prompted by an outsider to what is now the Chorotega reservation, six individuals from that community campaigned for it to be selected. The motivating factor for this was the promise that the government would purchase land from settlers from the *Meseta Central* (who migrated to the region in the 1960s) and redistribute it to locals of Indigenous ancestry.

To make a convincing case for this community's potential to merit reservation status, these individuals drafted a list of criteria that would prove Indigenous identity. The list included physical features ("looking Indian"); the presence of thatched-roof houses, known as *ranchos*, that served as housing for several families at that time and were similar to those built long ago (thus establishing a tie with history); the preparation of traditional (mostly corn-based) foods and drinks; an abundance of pre-Columbian artefacts in the area; the assertion that one person in the community made pottery; and the frequent selection of individuals from this community to serve as *mayordomos* – on the basis of local recognition of Indigenous ancestry – for the festival dedicated to the Virgin of Guadalupe, complete with its heavy dose of Indigenous lore. A final item on the list was a reputation for witchcraft, which has been discussed (on a local level) as having roots in Chorotega spiritual beliefs, perhaps because of their ideological placement in opposition to Catholicism.

Not all residents of the community that eventually became the Chorotega reservation agreed with that designation, nor did they appreciate the accusations of opportunism that were levelled against the community for seeking and attaining reservation status. Indeed, this formed a rift in the community. In 1993, in my first fieldwork foray into the community, it seemed fairly evenly divided on the issue. Approximately half of the community approved of its town's reservation status, and half resented it. There were no clear patterns in terms of age, gender, lineage, or religious affiliation, or any other salient division in terms of how people felt about the reservation. It seemed that opinions depended upon people's personal experience of being labelled as a resident of the reservation. For those who disliked the town's reservation status, their reasons included tremendous resentment at being the only community in the region officially designated as Indigenous when the whole area had Indigenous roots, and aversion to the stigma attached to Indigenous identity in a country that often projected an image of Whiteness and European heritage (see Wherry, 2006, p. 131).

In essence, at the same time that the declaration of the Chorotega reservation imposed Indigenous identity upon all its inhabitants (in accordance with the self-proclaimed identities of some residents, and in contrast to those of others), by default it also removed that label from all those people living outside of the reservation's borders. This is evident in the wording of Costa Rican folklorist and politician Miguel Salguero (1991) when he describes this reservation as a "nucleus" of Chorotega existence in the region (p. 170). Hypothetically, two cousins, one living inside the reservation and one outside it, who have similar worldviews, language, religion, and foodways, could be seen as having entirely different ethnic identities. One result of the reservation's designation was that it became unlawful to sell reservation land to anyone not of Indigenous heritage. However, in light of the common understanding that those who resided inside the reservation were those that bore official Indigenous identity, this meant that an individual residing in the reservation could only sell land to another individual from the reservation.

The Indigenous population that guidebooks and almanacs commonly cite as 1 per cent within Costa Rica also likely reflects the proportion of residents of the nation's twenty-three reservations to those outside of them.

Reflective of the process by which the Chorotega reservation came into being, there are no stark differences between culture inside and outside the reservation, for the most part. Most of the surrounding communities share customs (related to food and narrative) with inhabitants of the reservation. Inhabitants of the reservation speak Spanish, not an Indigenous language. Most residents of the reservation identify as Catholic, as do most residents of the surrounding communities. The largest difference is with one nearby community, located immediately outside the reservation, and largely populated by the predominantly White migrant population from the *Meseta Central*, which has established political and economic dominance over those from the reservation and other small nearby towns. In that community, for decades now, individuals from the reservation have met with discrimination in the clinic, high school, and areas of commerce.[4] There, the stigma attached to Indigenous identity (or labelling, in cases in which the label does not match individuals' self-identification) is brought into sharp focus. Resulting negative experiences have had considerable influence on how reservation insiders identify (or not) with the identity that the geopolitical boundary of the reservation has projected upon them. Indeed, it is upon knowing that someone comes from the reservation that an outsider might identify him or her as Indigenous and discriminate against that person. No other signs of indigeneity are taken quite so seriously as residence within the reservation. In fact, it is the lack of difference between those from the Chorotega reservation and those from the remaining majority of communities nearby (other than the one dominated by migrants from the *Meseta Central*) to which social scientists have pointed in order to decry Indigenous identity in the Chorotega reservation.

In contrast to the law that set the Chorotega reservation apart, thus implying difference, social scientists within Costa Rica have pointed to the reservation's lack of an Indigenous language and distinct customs separating its inhabitants from most of those outside of its politically created boundary as proof that it does not merit its reservation status. The nation's best-known anthropologist considers residents of the Chorotega reservation to be *campesino* or Mestizo (Bozolli de Wille, 1969, 1986). Her writings have been extremely influential among Costa

Rican social scientific circles, to the point that the Chorotega are not always listed among Costa Rican Indigenous groups (see, for example, Barrientos et al., 1982, p. 251). One result of this legal imposition of an ethnic label and subsequent questioning of that label by social scientists is that, for quite some time, inhabitants of the Chorotega reservation retained the stigma that accompanied the Indigenous label on a local level, but no longer received an equal proportion of funding to that accorded to reservations deemed more "legitimate" by social scientists. In spite of the negative effects that these views of watered-down indigeneity had on an economic level, most inhabitants of the reservation did little to dispel them.

According to interviews with residents of the reservation, when Peace Corps volunteers prompted local artisans (in nearby communities – see Wherry, 2006; Weil, 2004) to make pottery with designs drawn from pre-Columbian artefacts unearthed in this region, individuals from the Chorotega reservation declined to pursue the opportunity. Some residents of the reservation felt that performing Indigenous identity would solidify the stigmatized identity imposed upon them. This is in keeping with what Brayboy and Searle (2007) discuss as the "trap" of visibility (p. 173). Acting in accordance with local stereotypes, in a context in which Indigenous peoples were rarely represented as contributors to contemporary society, could create a form of visibility that would more deeply entrench stereotypical expectations and images of Indigenous peoples. In a system set up for purposes of acculturation, and in which Indigenous identity was heavily stigmatized, the Chorotega reservation was a "success story." Proving ethnic difference, in contrast, was likely to lead to local discrimination.

Local Definitions of Chorotega Identity

Immediately outside the reservation, stereotypes about the reservation and its inhabitants ran rampant from its imposition up to the early 2000s. Many local outsiders came to expect the reservation's inhabitants to act in accordance with stereotypes. Such expectations were so strong that some outsiders swore to me that they had heard the reservation's residents speaking in an Indian language, though Spanish is the language spoken both inside and outside the reservation (see Stocker, 2003). Some people suspected that residents of the reservation held rain dances (such images are probably drawn from expectations of generic, homogenized Indigenous practices in keeping with stereotypical images broadcast through the media). Many people associated the reservation with poverty, backwardness, danger, ugliness, and an odd simultaneous existence of violence and excessive timidity. "Positive" stereotypes that existed in some of the surrounding communities (positive only in their characterization, but still negative in their lack of attention to heterogeneity of thought and practice) linked inhabitants of the reservation to "authentic" cuisine and custom, and on that basis, still sought participation from reservation inhabitants in the festival dedicated to the Virgin of Guadalupe and its corresponding traditional food preparation. Some of these views of the reservation were in opposition to the views of reservation inhabitants, and some were not. All of them were tied to place of residence (within the reservation) as proof of indigeneity. In this manner, outsider and insider views shared some common ground.

To a degree, to speak of outsider views versus insider views, and academic or legal perspectives versus local ones, is to point to false dichotomies. These realms do not exist in isolation, but rather they interact in power-laden contexts. Thus, insider views of Chorotega identity at times reflect the discourses discussed earlier, and at other times contest them. In diverse ways, residents of the reservation internalized some elements of these outsider definitions, and at times they worked with them and adjusted them as needed. Such negotiation of identity was necessary given that many of the traditional markers of identity proved inappropriate to this particular situation. Consciousness of kind (Barth, 1969, p. 79; Schermerhorn, 1996, p. 17) and emic definition (Barth, 1969; Eriksen, 1993, p. 11) have proved insufficient. The first has been a less-than-effective way of defining ethnic identity in this context given that peoples from dominant groups often point to disagreement within subordinated groups as proof of weakness. In reality, no sizeable community could possibly count on full agreement among its members without some level of coercion, yet such lack of agreement (recognized as healthy or democratic in dominant society) is often upheld as a sign of disorganization or disunity within less powerful communities. Emic identification or consciousness of kind have also failed to work in this context in which social science and history have dismissed any insider opinion in their classifications of the Chorotega reservation as contradicting history or as not deserving its reservation status. Indeed, it appears that a combination of emic identification with outsider validation (in keeping with Jenkins, 1997, p. 17) is what has been needed to claim Indigenous identity and have that be believed by powerful discourses or dominant locals. Assertions of indigeneity have also relied upon reference to stereotypical views of race and ethnicity.

Ethnic Markers – Stereotypical and Traditional

In spite of social science's rejection of the biological basis of race in favour of a social constructionist perspective (an argument that perhaps was made best known by Omi & Winant, 1986), references to physical appearance still hold sway in discussions of ethnic identity (often discussed in racial terms outside of academe). While a focus on genes, per se, and on DNA testing or dental morphology to determine ethnic descent is still foreign to debates over indigeneity within the Chorotega reservation – although it has certainly been used in Costa Rican social scientific discourse (Brenes & Barrantes, 1983; Barrantes, 1993) – the language of heredity and phenotype is still used locally. Some youth from the Chorotega reservation whom I interviewed in 1993 and 1999 pointed to their skin colour in asserting their Indigenous identity. Just outside the community, a high school student asked me to verify a local rumour that the "last pure" Indian – as "evidenced" by his physical features, long hair, and affinity for horseback riding, in keeping with stereotypical images projected to prove Indianness and taken by this student as reality – existed within the reservation. A high school teacher who could have passed as a resident of the reservation, and whose Guanacastecan heritage almost certainly included Chorotega ancestry, repeatedly pointed out "prominent cheekbones" as evidence of Chorotega descent in some students from the reservation. Although a focus on "genes" may be Western in its inception, it has been acted upon as the basis for racial distinction for so long that it has entered Native discourse. This is, however, only one element of identity as it has been constructed in this context.

The role of place or homeland in the definition of ethnic identity has been especially salient in this particular context (see also Adams, 1991, p. 193; Alonso, 1994, p. 395; Geertz, 1973, pp. 262–3; Grosby, 1996, p. 51; Nagata, 1981, p. 94; Nederveen Pieterse, 1996, pp. 30–1; Wade, 1997, p. 18; Lawrence, chapter two of this volume). The internalization of the authority vested in a politically recognized boundary (Horowitz, 1975, pp. 133–4) has also been influential. Individuals from the reservation are labelled ethnically as a result of the place in which they live. That, in turn, affects identity. As various scholars assert, labels can, at once, be both imposed and projected (di Leonardo, 1984, pp. 22–3; Jenkins,

1997; Oboler, 1995; Wade, 1997, p. 66). That holds true for labels both local and scholarly, be they deliberately pejorative or unwittingly so.

Inside the reservation, some individuals (during the years of my research) identified as Chorotega, or as modern-day descendants of the Chorotega (thus rooting the Chorotega in the past), while some identified as "no longer Indian," alluding to the debates about lack of difference between their own community and those immediately outside of it (in keeping with Costa Rican anthropological definitions). According to some insider opinions, their categorization as Indigenous makes it so. This is in keeping with the view of Bonfil Batalla, who asserts that the commonality among all Indigenous peoples is their classification as Indigenous and the status that goes along with that (1972, p. 119). A related concept, presented by Marroquín, suggests that what connects Indigenous peoples to one another is a shared history of oppression or colonialism (1975, pp. 758–69). Those individuals from the reservation who identified as *campesino* did so in a way that reflected the work of several scholars who have written about the nexus between social class and Indigenous identity (Chapin, 1989, p. 11; Field, 1995, p. 792; Gould, 1993, 1998; Luykx, 1999, p. 265). This link is also evident in the Costa Rican social scientific accounts that reclassified the Chorotega of today as acculturated *campesinos* (Bozzoli de Wille, 1986, p. 75).

National Appropriation of Indigenous Culture

One result of scholarly labelling (or scholarly critique of legal labels) has been what one scholar calls *desindianización* (de-Indianization). Bonfil Batalla (1989) defines this term as "loss of original collective identity as the result of the colonial domination process" (p. 13; translation mine). In the case of the Chorotega, as we have seen, history denied Chorotega identity, law imposed it and delimited it within specific places, and social science decried its authenticity. At the same time, the nation-state adopted Chorotega custom and called it "*lo típico*" – "typical" Costa Rican culture – to be displayed to tourists and manipulated to provoke nostalgia and patriotism. Wherry (2006) argues, "In the national imagination, the country folks, *not* the Indians represent the nation" (p. 127). He goes on to cite, as evidence of this assertion, the woodworking tradition (whose origins lie in the *Meseta Central*) that is marketed to tourists as Costa Rican national culture.

However, I argue that performative elements of culture – as opposed to material culture, which is also "sold" to tourists as spectators – have different origins. The foods, folkloric dance, and oral traditions upheld as *lo típico* originate from Chorotega traditions (Guevara Berger & Chacón, 1992, p. 18), although they are represented as non-Indigenous, *campesino* culture and promoted as national culture. Ironically, then, when residents of the Chorotega reservation practise customs that have been appropriated as "national" or "typical," they seemingly prove assimilation. One result is that these practices ceased to be read as symbols of indigeneity, but rather came to represent national (*campesino*, Mestizo, or non-Indigenous, White) belonging. This is one reason that individuals wishing to symbolize the Indigenous roots of an event must return to stereotypical icons (as in the case of the poster described at the outset of this chapter) in order for outsiders to validate its Indianness. To prove Indigenous identity to those less willing to listen to insider views, individuals asserting Indigenous identity have had to portray themselves or their community in accordance with people's stereotypes about them, given that the current reality lived by Indigenous peoples in the Chorotega reservation has been dismissed by social science discourse in Costa Rica (which has seeped into common opinion) as truly or recognizably Indigenous. In contrast, locally speaking, in the communities immediately outside the reservation, residing within the reservation has been sufficient to label one as Chorotega.

One exception to this appropriation of Guancastecan or Chorotega cultural practices by the nation (as well as to Costa Rican social science's denial of Indigenous existence in this region) is the production of pottery. Bozzoli de Wille cites ceramics production as the one element of Indigenous custom remaining in the Chorotega reservation (1969, pp. 4–5; 1986, p. 75) in spite of the fact that this has not, by any means, been widespread within the reservation. Those that pushed for this community to become the Chorotega reservation cited only one member of the community that practised the art. Only one person in the reservation currently does so (and this fact was masked for nearly a decade). This mention of pottery is interesting given the history of ceramics production in the region. While it does have ancient roots, that tradition was severely limited, if not truncated, until Peace Corps volunteers reinvigorated it in 1969 and 1970 (Wherry, 2006, pp. 140–1). Weil (2004) refers to these products as "Chorotega revival ceramics" (p. 240). These artisans incorporated the official, scholarly view of the Chorotega past by citing archaeological interpretations of the symbols on their wares (Weil, 2004, p. 245). Here, too, certain academic definitions have filtered into local ones. The authority vested in place comes into play once again, in that these wares have, at times, been sold throughout the country bearing the name of the Chorotega reservation, where they were not produced. By inscribing upon these objects a perceived (calculated) authenticity rooted in place, tourists may believe they are buying a piece of ethnicity or a piece of culture. Certainly, artisans in the community that do produce these wares cite Indigenous heritage as a part of their marketing tactics.

Wherry (2006, p. 125) asserts that this artistic practice is used to show Indigenous identity in light of the prevalence of a non-Indigenous language and of the Mestizo makeup of the region where they are produced. Here, artisans have gotten around the paucity of traditionally accepted (or perhaps stereotypically recognized) ethnic markers by presenting the material product of a tradition marketed as unbroken and rooted in an Indigenous past. Weil (2004) suggests that "the ethnic arts market … valorizes indigenous culture" (p. 248). So, too, does the tourism industry.

The Tourism Industry and Its Implications for Ethnic Identity

Those from the Chorotega reservation once eschewed demonstrations of Indigenous identity in keeping with stereotypes as a measure of self-protection. However, the context is changing now. In earlier years, Indigenous peoples in Costa Rica (not only from the Chorotega reservation) had to fight to get recognition as Costa Rican citizens (G. Rodríguez, personal communication, 1993). This may have stalled a movement towards autonomy in a time when Indigenous peoples of other nations strove for that. The assimilationist motives behind the creation of reservations may also have stunted such a movement. Now, however, Indigenous communities may be poised on a precipice of change. Wherry (2006, p. 132) notes that since the 1990s, the nation has embraced a more multicultural image. Friedlander (2006, p. 183) echoes this idea for Mexico and other parts of Latin America. While this was not evident among Costa Ricans, in general, during my research there in 1999 (see Stocker, 2005), appreciation of ethnic pluralism has been something intriguing to tourists. Just as tourists have valued ceramics tied to Chorotega tradition, many also have a romanticized fascination with Indigenous existence. This has led to the development of websites announcing zoo-like tours to select reservations and performances that approximate stereotypical expectations in some communities. In the Chorotega reservation, it has not reached that extreme. Nonetheless, tourism may be key to a change in the local value placed on Indigenous identity.

In 1999, some residents of the reservation resented a surprise visit by three busloads of national tourists. This tourist visit appeared to be an isolated incident. In 2006, in contrast, there was talk of reservation residents courting tourism. In 2007, clear plans were underway to invite tourism into the community. Tourism is not new to the region, on the whole, but it has not usually included residents of the reservation as its beneficiaries. There is a bar in a nearby beach town that bears the name of the reservation, as well as a coffee plantation tour located just outside the reservation that does the same. Likewise, in another nearby town and hub for beach-bound tourists changing buses, businesses boast names that allude to Indigenous history. In all of these examples, the aim seems to be to draw tourists that might value such an identity, in contrast to many locals who have belittled it. However, tourism has drawn closer to the reservation now, and is finally beginning to include its residents.

International tourism has now reached the neighbouring community in which Chorotega residents have long felt discrimination. One result is that the local folkloric dance group (performing "typical" dance to marimba music, not an embellished, hyperbolized performance of Indian stereotypes) has been invited, repeatedly, to perform. The dances they perform are those that have been claimed as national dances, purportedly emblematic of *campesino* culture and identity. For the most part, they are not unique to the reservation, yet it is the reservation dance group that has been invited to perform. I assert that this is not coincidental. Thus, even in a town that has scorned indigeneity for decades, a tourist-inspired, economic value placed on Indigenous identity may be starting to have positive consequences. In this case, what lends "authenticity" to the performers, in the eyes of a tourist audience, is an identity rooted in place; residence within the reservation lends authority to their stance (see also Deloria, 1998, pp. 143–4, 148). Recognition of the influence of tourism on commonly held perceptions of what counts as traditional is not new (see Babcock, 1997; Wherry, 2006, p. 126). However, the effects of this for those designated as Chorotega through place of residence have been less visible than the effects of national and scholarly discourse on Indigenous identity.

Friedlander (2006, p. 208) implies that as benefits for being Indigenous rise (in a context of multicultural appreciation), so too might the numbers of those who self-identify as Indigenous. This reasoning became evident in the Chorotega reservation when individuals there were charged with opportunism for receiving reservation land in exchange for professed identity. As Friedlander (2006) states, "In the old days, villagers learned to take the Indian out of their everyday lives. Now they are learning to put it back in" (p. 218). She goes on to explain, "There is no contradiction between the growing interest today in Indian cultures and the expanding influence of global capitalism" (p. 218). According to Wherry, it is the Costa Rican state that is cashing in on multiculturalism: "With reluctance, the Costa Rican state has recognized indigenous culture as a national asset and has thereby given the artisans a basis to make claims on the state" (Wherry, 2006, p. 147). I would extend this argument to note that this may later have an effect upon local values of Indigenous culture. It could also, potentially, lead to the growing "industrialization of identity" (see the introduction to this volume). In keeping with what Weil (2004) notes for a different community, the residents of the reservation have begun to "engage with tradition as a *resource*" (p. 245).

While individuals have not flocked to claim Chorotega Indigenous identity in the past, were the rampant discrimination against those labelled as such curbed – or if this identity were to become valued (not only on an international level, but on a local level) – this could soon change. Those who have long borne the brunt of the negative effects of ethnic labelling, evident in schools, clinics, and elsewhere, might be reluctant to allow people outside the reservation (and thus formerly protected from the stigma attached to such an identity) to enjoy its newfound benefits without receiving additional perks themselves. In claiming their place as beneficiaries of this new identity market, not only have residents of the reservation expanded the reach of their performances, but they have added to the repertoire, as well.

Some aspects of identity performed for audiences reflect actual practices within the community and some draw from reinvented traditions (Hobsbawm & Ranger, 1983). Music and dance were practised within the community before the rise of tourism, and the foods marketed to outsiders have long been included in local practice. Those performative elements of culture that have been added include the presentation of an annual cleansing ritual once carried out only in private, and the addition of costumes based on descriptions left by the Spaniard chroniclers at the time of contact. While the chronicles refer to "painted" bodies, the documents to which the performers' leader had access did not provide as thorough a description as other sources. The performer appeared with paint made from local resources, but applied in a fashion reminiscent of U.S. film renderings of Plains Indians. Thus, globalization has infused local imaginings and interpretations of historical descriptions.

These additions to the performers' repertoire do not reflect common, current practice, but community members appear to accept their performance because, as one individual commented, they are presented as customs from the past, not as current daily life. They are not intended to dupe audiences into believing that the reservation's inhabitants still live as they did centuries ago, but are carried out in a way that strives for accuracy and authenticity, in keeping with what people expect tourist audiences to enjoy. In this manner, the community can "own" elements of the Indigenous past at the same time that they assert themselves as members of modern society. In keeping with Deloria's (1998, p. 8) thoughts, through such performances that include stereotypical expectations mixed with autonomous self-presentation, "native people have been present at the margins, insinuating their way into Euro-American discourse, often attempting to nudge notions of Indianness in directions they found useful." Greene (2004, p. 223) adds, "this does not … make indigenous peoples innocent pawns of more powerful players but rather demonstrates their active engagement in wider networks of power as political strategists whose decisions have direct repercussions on their legitimacy as indigenous representatives."

Furthermore, community members have begun discussions around making the reservation name a registered trademark so that all products made there might bear a formal (and legal) stamp of authenticity rooted in place, thereby turning culture into a product (see also Hutchins, 2007, p. 46; Greene, 2004, p. 223). In this manner, in keeping with what Greene (2004, p. 213) asserts, "indigenous people are struggling to monitor and assert more direct control over their cultural property by challenging and politicizing its use by nonindigenous actors." While place of residence has long been stigmatized, through tourism it might become a badge that lends higher status, at least in some circles, to those officially identified as Chorotega.[5]

This marketing of Indigenous identity may smack of opportunism to some, perhaps, that view the commodification of culture as selling out or as rooted in economic interests alone. This assumes, however, that economic motives and efforts at community building are necessarily at odds, and that such economic concerns preclude genuine expressions of identity. The presentation of culture for financial gain is often judged negatively, while motives related to community building are not. In the present case, the two impetuses are merged. In the recent past, residents of the reservation had to leave the community to seek employment in urban areas or plantations far away, sometimes dividing families in the process (see Stocker, 2007). This new economic opportunity allows individuals to stay in the community. Furthermore, as Hutchins (2007, p. 93) notes for a different context, opening Indigenous practice to tourist audiences does not necessarily sap them of meaning for Indigenous participants. Deloria (1998, p. 146), too, found that the performance of culture for U.S. Native peoples "may have helped some Indian people consolidate a native sense of self." In this regard, marketing identity does not inevitably run counter to a community's identity. Rather, it might serve to solidify a sense of community at the same time that it presents new livelihoods. This, as Greene (2004, p. 223) asserts, "is another strategy used in broader politics of self-determination that emerges in connection with the economic demands of a global market." Thus, the marketing of Indigenous customs through performance, trademarked goods, and other "authenticating practices" (Bodinger de Uriarte, 2003, p. 556) is no different from nation-building activities in other contexts. Anderson (1983, pp. 11–12) points out that nations "loom out of an immemorial past, and, still more important, glide into a limitless future." I argue that Chorotega self-presentation and marketing of identity is an act of nation-building writ small.

Conclusions

Just as outsider definitions have always played into insider definitions (while the reverse has not always been the case), an impending "identity industry" is likely to have repercussions for those individuals that reside within the Chorotega reservation. Traditionally, the negative effects of local definition as Indigenous have far outweighed the potential benefits for many inhabitants of the reservation. On the cusp of tourism, however, that might change. Friedlander (2006) notes, "while the cultural markers [of indigeneity] were frequently changing, the social position of Indians in Mexico stayed essentially the same" (p. 182). While a parallel argument could be made about the status of the Chorotega of Costa Rica in spite of changing definitions of Indianness, in tourism – the newest iteration of labelling and implied definition – residents of the reservation might have more say in their involvement with it.

What runs throughout this entire history of labelling – historical, legal, social scientific, local pejorative, insider, and now tourist – is the idea of place as key to the perceived authenticity of Indigenous identity, whether it is to the benefit or the detriment of the inhabitants of the Chorotega reservation. Indeed, rarely have the positive or negative effects of such labelling been up to residents of the reservation. More often, the debates surrounding Indigenous identity for those labelled as Chorotega based on their place of residence have excluded insider opinions. Insiders have been left with the task of accepting, contesting, negotiating, or responding to those labels in some fashion. At times the labels have been manipulated to obtain benefits, and at other times the negative effects of labelling have outweighed any positive outcomes that might have come with these labels and their corresponding stereotypes.

It is at this moment – in light of the encroachment of tourism on the reservation – that those who identify themselves as Chorotega or are labelled as such by others may be able to use the label to their benefit in a way that does not necessarily require a performance of stereotypes presented as reality. Rather, as of 2007, it involved the continued practice of cultural forms once appropriated by the nation as non-Indigenous, as well as proportionally lesser displays of past custom presented as just that. By virtue of its performance for an international tourist audience eager to appreciate indigeneity, and as a result of its presentation by individuals whose place of residence lends authority to claims of Indigenous identity, the result might be one of solidifying the location of the Chorotega within the nation rather than at its margins.

This shifting of "cultural markers," as Friedlander (2006, p. 182) calls them, might allow the continuance of practices long done in the reservation – perhaps in assertion of national belonging, perhaps as an expression of culture rooted in Chorotega origins – as both national *and* Indigenous culture. This reclassification of dance as *campesino and* Indigenous – no longer separating the two identities in such an artificially distinct manner – and the value placed on this and other cultural elements through tourism, might then lead to a greater valuing of Chorotega identities on a local level. Just as outsider labels and their connotations have filtered down to the local level in the past, so too might some of the positive connotations of Indigenous identity as sought by tourists. Bodinger de Uriarte (2003, pp. 561–2) reminds us that "attempts at self-definition and autonomy must be understood as often antagonistic – but always related – processes of contestation between local definitions and discourses of self and the dominant narratives of racial essences and cultural stereotypes." Rather than returning to stereotypical images, those labelled as Chorotega in Costa Rica might be able to use their own symbols and practices, instead of exaggerating those unrelated to local culture but read as Indigenous by outsiders, to push tourist expectations in more realistic directions and to express Indigenous cultural practices once interpreted as proof of assimilation, and now perhaps viewed as authentically their own.

NOTES

1 A variety of terms exist to label First Nations or Indigenous peoples. Terms that are innocuous in some contexts may be derogatory in others. The labels most often used by residents of the Chorotega reservation in Costa Rica are "*Indio*" and "*indígena*." I will use the English translations of these terms (Indian and Indigenous, respectively), with the connotations they have when spoken respectfully by residents of the Chorotega reservation.

2 For a more complete discussion of the history of the Chorotega reservation and of Chorotega Indigenous identity as well as other issues addressed in this chapter, see Stocker (2005).

3 Throughout this chapter, I, too, have chosen to use the past tense. However, I do so to reflect the fact that these assertions relate to research conducted within a specific time frame (1993–7), not as an implication that the Chorotega no longer exist or have remained unchanged through time.

4 See Stocker (2005), for a thorough account of this discrimination.

5 This is not to say that tourism is unproblematic in other regards or that its effects would all be positive. However, a full discussion of those dynamics lies beyond the scope of the current chapter.

REFERENCES

Adams, R.N. (1991). Strategies of Ethnic Survival in Central America. In G. Urban & J. Sherzer (Eds.), *Nation-States and Indians in Latin America* (pp. 181–206). Austin, TX: University of Texas Press.

Alonso, A.M. (1994). The Politics of Space, Time and Substance: State Formation, Nationalism, and Ethnicity. *Annual Review of Anthropology*, *23*(1), 379–405. http://dx.doi.org/10.1146/annurev.an.23.100194.002115

Anderson, B. (1983). *Imagined Communities*. New York: Verso.

Babcock, B.A. (1997). Mudwomen and Whitemen: A Meditation on Pueblo Potteries and the Politics of Representation. In L. Lamphere, H. Ragoné, & P. Zavella (Eds.), *Situated Lives: Gender and Culture in Everyday Life* (pp. 420–39). New York: Routledge.

Barrantes, R. (1993). *Evolución en el trópico: los amerindios de Costa Rica y Panamá*. San José, Costa Rica: Editorial de la Universidad de Costa Rica.

Barrientos, G., Borge, C., Gudiño, P., Soto, C., Rodríguez, G., & Swaby, A. (1982). El caso de los Bribris, indígenas talamanqueños. Costa Rica. In Guillermo Bonfil Batalla et al. (Eds.), *América Latina: etnodesarrollo y etnocidio* (pp. 249–55). San José, Costa Rica: Ediciones FLACSO.

Barth, F. (1969). *Ethnic Groups and Boundaries: The Social Organization of Culture Difference*. Boston, MA: Little, Brown and Co.

Bodinger de Uriarte, J. (2003). Imagining the Nation with House Odds: Representing American Indian Identity at Mashantucket. *Ethnohistory*, *50*(3), 550–65.

Bonfil Batalla, G. (1972). El concepto del indio en América: una categoría de la situación colonial. *Anales de Antropología 9*, 105–24.

Bonfil Batalla, G. (1989). *México profundo: una civilización negada*. D.F., Mexico: Grijalbo.

Bozzoli de Wille, M.E. (1969). *Localidades indígenas costarricenses 1960–1968*. San José, Costa Rica: Publicaciones de la Universidad de Costa Rica.

Bozzoli de Wille, M.E. (1986). *El indígena costarricense y su ambiente natural*. San José, Costa Rica: Editorial Porvenir.

Brayboy, B.M.J., & Searle, K.A. (2007). Thanksgiving and Serial Killers: Representations of American Indians in Schools. In S. Books (Ed.), *Invisible Children in the Society and Its Schools* (pp. 173–92). Mahwah, NJ: Lawrence Earlbaum Associates, Publishers.

Brenes, W., & Barrantes, R. (1983). Salud oral y morfología dental de los amerindios guaymí del Limoncito. *America Indigena*, *43*(1), 215–27.

Chapin, M. (1989). The 500,000 Invisible Indians of El Salvador. *Cultural Survival Quarterly*, *13*(3), 11–16.

de Peralta, M.M. (1893). *Etnología centro-americana: Catálogo razonado de los objetos arqueológicos de la República de Costa Rica*. Madrid, Spain: Hijos de M. Gines Hernández.

Deloria, P.J. (1998). *Playing Indian*. New Haven, CT: Yale University Press.

di Leonardo, M. (1984). *The Varieties of Ethnic Experience*. Ithaca, NY: Cornell University Press.

Eriksen, T.H. (1993). *Ethnicity and Nationalism: Anthropological Perspectives*. London: Pluto Press.

Field, L.W. (1995). Constructing Local Identities in a Revolutionary Nation: The Cultural Politics of the Artisan Class in Nicaragua, 1979–1990. *American Ethnologist*, *22*(4), 786–806. http://dx.doi.org/10.1525/ae.1995.22.4.02a00070

Friedlander, J. (2006). *Being Indian in Hueyapan: A Revised and Updated edition*. New York: Palgrave Macmillan. http://dx.doi.org/10.1057/9780230601659

Gagini, C. (1917). *Los aborígenes de Costa Rica*. San José, Costa Rica: Trejos Hermanos.

Geertz, C. (1973). *The Interpretation of Cultures*. New York: Basic Books.

Gould, J.L. (1993). ¡*Vana ilusión*! The Highlands Indians and the Myth of Nicaragua Mestiza, 1880–1925. *Hispanic American Historical Review*, *73*(3), 393–429. http://dx.doi.org/10.2307/2517696

Gould, J.L. (1998). *To Die in This Way: Nicaraguan Indians and the Myth of Mestizaje, 1880–1965*. Durham, NC: Duke University Press.

Greene, S. (2004). Indigenous People Incorporated? Culture as Politics, Culture as Property in Pharmaceutical Bioprospecting. *Current Anthropology*, *45*(2), 211–37. http://dx.doi.org/10.1086/381047

Grosby, S. (1996). The Inexpungeable Tie of Primordiality. In J. Hutchinson & A.D. Smith (Eds.), *Ethnicity* (pp. 51–6). Oxford: Oxford University Press.

Guevara Berger, M., & Chacón, R. (1992). *Territorios indios en Costa Rica: orígenes, situación actual y perspectivas*. San José, Costa Rica: García Hermanos, S.A.

Hobsbawm, E., & Ranger, T. (1983). *The Invention of Tradition*. Cambridge: Cambridge University Press.

Horowitz, D.L. (1975). Ethnic Identity. In N. Glazer & D.P. Moynihan (Eds.), *Ethnicity: Theory and Experience* (pp. 111–40). Cambridge, MA: Harvard University Press.

Hutchins, F. (2007). Footprints in the Forest: Ecotourism and Altered Meanings in Ecuador's Upper Amazon. *Journal of Latin American and Caribbean Anthropology*, *12*(1), 75–103. http://dx.doi.org/10.1525/jlat.2007.12.1.75

Jenkins, R. (1997). *Rethinking Ethnicity: Arguments and Explorations*. London: SAGE.

Luykx, A. (1999). *The Citizen Factory: Schooling and Cultural Production in Bolivia*. Albany, NY: State University of New York Press.

Marroquín, A. (1975). El problema indígena en El Salvador. *América Indígena* *35*(4), 747–71.

Matamoros Carvajal, A. (1990). *Acción indigenista en Costa Rica*. San José, Costa Rica: CONAI.

Monge Alfaro, C. (1960). *Historia de Costa Rica*. San José, Costa Rica: Imprenta Trejos.

Nagata, J. (1981). In Defense of Ethnic Boundaries: The Changing Myths and Charters of Malay Identity. In C.F. Keyes (Ed.), *Ethnic Change* (pp. 88–116). Seattle, WA: University of Washington Press.

Nederveen Pieterse, J. (1996). Varieties of Ethnic Politics and Ethnicity Discourse. In E.N. Wilmsen & P. McAllister (Eds.), *The Politics of Difference:*

Ethnic Premises in a World of Power (pp. 25–44). Chicago, IL: The University of Chicago Press.

Oboler, S. (1995). *Ethnic Labels, Latino Lives: Identity and the Politics Of Re(Presentation) in the United States*. Minneapolis, MN: University of Minnesota Press.

Omi, M., & Winant, H. (1986). *Racial Formation in the United States: From the 1960s to the 1980s*. New York: Routledge.

Salguero, M. (1991). *Cantones de Costa Rica*. San José, Costa Rica: Editorial Costa Rica.

Schermerhorn, R. (1996). Ethnicity and Minority Groups. In J. Hutchinson & A.D. Smith (Eds.), *Ethnicity* (pp. 17–18). Oxford: Oxford University Press.

Stocker, K. (2003). "Ellos se comen las heces/eses": The Perceived Language Difference of Matambú. In S. Wortham & B. Rymes (Eds.), *Linguistic Anthropology of Education* (pp. 185–211). Westport, CT: Praeger.

Stocker, K. (2005). *"I Won't Stay Indian, I'll Keep Studying": Race, Place, and Discrimination in a Costa Rican High School*. Boulder, CO: University Press of Colorado.

Stocker, K. (2007). Identity as Work: Changing Job Opportunities and Indigenous Identity in the Transition to a Tourist Economy. *Anthropology of Work Review*, *28*(2), 18–22. http://dx.doi.org/10.1525/awr.2007.28.2.18

Wade, P. (1997). *Race and Ethnicity in Latin America*. London: Pluto.

Weil, J. (2004). Virtual Antiquities, Consumption Values, and the Cultural Heritage Economy in a Costa Rican Artisan Community. In C. Werner & D. Bell (Eds.), *Values and Valuables: From the Sacred to the Symbolic* (pp. 231–56). Walnut Creek, CA: AltaMira Press.

Wherry, F.F. (2006). The Nation-State, Identity Management, and Indigenous Crafts: Constructing Markets and Opportunities in Northwest Costa Rica. *Ethnic and Racial Studies*, *29*(1), 124–52. http://dx.doi.org/10.1080/01419870500352454

6 Carib Identity, Racial Politics, and the Problem of Indigenous Recognition in Trinidad and Tobago

MAXIMILIAN C. FORTE

The history of the formation, interpretation, and resurgence of Carib identity in Trinidad and Tobago, as elsewhere in the Caribbean, is a story of race, place, and the politics of recognition. In this chapter, I focus on the Santa Rosa Carib Community in the Borough of Arima, on the island of Trinidad, a community that has taken the name of St Rose, after whom the old Catholic Mission of Arima was named. Racializations of identities in Trinidad were institutionalized and regulated in conjunction with the broader political economic processes that shaped the establishment of British colonial rule as Britain took over from Spain from 1797 onwards. Indigenous identity was strictly governed, given the economic status associated with Mission Indians – that they were nominally free labourers (a status shared with White colonists), yet confined to a specific place (a status shared with slaves and indentured labourers). Miscegenation was a formal basis for excluding individuals from the rights and status pertaining to mission residence. Purity of blood ("diluted" through "intermarriage") became the norm for assigning or officially rejecting Indigenous identity. Over a century later, while racial notions of identity persist, current Carib self-identifications stress indigeneity as a cultural heritage, a body of practices, and a recognition of ancestral ties, partially circumventing the racial ideologies that would deny their Indigenous identity. They do so in the face of ongoing, continually modified narratives of the Caribs' alleged "extinction." Asserting extinction is one blunt way of not even having to answer the question of "who is an Indian"; asserting Indigenous presence places that question back on the books.

The resilience of Carib identity in places such as Trinidad and Tobago is remarkable, not to mention the renewal, resurgence, and social revalidation of this identity. This resilience is remarkable not only when one considers the consistent pattern of European colonial military onslaughts, enslavement, expropriation of lands, and social marginalization, but also in light of the cultural stigma historically attached to Caribness (primitive, poor, ignorant, alleged "man eaters"), which often drove even surviving Caribs and persons with Indigenous ancestry to seek refuge in other identities, as some still do. Even if left at this, the situation is clearly a historically complex one. What renders it even more complex is the pattern of racial thinking that was imposed by European colonizers through all sorts of residential and labour segregations and legislation that would control and delimit who was deemed to be Indigenous. The introduction of foreign labour from Africa, the French Caribbean, and Asia, from the late 1700s onwards, was subject to the administration of identities and the "rights" which the colonial administrations would allot to these diverse groups. Colonial administrators' calculations of the "values" to be assigned to the diverse "races" were aimed at shoring up the dominance of European colonists. Afterward, the rise of nationalism, independence, and the emergence of party politics organized along an ethnic divide between Trinidadians of East Indian and African descent further cemented racial thinking. More recently, there has been positive validation of Carib identity and history by leading elements of the wider society, but this has not resolved the question of where Caribs fit within the larger scheme of racialized divisions between the country's two leading groups, East Indians and Africans. Thus, recognition becomes a problematic political issue, and here I will focus on the racialization of Caribness in order to highlight how Caribs are recognized, and how they recognize themselves.

The structure of this chapter follows three basic lines of argument: First, that the political economy of the British colony dictated and cemented racializations of identity. Second, that the process of ascribing Indigenous identities to individuals was governed by the economic rights attached to residents of missions, which were denied to any miscegenated offspring. There were thus political and economic interests vested in the *non*-recognition of Caribs, and race provided the most convenient justification – a justification that took the form of a narrative of extinction. Third, over a century later, while racial notions of identity persist, current Carib self-identifications stress indigeneity as a cultural heritage, an attachment to place, a body of practices, and a recognition of ancestral ties that often circumvent explicitly racial schemes of self-definition. State recognition of the Caribs occurs within this historical and cultural context, and therefore imposes limits and conditions that simultaneously create new forms of non-recognition.

Race: A Non-Indigenous System of Categorization

In thinking about race and Caribness, I should probably start by noting how racial thinking about Caribness emerged in the first place, since such thinking is not itself rooted in the Indigenous cultures of the Caribbean. Ethnohistorians have already indicated the tendency of island Caribs to acquire European and African captives from Puerto Rico and other territories and amalgamate them into their society, culturally adopting and assimilating them. For example, there were "estimates of there being up to three hundred European and African captives on Dominica" by the late 1500s (Whitehead, 2005, p. 232; Hulme & Whitehead, 1992, p. 38). In the account of Luisa de Navarrete, a creole woman captured from Puerto Rico in 1576, she testified that Caribs made their captives "work and go about naked by day and night, and they paint them like themselves" – captives who were "already as much *caribes* as the rest of them, and the women say that they no longer remember God, and the man neither more nor less so … and they do just as the Indians do" (quoted in Hulme & Whitehead, 1992, pp. 40, 42–3). As Whitehead also notes, "the presence and social integration of black runaway slaves within the Amerindian societies of the Caribbean certainly had begun as early as the mid-sixteenth century" (2005, p. 234). The Caribs of the early sixteenth century were thus a cosmopolitan mixture of peoples, yet all assembled under the label of Carib and all engaged in the lifeways associated with island Aboriginals (Whitehead, 2005, p. 225). From this early point, in other words, there is no evidence to suggest that race and racial purity were Indigenous concerns or were part of a philosophy rooted in Indigenous culture. This is not to suggest that Caribs could not or would not find various ways to exclude others; rather, it is that they did not exclude others on a basis that we could in any way identify as *racial*.

In the case of Trinidad specifically (Tobago lies largely beyond the scope of my work, and remained a separate colony until the late 1800s), we see a similar pattern of intercultural and interethnic amalgamation between long-time Spanish settlers and Indigenous inhabitants, in an underdeveloped colony long neglected by Spain (Newson, 1976). While there is no doubt that the Indigenous population acquired some of the cultural practices and beliefs of their Spanish cohabitants, what is most often remarked upon is that the housing, dress, and material sustenance of the Spanish settlers were barely distinguishable from those of the Aboriginals (see Ottley, 1955). As Ottley pointed out, in order to ensure their own survival under adverse conditions in a peripheral colony ignored by Spain, Spanish settlers had to adopt the lifeways of their Indigenous cohabitants (1955, p. 50). Port of Spain, site of the nation's future capital, was described in 1757 as consisting of "a mixture of Indianised half-breed Spaniards" and its "streets were bordered by the mud-huts of the Spaniards and half-breed Indians," huts that were thatched (Ottley, 1955, pp. 51, 52, 53).

This Spanish-Indigenous fusion became ingrained to the extent that even today, many of those who could be called Carib, and who in different situations identify themselves as Carib, go by the ethnic label of "Spanish" or "Payol" (from Español, sometimes also "Panyol") (Moodie-Kublalsingh, 1994). When the Spanish colonial regime ended at the close of the 1700s, with Britain's occupation of Trinidad and the arrival of French Caribbean planters and their slaves, ideas of racial hierarchy, exclusion, and concerns with purity came to the fore, as did the narrative of extinction. Race would now matter more than ever, as Trinidad was turned into a slave colony producing a lucrative export. The Indigenous populations, especially those that were clustered in settlements on lands suitable for sugar production, were relocated and reorganized as mission villages run by the Catholic Church. These missions produced mainly cocoa (being at higher elevations) and crops for their own needs.

The Colonial Administration of Race

In the nineteenth century, under British domination, the territory became predominantly an African slave colony; this was soon followed by African emancipation and the importation of indentured labourers, primarily from India. We clearly see, in government records and in the writings of the local elites who produced the first historical and social commentaries on the island, a definite concern with assigning particular "kinds" of people to particular commercial crops, in particular zones of the island, each of which existed under very different labour regimes.

For the first four decades of British rule, Africans were enslaved. Amerindians, on the other hand, were nominally free labourers. Both were confined populations: Africans were confined on sugar estates, and Indigenous residents were confined to missions, where they cultivated cocoa. After the late 1830s, Africans moved off the plantations and formed the basis for an urban work force. East Indians who replaced Africans were also assigned to sugar estates in south and central Trinidad, and as indentured workers their labour was not free – until the end of their indenture contracts, when most opted to remain in Trinidad and acquired plots of land as part of their contract. Yet another group of free labourers came with a large influx of Venezuelan Mestizos and Amerindians from the 1870s to the 1920s, blending in with local Mestizos and local Indigenous people – who by that time had been divested of their collectively owned mission lands by the British authorities and those seeking access to cocoa-growing lands once that commodity's value began to boom.

There were thus specific colonial conditions under which "Indian"[1] was allowed to exist, for a time: to Indians were attached rights to collective, inalienable land; nominally free labour; residential exclusivity; and, of course, the prospect of Christian redemption. Under colonial administration, these rights were relatively unique, and second only to those of the small White population. (Indeed, in some local censuses, "Indians after 1823 seemed to have been included in figures given for the number of 'white people'" [Leahy, 1980, p. 104]). In this crucible, where the British ranked and scaled peoples according to their material rights and economic obligations, race became the favourite way to normalize and naturalize, and to ideologize identity.

Colonial Exclusions: Purity and Liberty, Land and Labour

Under the colonial regime, who got what was determined according to a finely graded scale of racial identity. Those who were White, and closest to being White, could expect property rights and ownership of their own labour, unlike African slaves, and unlike indentured East Indians. The "inferior peoples" were *lower* – as in subjugated and subordinated – in material terms, and were kept that way for as long as was practical, with the added injury that their condition was ideologized as inherent to their natural biological properties. In addition, moral qualities and character traits were also divided up according to the different values assigned by the British rulers: "There were certain cultural proclivities linked to each 'race' stemming from the justifications of colonial labour schemes (slavery and indenture), where, not only were Whites considered respectable, Blacks [were] considered fun-loving, profligate and in need of cultural education, and East Indians considered clannish and avaricious (and later entrepreneurial) under the colonial order" (Yelvington, 1995, p. 25).

Not only were the biological and cultural traits of workers classed according to the ways the different "races" were valued, but so were the crops that they cultivated. As Henry Nelson Coleridge wrote in the early 1800s,

> If I ever turn planter ... I shall buy a cacao plantation in Trinidad ... The cane is, no doubt, a noble plant, and perhaps crop time presents a more lively and interesting scene than harvest in England; but there is so much trash, so many ill-odored negros, so much scum and sling and molasses that my nerves have sometimes sunken under it ... Sugar can surely never be cultivated in the West Indies except by the labour of negros, but I should think white men, creoles or not, might do all the work of a cacao plantation. (Coleridge, 1991 [1826], p. 72)

Thus, with Trinidad under British control from 1797 onwards, we see a more efficiently wrought and enforced formal regimentation of ascription practices, especially with the development and regulation of African slavery and East Indian indenture. The racial division of labour was reflected in the way specific categories of people were tied to particular cash crops: Africans and East Indians with sugar, Amerindians with cocoa. Moral values were attached to crops: cane, cane trash, smoke and sweat were to be sneered at; cocoa, in the hills, on cool, green estates bordered by rivers, was seen as affording work for noble and independent people. Race was a measure of one's social rank in the colony, an overall index of one's rights and privileges, and an indicator of one's value as a person.

Keeping the races "pure," thereby more effectively and efficiently administering who got what, was a paramount concern among the White ruling class. With White purity came White liberty. Obscurity (i.e., "mixture") meant a decline into increasing "inferiority," until a perverse new "purity" was designated: Blackness and utter dispossession. No wonder, then, that women, as gatekeepers to the next generations of offspring, became so critical to racial theorists and colonial legislators.

When it became desirable to dispossess the Caribs of lands that were theirs, and were inalienable, the colonial project became one of defining them out of existence, so that their lands could be put up for sale. No racial purity meant there were no Caribs, which meant that there were no lands to be reserved for Caribs. Residence in the Mission of Santa Rosa in Arima was determined by race: mixed-race offspring were no longer bound to the mission and could not in the future lay any claim to the mission lands. It mattered not that they were raised by Indigenous mothers, and may have felt more attachment to their Indigenous ancestry and the cultural practices it bequeathed; what mattered for the authorities was their "racial mixture."

The concern for one's place in the labour system, one's relative degree of freedom from coercion, and, in the case of Amerindians, access to inalienable, collective lands within Catholic Mission villages, mandated documentation and regulation of who was, or was not, "Indian." Indigenous identity was strictly governed, given the economic status associated with Mission Indians. While the Mission system lasted, baptismal registers clearly indicated whether a child was "Indio" or "India," as this would mean that the child would have rights to residence in the Mission as an adult and would have rights to land. It was noted in the register whether the parents were both native "Indian" or not, although in some cases, only the mother would present herself at the baptism, and no note was made of who the father might have been. Miscegenation was a formal basis for excluding individuals from the rights and status obtaining to mission residence, and this would be just one mode of erasing Indigenous identities from the cultural and political landscape.

The subject of miscegenation and land rights was formally discussed in a recorded session of the Burnley Commission of 1841, which was appointed by the colonial government (Burnley was otherwise the Chairman of the Agricultural and Immigration Society in Trinidad). In its pages, we witness the following exchange between the commissioners and Martin Sorzano, the *corregidor* of the Mission of Arima (Burnley, 1842, p. 109):

> 561. Have they [the Amerindians of the Mission] not always met with the most liberal treatment from the colonial government, and have laboured only for their own benefit?
>
> Sorzano: Always; they were even *exempted from taxes paid by other free classes* in the community, and had medical attendance furnished to them gratis.
>
> 562. To what, then, do you ascribe the gradual and rapid diminution in their number?
>
> Sorzano: Chiefly to *the gradual mixture of the races*. As *pure Indians* they were *compelled to remain at the mission*, and conform to the regulations;

but the children born of Spanish and Creole fathers could not be so classed, and would not submit to the restraint of remaining there.

564. As they appear to have emancipated themselves from the regulations of the mission, do you think they have any legal claim to either the cocoa or the land at present?

Sorzano: I should think not; but it is a legal question, which I am not competent to answer. (Emphases added)

Sorzano chose to cast his answers to question 562 in terms of freedom of choice: the reality was that Mission Indians could leave at any time, but would forfeit rights to collectively owned lands. In addition, "mixed" offspring had no such rights, rendering the "choice" of remaining at the mission quite untenable. The fact that legal questions underlining claims to cocoa and land were raised in such close proximity to issues of miscegenation is also very instructive.

By the 1850s, the Mission was dissolved in de facto terms, and as "Indio" had been undermined as a category of racial purity with certain labour and land rights attached, no longer were any individuals baptized and noted by priests as Indian; it was as if they had all simply vanished one night in 1852 (the year of the last recorded entry that I found in the baptismal registers of the Mission). Lands were expropriated; therefore, there could be no Indians. The pure Indian had indeed become the dead Indian, as a matter of definition. Any claimants to the identity would have to live up to tangible benchmarks of Indian identity, such as "purity of blood." Images of the "true Indian" became monumentalized and began to serve as informal, everyday visual benchmarks for measuring indigeneity.

Extinction by Miscegenation and the Role of Scholarly Expertise

Throughout the 1800s in colonial Trinidad, writers hailing from the elite classes of local society (and/or from abroad) produced various theories and myths of Indigenous extinction in Trinidad (for more, see Forte, 2004–2005, 2006). Whether intentionally or not, these narratives served to bolster and justify the dominant order based on expropriating collective Indigenous lands, furthering private property ownership, and realigning northwestern Trinidad with the increased demand in the world market for cocoa. As sugar declined in value on the world market, Indigenous cocoa-growing lands lands became more valued by private interests supported by the state.

One of the dominant myths of extinction, wrapped in the terms of the then-dominant doctrine of evolutionism, had to do with *extinction via miscegenation*, a purely racial argument, one which we heard echoed in Sorzano's statements above. The idea here is that the only *real* Carib is a *pure* Carib – and the only *pure* Carib is a *dead* Carib. One of the first expressions of this idea appeared in the writing of E.L. Joseph, which was perhaps the first attempt at writing a history of Trinidad in the English language:

> This indolent harmless race is here fast merging on extinction – from no fault of the local government, nor from any disease: the births amongst the Indian women exceed the deaths in the usual ratio; the fact is, that the Indian men, since they are obliged to live in society, choose mates of other races, and the women do the same … hence out of every seven children born of an Indian mother during the last 30 years, there are scarcely two of pure blood, as I have been informed; this will of course decrease their population; for those of the mixed race, whether they be Samboes (between Negroes and Indians), or Mustees (between Europeans and Indians), or the countless castes that the admixture between the African, European, and Indian tribes produce, they are *not the real aboriginal race*, and leave the inactive community of Indians as soon as they reach the age of discretion. (Joseph, 1970 [1838], pp. 102–3, emphasis added)

Another of my favourite quotes in this regard comes from a French historiographic text, published in 1858 and containing a lot of material about Trinidad's Aboriginal population:

> At present there cannot be above 200 or 300 Indians in the colony, so that the aborigines may be said to be almost extinct … finally sunk under the ascendancy of a more intelligent race … but I also coincide in opinion with some judicious observers, who trace the approximate extinction of those tribes to the marked preference manifested by the Indian women towards the negroes and the whites, by whom they were kindly treated, whilst they were regarded by their husbands, of kindred race, more as slaves and beasts of burden, than as equals or companions. As a consequence of those connections, there exists at present, in the colony, a certain number of individuals of Indian descent, but of mixed blood. (De Verteuil, 1858, p. 172)

Their "approximate extinction" occurred as a result of (to use questionable language) mixing with other races. Mixing produces impurity, and hence the "real Indian" vanishes.

Extinction via miscegenation, coupled with regular allusions to the imported motif of American Plains Indians, also featured in texts of the latter half of the century. In the 1880s, James Henry Collens, author of a series of handbooks on Trinidad, wrote that, "as in most other similar cases, persecution or civilization, perhaps both, have driven before them these wild children of the plains, until they have become, so far as Trinidad is concerned, all but extinct" (Collens, 1886, p. 7). Collens is clearly drawing inspiration for his ideas of extinction from other contexts ("as in most other similar cases"), namely, that of the U.S.: what few "plains" existed in Trinidad had been created for sugar cultivation; Indigenous peoples inhabited either the coastlines or the mountainous interior. Writing in the same period, and again with references to North American Indians, another writer, L.M. Fraser, stated:

> There are few traces left of those to whom the hills and forests once belonged. As in North America the Red Indians have gradually disappeared before the encroaching white races, so in Trinidad the Aruacas and the Chaymas, the Tamanacos and the Cumanagotes have little by little faded away out of the community, and are now barely represented by a few families of mixed descent. (Fraser, 1971 [1891], p. 1)

The latter is, like Collens's, an argument of virtual extinction, specifically based on a conception of extinction via miscegenation, which in turn is logically rooted in notions of racial purity. Another noted author asserted that it was as early as 1797, when the British seized the island from the Spanish, that many of the Indigenous peoples of Trinidad had become extinct: "Probably many of them had been absorbed by intermarriage with the invaders. At present, there is hardly an Indian of certainly pure blood in the island, and that only in the northern mountains" (Kingsley, 1877, p. 74). The significance of Kingsley's last statement is that it serves as a preview for a much more recent narrative: that all of Trinidad's real Indians have died out, *except in a specific place.* More on this later.

The importance of these texts is that they produced a base upon which later historical narratives were built, sometimes with little modification. In the 1940s, a key figure in Trinidad's Historical Society asserted with confidence, "[T]o this day we speak of the Queen of the Caribs at Arima, yet I doubt if there is much – if any – Carib blood in her or her race" (Bullbrook, 1940, p. 4). In a society that privileged learning and expertise, the written text achieved a prominence out of proportion with the intellectual merit of its contents, with some writers defiantly refusing to even mention their sources: "[A]nyone who questions any of my facts or conclusions may get in touch with me, and I shall be happy to refer him to the relevant authority," declared Ottley (1955, p. v) – which presents a serious problem, as he is now deceased. Ottley's book was endorsed by the Governor and Commander-in-Chief of Trinidad, Major General Sir Hubert Elving Rance. Thus, when Ottley stated that "but for a handful of them at Arima, these first inhabitants of Trinidad have gone" (1955, p. 4), it came with the added imprimatur of official approval. Even much later, Bridget Brereton, Trinidad and Tobago's leading contemporary historian, for a time argued in these terms: "[T]he Amerindians gave way to newer and sturdier people. Their day was nearly done, and they had no role to play in the development of Trinidad by the later nineteenth century" (Brereton, 1979, p. 131). (She has substantially revised this more recently – see Brereton, 2007, pp. 178–80.)

Even a local historian in Arima, with some attachment to the contemporary Carib community itself, could write in absolute terms of the "the tragedy of total extinction," and in racial terms of "the racial extinction of the Amerindians and the subordinate nature of their cultural system," with the result being that "these first Trinidadians, the Amerindians, have all but disappeared" (Elie, 1990, pp. 1, 2, 3, 5) – a statement truly remarkable for also demeaning the Aboriginal culture. This also shows how deeply pervasive and influential these portrayals are. Nor has this stopped. In a recent article that occasioned much discussion in the pages of the *American Ethnologist*, Viranjini Munasinghe (2002, p. 668) referred to "the almost total annihilation of the indigenous population." It was thanks to an anonymous reviewer, as she admitted, that she added this footnote: "There are persons who claim indigenous Carib ancestry in contemporary Trinidad," but the note went on to include a very debatable justification of her own act of literal marginalization: "but for the most part they continue to be symbolically erased in terms of national significance" (Munasinghe, 2002, p. 687n12). One might also note the skepticism in Munasinghe's tone: she speaks of "persons who claim indigenous Carib ancestry," rather than just *recognizing* them as Caribs, and calling them Caribs, without the prickly qualifications and modifiers.

Self-Extinction: Shame and Hidden Identities

Another mode of erasing indigeneity from the cultural landscape was to instill shame in children of Indigenous ancestry, a process guided by the Catholic Church, state-run schools, and also, it has to be said, by the parents of these same children. Caribs were routinely cast as cannibals, as savages, as poor and illiterate, backward, and out of step with modernity and White Christian righteousness.

I have accumulated many stories during the course of my fieldwork, from individuals in the 50-to-75-year age bracket, of parents who refused to elaborate on family histories, of everyday household practices with unexplained origins, and of somewhat odd family self-identifications as "Spanish" or even, in some cases, "French" (despite complexions and features that gave evidence of more diverse origins). This accounts for what might otherwise be seen as a paradox: active members of the Carib Community on Calvary Hill in Arima attest to the fact that many of their relatives and neighbours today, who would most likely be seen by many in the wider society as "pure blood Amerindians," nevertheless renounce any self-identification as Carib, preferring to refer to themselves simply as mixed, or Spanish, or just Trinidadian. Those who might be seen as less than "pure" are often the ones who are committed to maintaining the culture. The highest expression of this disconnection between race/blood and cultural survival is offered by the Garifuna of St Vincent and the Caribbean coast of Central America, who are the last speakers of the Island Carib language and who have retained many Carib traditions intact, while appearing as a wholly Afro-Caribbean population.

There is, therefore, recognition in the Carib Community of the fact that "blood" does not imply public commitment or even personal affective attachment to a cultural heritage. Moreover, individuals whose own genealogical history is quite diverse, comprising multiple ethnic ancestries, are some of the people who are most committed to making the resurgence of Carib identification a reality today – challenging the stigma, shame, and silence of the past. These realizations, among active members of the Carib Community, have helped to further open the door to different ways of conceptualizing who the "real Carib" is, and to the minimization of the role of "blood purity" in cultural survival and resurgence.

The Rule of Race: National Independence and Party Politics

With Trinidad's achievement of internal self-rule in 1956, and eventual independence in 1962, the country witnessed the organization of political support along ethnic lines with two parties traditionally vying for power, one dominated by urban African-descended Trinidadians, and the other by more rural, East Indian-descended Trinidadians, locked for decades now in what can seem like a virtual Cold War.

Long in power, the African-dominated People's National Movement (PNM) cultivated patron–client relationships to ensure electoral support, and one of its clients was the Santa Rosa Carib Community in Arima, which it pushed towards formal incorporation and official recognition beginning in the mid-1970s. Members of the Carib Community not only live in close proximity with Afro-Trinidadians, with Arima long a bastion of support for the PNM, but have also intermarried with them. This is not to say that one never hears stigmatizing statements against Africans from members of the Carib community, but then that would be true in an Afro-Trinidadian community as well. The people who seem most alien to members of the Carib Community, especially to the older generation, are East Indians; one Carib elder I spoke with went as far as mistrustfully referring to East Indians as "that other nation," a strong statement which I had not before encountered in my time in Trinidad. Nonetheless, members of the Carib Community have also intermarried with persons of East Indian descent.

To some extent, at least for some members of the older generation of Caribs (those over fifty years of age), "racial mixture" is a problem when it comes to asserting an identity as Carib. They are commonly forced to answer what is virtually an accusation: that they are not "pure." Some accept this designation, repeating the propaganda about racial purity – what are now the society's official rules – even while their everyday customary practice runs counter to these rules. As a researcher who is a member of the Carib Community wrote, "[T]hey know that none of them is a pure blooded Amerindian as they are mixed with other ethnic groups" (Almarales, 1994, p. 3). She quotes the chief of the Carib Community, Ricardo Bharath Hernandez, who told her that "some of the Carib descendants were ashamed of their ancestry, 'having lost all pride in their bloodline'" (Almarales, 1994, p. 3). What remains unsettled is Carib as a cultural identity, not a racial one, and it is extremely difficult to convince a Trinidadian audience that culture is not something that is "in the blood," that it is not something that should be seen on one's face. Indeed, it is even difficult for some Caribs to accept that.

What Makes a Carib?

For most members of the older generation, a Carib is someone with proven ancestry to the Amerindians of Arima. Kinship matters foremost, but not always exclusively. Caribs are those you know as Carib, those who have always known themselves to be Carib, and those who are referred to by other Caribs as Carib. This seems relatively simple and unproblematic, except that it covers over the routine exclusions of those who are "too dark" to be considered "real" Caribs. It is still not uncommon to hear members of the community refer to someone, casually and informally, as a "true" or "pure" Carib, based entirely on that person's appearance. The concept of a "Black Carib" is a novel innovation for Trinidad, even if in St Vincent it dates to the 1700s, and even though some members have Vincentian Carib ancestry.

One of the challenges of identity and belonging, taken up with greater vigour by the Carib community, is to realign Caribness with the practice, beliefs, and lifeways that mark Indigenous belonging. This is a big challenge to the dominant way of understanding identity, and one that may contribute to efforts elsewhere in the society to overcome race by transcending it. While some members of the community told me that a Carib is someone with a specific genealogy, others also held that Carib is something one *feels*, a sense of being rooted *here*, or being totally at home in the nation's forests, mountains, rivers, and beaches – a notion of belonging to *this place*, where there is no other place that beckons.

Everyone Has Some Carib in Them

Rather than simply leaving things at "Caribs are mixed with," say, Africans, spokespersons for the Carib Community have tried to take their discourse further by flipping the direction of the narrative of mixture. Capitalizing on an institutionalized discourse of national identity and national belonging, and official depictions of Trinidad as a mixed, cosmopolitan, or creolized society, Carib spokespersons will not deny that they are an amalgam of the wider society's multiethnic influences – instead, they will assert that there is, as a result, "some Carib blood" in everyone else. The late Elma Reyes, a research and public relations officer for the Santa Rosa Carib Community, wrote an extensive newspaper article that argued this very point (Reyes, 1995). Carib Breweries, which appropriated the name of the people and for a while even funded the Carib Community, subsequently used the idea that "everybody has some Carib in them" as a marketing slogan.

Culture is still objectified as race, as a biological essence, but at least the diminishing zone of exclusion around Carib identity is disrupted. Rather than being framed in terms of "decline," now the Caribs' argument is about diffusion and dissemination, about how the rural lifeways of the Caribs shaped and influenced those of many Trinidadians, East Indians, and Africans, and have thus been perpetuated. Rather than extinction via miscegenation, this is survival via miscegenation which facilitated cultural diffusion. The problem remains one of arresting common, everyday, taken-for-granted practices and reassigning a Carib label to them.

Over a century after the demise of the mission of Arima, current Carib self-identifications are beginning to frame indigeneity as a cultural heritage and a body of practices. This is not to say that racial notions of identity no longer persist in the wider society. By and large, however, the response of the Trinidadian state, mass media, and schools, and of Indigenous visitors from other Caribbean territories and even Canada, has been to make little or no remark about physical appearance, generally accepting and recognizing the community as Carib. This is rather novel, I think, and it possibly represents an opening for the decolonization of prior modes of ascription and self-identification as Indigenous.

Today it seems that certain practices, objects, rituals, beliefs, affiliations, and clusters of family connections help to render indigeneity broader, less formulaic, and more open than previous forms of racialization. It is not even a question of members of the Carib community rejecting notions of race – it is more that in the process of fostering cultural renewal, they have complicated their own perspectives of what it means to be Indigenous. In effect, indigeneity has been rendered by them as a process and practice, a project of always becoming. I do not wish to make too bold an assertion here: I am not suggesting that racialized notions of Carib identity are gone from the wider society, or from some Caribs themselves, only that matters now seem even more unsettled than in the past couple of centuries, with previously dominant discourses now suffering from increased neglect, dissolution and confusion.

One of the clearest ideological challenges facing the Caribs in Trinidad today stems from the multiplicity of narratives of identity – all simultaneously present, each with its internal contradictions, partially transmitted, selectively read, and incompletely understood – producing a situation that from this angle looks like a much-awaited transition, and from that angle appears to be a retreat to the hardened arteries of racial orthodoxy. Adding to the accumulation of ideological conflicts, and to the blurring of dividing lines, is the state's extinctionist form of recognition of the Carib presence.

Extinction by Recognition

In a 2004 address at the Arima Town Hall, at which the President of the Republic of Trinidad and Tobago, members of the media, and Indigenous delegates from the Caribbean region were present, Ricardo Bharath-Hernandez, the chief of the Santa Rosa Carib Community, made the following statement:

> ... among us there are many well-intentioned, informed and respected academics, politicians and ordinary citizens who are still doubtful about our existence. Many assumed that the "mixing of blood" and the process of assimilation all but wiped out our distinctive identities and valid claims to Aboriginal or Indigenous status in this land ... some of those who concede that we exist see us as leftover or unfinished business of the process of civilization and assimilating of the primitive people. We affirm that we are not a people of the past. We are a people with a past. (Bharath Hernandez, 2004, n.p.)

Here the chief clearly addresses issues of extinction – of the production of "non-Indians" by way of miscegenation and assimilation, or their reduction to archaeological relics.

Presumably, state recognition, which has been much sought after by the Carib leadership over the past forty years, would have advanced the group's claims against such ways of diminishing and erasing their identity. First, we need to address what recognition there has been from the state. While successive PNM governments, beginning in the early 1970s, recognized and acknowledged the presence of the Caribs in Arima by providing them with funds, it was also under government direction that the Carib Community was formally incorporated as a limited liability company. This is already an act of misrecognition – imposing the status of a business on what was actually a kin-based community whose purpose was not profit. The second, more formal act of recognition came on 8 May 1990, when it was announced that the cabinet of Prime Minister A.N.R. Robinson, who led the National Alliance for Reconstruction (NAR), "decided that the Santa Rosa Carib Community be recognized as representative of the indigenous Amerindians of Trinidad and Tobago, and that an annual subvention of $30,000 be granted to them from 1990" (Office of the Prime Minister, 1990, n.p.).

The wording of the above, and further instruments of recognition (Hansard, 1991, 1992, 2000; and Forte 2007a, 2007b, 2007c, 2009) is both consistent and significant, for these claims by successive governments that one group was representative of all "indigenous Amerindians" served to contain indigeneity (representing all, thereby eliminating other claimants), and indeed to contain it in one place (Arima) and one form (a company). Yet, while claiming to recognize the Indigenous presence, the government of Trinidad and Tobago has no legal definition of the term "Indigenous Peoples." Nor has the state admitted Indigenous identification into the national census (more on this below).

Extinction by Localization

The SRCC is a formally constituted group; it cannot be equated with, nor stand for, all persons of Indigenous descent in Trinidad, and to my knowledge its leadership has never made such a claim. Yet, typically, we find in most Trinidadian publications – whether these be locally self-published books and pamphlets, tourist brochures, Trinidadian websites, newspaper articles, or school texts – that Arima is routinely hailed as the "home of the Caribs," or the home of the *last remaining* Caribs.

This form of localized recognition, besides being unsupported by ethnohistoric research, functions either deliberately or by accident to delimit and contain indigeneity in Trinidad and Tobago. Spotlighting Arima as the home of the island's last remaining Caribs also defies logic. The Indian Mission of Toco on the north coast survived virtually as long as that of Arima, as did that of Siparia in the south. Why would Indigenous descendants have mysteriously disappeared in those places and not at Arima? Indeed, many Indigenous descendants in Arima, being of so-called mixed race, were effectively barred from the mission and thus forced to leave Arima. The de facto dissolution of the mission of Arima meant that many Caribs had to move elsewhere and squat on other lands. So it is not just the ex-mission towns that have Amerindian descendants, but a whole range of small rural villages and hamlets, including Talparo, Brazil, Rio Claro, and Paria, among others. Dislocation, of course, also facilitated cultural diffusion.

To limit recognition to Arima, and to the Santa Rosa Carib Community, is to wipe the rest of the face of Trinidad clean of the possibility of Indigenous identification. This is reinforced by the deliberate omission of Indigenous identity from any censuses. Localization of recognition in Trinidad effectively serves to neutralize indigeneity by evading the widespread dissemination of Amerindian ancestry, family lines, and cultural practices throughout the country.

Discounting Indigeneity

The absence of a Carib, Amerindian, Native Indian, or Indigenous category on the census renders extraordinary the statement made by the Minister for Community Development, Culture and Gender Affairs, Joan Yuille Williams, on 23 September 2006, in the Carib Community Centre itself, that people of Amerindian and "mixed Amerindian" descent in Trinidad are "a very small minority." In the absence of a census that allows for such identification, how would she have proved this assertion?

In June of the same year, the government of Trinidad and Tobago was confronted with this issue by the United Nations Committee for the Elimination of Racial Discrimination (CERD), as outlined in a report on the countries of Latin America and the Caribbean, in which CERD states:

> 351. The Committee expresses its concern at the absence ... of specific information on the indigenous population as well as other relatively small ethnic groups of the State party in the report, and particularly the absence of a specific categorization of the indigenous population as a separate ethnic group in official statistics on the population. The Committee encourages the Government to include the indigenous population in any statistical data as a separate ethnic group, and actively to seek consultations with them as to how they prefer to be identified, as well as on policies and programmes affecting them. (CERD, 2006, p. 534)

In a supplement, CERD makes specific reference to the Caribs:

> 34. Members of the Committee asked why the Caribs had all but disappeared, exactly how many were left, why they were not treated as a separate racial group and whether measures were being taken to help them, particularly in the economic and educational fields, so as to compensate them for the injustices they had suffered. (CERD, 2006, p. 536)

We do not know how members of the CERD delegation even came to know of the Caribs, but we know that representatives of the government of Trinidad and Tobago had told them that the Caribs were virtually extinct, and had apparently suggested they were a non-distinctive "mixed race" group. For example, in 1980, representatives of the Trinidadian government stated to CERD that "the Carib-Indian population was extremely small, numbering less than 300, and had almost disappeared as a separate group" (CERD, 2006, p. 546). Yet, as they admitted, there was no Carib category in the census, and thus the number is furnished without support. Interestingly, 300 is also the number offered by De Verteuil in 1858, which makes the government's current number all the more suspicious; it appears either to be an unconsciously proffered echo, or to advance the incredible idea of total non-growth in the Indigenous population over 150 years (for more on CERD, the UN, and the Trinidadian government on the subject of the Caribs, see Forte, 2012).

In terms of international covenants on the rights of Indigenous Peoples, Trinidad has had a mixed record of acceptance, even as it has boasted of its state recognition of the Caribs. While Trinidad voted to approve the UN Declaration of the Rights of Indigenous Peoples in 2007, it never signed Convention No. 169 of the International Labour Organization, on Indigenous and Tribal Peoples, which came into being in 1989. In its refusal to sign, Trinidad was accompanied by Canada, the U.S., Belize, and Guyana, all of which also claim to recognize their Indigenous populations.

Two of the biggest and most immediate challenges for the resurgence of Carib identification in Trinidad are (1) to transcend the ideologically constructed and culturally mediated limitations of "race" as a way of understanding Carib indigeneity, a discourse that has produced narratives of extinction that even now persist in various forms; and (2) to compel the Trinidadian state to begin to count self-identifying Indigenous persons on the national census, and subsequently to move past localized recognition of one community alone. Without these measures, it is difficult to see how the Caribs can escape complete statistical elimination and continued treatment as relics of a distant past. In addition, the recognition of one group alone has already begun to create significant tensions and arguments, as another organization, called "Partners for First Peoples' Development," has been created in Arima itself, and has contested the sole recognition granted to the Santa Rosa Carib Community. As a spokesman for Partners declared to the national press, "Our group is about all people who have indigenous blood, regardless of how you look or your religious persuasion. The Government … through its wisdom or non-wisdom has seen it fit to recognize only the Santa Rosa mission [*sic*] as the representative body of peoples with indigenous blood" (Ramdass, 2010, n.p.). Unfortunately, Carib descendants may find themselves in a fight that the state created.

NOTES

1 "Indian" in colonial Trinidad always referred to Indigenous peoples, while people from India were routinely referred to in official documents and everyday discourse as "Coolies." In recent decades, and especially with the advent of national independence, labels have shifted. Now "Indian" almost always refers to people from India, while "Carib" has become the recognized label for designating Indigenous identity in Trinidad, based on both historical sources and local naming conventions in Arima.

REFERENCES

Almarales, B. (1994). *The Santa Rosa Carib Community from 1974–1993*. Unpublished Bachelor's Thesis, University of the West Indies, St. Augustine, Trinidad.

Bharath Hernandez, R. (2004). First Peoples of Our Nation. Address on the occasion of a symposium held at the Arima Town Hall, Arima, Trinidad and Tobago, 14 October.

Brereton, B. (1979). *Race Relations in Colonial Trinidad, 1870–1900*. Cambridge, UK: Cambridge University Press.

Brereton, B. (2007). Contesting the Past: Narratives of Trinidad & Tobago History. *New West Indian Guide / Nieuwe West-Indische Gids, 81*(3–4), 169–96.

Bullbrook, J.A. (1940). The Ierian Race. A lecture delivered at the meeting of the Historical Society of Trinidad and Tobago held in the hall of the Victoria Institute at 8:30 p.m on Friday, 3 March 1939. Port of Spain, Trinidad: Historical Society of Trinidad and Tobago.

Burnley, W.H. (1842). *Observations on the Present Condition of the Island of Trinidad, and the Actual State of the Experiment of Negro Emancipation*. London: Longman, Brown, Green, and Longmans.

CERD. (2006). Compilación de observaciones finales del Comité para la Eliminación de la Discriminación Racial sobre países de América Latina y el Caribe (1970–2006). Santiago, Chile: Alto Comisionado de las Naciones Unidas para los Derechos Humanos, Representación Regional para América Latina y el Caribe. http://web.archive.org/web/20110219082203/http://www2.ohchr.org/english/bodies/cerd/docs/CERD-concluding-obs.pdf

Coleridge, H.N. (1991 [1826]). Six Months in the West Indies. In G. Besson & B. Brereton (Eds.), *The Book of Trinidad* (pp. 117–26). Port of Spain, Trinidad: Paria Publishing.

Collens, J.H. (1886). *Guide to Trinidad: A Handbook for the Use of Tourists and Visitors*. Port of Spain, Trinidad: n.p.

De Verteuil, L.A.A. (1858). *Trinidad: Its Geography, Natural Resources, Administration, Present Condition, and Prospects*. London: Ward & Lock. http://dx.doi.org/10.5962/bhl.title.28272

Elie, J.P. (1990). Five Hundred Years of European Domination of The Caribbean – The Achievements of the Subjugated Peoples – The Amerindians. Paper presented at the 15th Annual Conference of the History Teachers' Association of Trinidad and Tobago.

Forte, M.C. (2004–2005). Writing the Caribs Out: The Construction and Demystification of the "Deserted Island" Thesis for Trinidad. *Issues in Caribbean Amerindian Studies, 6*, August 2004–August 2005. http://www.centrelink.org/forteatlantic2004.pdf

Forte, M.C. (2006). Extinction: Ideologies against Indigeneity in the Caribbean. *Southern Quarterly*, *43*(4), 46–69.

Forte, M.C. (2007a). Does Trinidad Recognize Its Indigenous People? *Review of the Indigenous Caribbean*, 10 March. http://indigenousreview.blogspot.com/2007/03/does-trinidad-recognize-its-indigenous.html

Forte, M.C. (2007b). Does Arima Matter? *Review of the Indigenous Caribbean*, 11 March. http://indigenousreview.blogspot.com/2007/03/does-arima-matter.html

Forte, M.C. (2007c). News about Trinidad's Caribs and the State. *Review of the Indigenous Caribbean*, 31 August. http://indigenousreview.blogspot.com/2007/08/news-about-trinidad-caribs-and-state.html

Forte, M.C. (2009). Forgetting the Caribs of Trinidad. *Review of the Indigenous Caribbean*, 24 October. http://indigenousreview.blogspot.com/2009/10/denigrating-celebrating-remembering-and.html

Forte, M.C. (2012). Racial Discrimination: The Caribs, the Government of Trinidad and Tobago, and the United Nations. *Review of the Indigenous Caribbean*, 2 February. http://indigenousreview.blogspot.com/2012/02/racial-discrimination-caribs-government.html

Fraser, L.M. (1971 [1891]). *History of Trinidad (First Period), from 1781 to 1813* (Vol. I). London: Frank Cass and Co.

Hansard. (1991). House of Representatives, 15 March. Port of Spain, Trinidad and Tobago: Parliament of the Republic of Trinidad and Tobago. http://www.ttparliament.org/hansards/hh19910315.pdf

Hansard. (1992). House of Representatives, 16 October. Port of Spain, Trinidad and Tobago: Parliament of the Republic of Trinidad and Tobago. http://www.ttparliament.org/hansards/hh19921016.pdf

Hansard. (2000). Senate, 18 July. Port of Spain, Trinidad and Tobago: Parliament of the Republic of Trinidad and Tobago. http://www.ttparliament.org/hansards/hs20000718.pdf

Hulme, P. & Whitehead, N.L. (Eds.). (1992). *Wild Majesty: Encounters with Caribs from Columbus to the Present Day*. Oxford: Oxford University Press.

Kingsley, C. (1877). *At Last: A Christmas in the West Indies*. London: Macmillan and Co. http://dx.doi.org/10.5962/bhl.title.4323

Leahy, V. (1980). *Catholic Church in Trinidad, 1797–1820*. Arima, Trinidad: St. Dominic Press.

Moodie-Kublalsingh, S. (1994). *The Cocoa Panyols of Trinidad: An Oral Record*. London: British Academic Press.

Munasinghe, V. (2002). Nationalism in Hybrid Spaces: The Production of Impurity out of Purity. *American Ethnologist*, *29*(3), 663–92. http://dx.doi.org/10.1525/ae.2002.29.3.663

Newson, L. (1976). *Aboriginal and Spanish Colonial Trinidad: A Study in Culture Contact*. London: British Academic Press.

Office of the Prime Minister. (1990). News Release No. 360, 8 May. Port of Spain, Trinidad and Tobago: Information Division.

Ottley, C.R. (1955). *An Account of Life in Spanish Trinidad (From 1498–1797)* (1st ed.). Diego Martin, Trinidad: C.R. Ottley.

Ramdass, R. (2010). Argument Erupts between 2 Groups. *Trinidad Express*, 15 October. http://www.trinidadexpress.com/news/Argument_erupts_between_2_groups-105006909.html

Reyes, E. (1995). Carib Blood May Run in Your Veins. *Trinidad Guardian*, 31 May, p. 8. http://guanaguanaresingsat.blogspot.com/2010/06/carib-blood-may-run-in-your-veins.html

Whitehead, N.L. (2005). Black Read as Red: Ethnic Transgression and Hybridity in Northeastern South America and the Caribbean. In M. Restall (Ed.), *Beyond Black and Red: African-Native Relations in Colonial Latin America* (pp. 223–43). Albuquerque, NM: University of New Mexico Press.

Yelvington, K. (1995). Cricket, Colonialism, and the Culture of Caribbean Politics. In M.A. Malec (Ed.), *The Social Roles of Sport in Caribbean Societies* (pp. 13–51). London: Gordon and Breach.

7 Encountering Indigeneity: The International Funding of Indigeneity in Peru

JOSÉ ANTONIO LUCERO

In Latin America, what we might call the regimes of indigeneity – the rules, expectations, assumptions, and other explicit or implicit understandings that regulate the distinctions between Indigenous and non-Indigenous identifications – have not relied on the kind of blood quantum requirements that are common in North America. Part of the reason for this difference in "blood politics" lies in the fact that, generally speaking, "blood" is already part of the national ideologies of racial mixture that incorporate the mixing (and spilling) of African, European, and Native blood as foundational narratives. Thus, in a region where "everyone" has Native blood but not everyone is "Indian," the social category and social fact of Indianness necessarily rely less on biology or blood than on the intersecting sociocultural workings of politics, language, place, class, and gender.[1]

In the Andean region, the so-called Indian problem was one of incorporating the rural highland and Amazonian populations into the imagined community of the national state. For such an undertaking, elites turned to the art and politics of *indigenismo*: the literature, the paintings, and the policies about and designed for Indigenous people, but not produced by them. Eventually, progressive mid-twentieth-century state reforms sought to solve the Indian problem by making it a peasant problem, a problem of land reform and economics. Yet, throughout the region since the 1960s, Indigenous people have politically reconstituted themselves through powerful acts of organization, mobilization, and other forms of self-representation both locally and globally. As many scholars have noted, an important part of this political construction of indigeneity has involved non-Indigenous networks that include transnational actors like churches, non-governmental organizations (NGOs), and international development agencies (e.g., Albó, 1991; Brysk, 1994; Yashar, 2005). As Arturo Escobar has noted, it is in this way that "development operates as an arena for cultural contestation and identity construction" (Escobar, 1995, p. 15).

This essay is part of a larger project that seeks to understand how international non-governmental organizations (INGOs) and Indigenous actors negotiate the meanings of indigeneity and the terms of "international cooperation." It takes its case studies from the experiences of Oxfam America, an especially important funder of Indigenous political activity in Latin America. While Oxfam America's grants are small compared to multilateral programs, as an early funder of and producer of knowledge about Indigenous activism, lessons from its encounters with indigeneity are especially important.

Specifically, this essay examines two different moments in the interactive process of legitimation between INGOs such as Oxfam America and Indigenous political organizations in Peru, as actors on both sides of the development encounter shape discourses over the meanings of development and indigeneity across local and global scales. The following section provides an introduction to the challenges of understanding indigeneity in Peru, then proceeds to a discussion of two moments in the relationship between Oxfam America and Indigenous actors in Peru. Finally, this essay concludes with a discussion of the importance of multi-scalar approaches to the understanding of Indigenous identities and politics in Latin America and beyond.

Peru: The Place of Indigeneity (or Indigeneity Out of Place?)

Peru shares with other Latin American states a contradictory position of celebrating its pre-Columbian Indigenous past while simultaneously marginalizing the large existing populations of Native people. Even the 2001 election of President Alejandro Toledo, who emphasized his impoverished Andean upbringing during his campaign and inaugurated his presidential term with a neo-Incan ceremony at Machu Picchu, represented less of an opening for Indigenous politics than a continuation of the longstanding tradition that Cecilia Méndez (1996) summarizes as "*Incas sí, Indios no.*"[2] Though statisticians and economists dispute the count of Indigenous people in Peru, a recent World Bank study confirms what many suspect: that the Indigenous population in Peru is significant (between 25 and 48 per cent of the national population), and that it is extremely poor (62 per cent of all poor and extremely poor people are Indigenous) (Hall & Patrinos, 2005; Trivelli, 2005). The Peruvian state has not asked about indigeneity in any census since 1940 when it determined that 45 per cent of Peruvians were Indian (Huber, 2007, p. 2n1).

Indianness in Peru has been expressed in ways that reflect the importance of the idioms of class and region. Officially, there are no "Indigenous" communities in Peru, but rather *comunidades campesinas* (peasant communities) in the largely Quechua and Aymara highlands, and *comunidades nativas* (native communities) in the Amazonian lowlands. These labels of "peasant" and "native" were institutionalized by the leftist Revolutionary Government of the Armed Forces of General Juan Velasco Alvarado (1968–75) and the emergence of peasant federations like the (Communist-created) Peasant Confederation of Peru (CCP) and the (officialist) National Agrarian Confederation (CNA). Though these federations articulated many Quechua and Aymara communities, the prevailing view of Andean rural organizing was that class overshadowed race. Xavier Albó captures this view when he states that "the great difference [between Peru] and the other Andean countries ... is that rural organizations of the rural Andes have made little progress in reclaiming their ethnic identity" (1991, p. 325). The situation is different in the Amazonian lowlands, however, as the "native communities" have organized explicitly on "ethnic" grounds since the 1960s, and have created supra-local organizations like AIDSEP (the Inter-Ethnic Association for the Development of the Peruvian Jungle).

This alleged "lack" of Andean Indigenous political identification has been used to highlight Peru as a place where Indigenous politics seems to lie dormant in contrast to the explosion of Indigenous mobilizations that have taken place in Ecuador and Bolivia. While this is not the place to review this line of argumentation,[3] it is important to note that – setting aside the conceptual debate over whether there is or is not an "Indigenous movement" in Peru, or whether "*campesino*" is or isn't a racialized category – as an empirical matter, within various sectors of Peruvian society, "Indigenous" identities are problematic because they are considered dangerous.

The essential and tragic context for every discussion of contemporary Peruvian politics is the long, racialized, and regionalized war between the forces of the Shining Path (and other leftist guerillas) and the Peruvian state. The war, which began in 1980 and took nearly 70,000 lives, entered its last phase when the government of Alberto Fujimori captured Sendero's leader Abimael Guzman in 1992.[4] Arguably, the slow response of President Belaunde (1980–5) and the increasingly and indiscriminately violent counter-insurgency policies of the first Alan García government (1985–90) had something to do with perceptions of the violence as something distant from coastal Lima. Mario Vargas Llosa provides a particularly clear illustration of this view:

> That there is a nation completely separate from the official nation is, of course, the great Peruvian problem. That people can simultaneously live in a country who participate in the 20th century and people like the *comuneros* of Uchuraccay and all the Iquichano communities who live in the 19th – if not to say the 18th. This enormous distance which exists between the two Perus is behind the tragedy we have just investigated. (Vargas Llosa, 1983)

Vargas Llosa's view has been extensively and thoroughly criticized by anthropologists inside and outside of Peru (e.g., Mayer, 1991). Yet, there remains a strong strain of this kind of thinking in both conservative elite and even progressive intellectual segments of Peruvian society. Consider the response given by Julio Cotler, one of Peru's most distinguished social scientists, when asked by television journalist Cecilia Valenzuela whether Indigenous demands based on race and ethnicity actually pose a threat to the Andean region:

> Increasingly, these ethnic groups or the leaders of these groups begin to make demands based on ethnic or racial problems. Now, what is the danger that this can lead to? We already know the dangers; it can end in divided countries, in civil wars, in massacres. The Balkans is a good example ... This is no joke. (Cotler, 2005)

It is important to put these comments in context. They were made in the midst of an electoral campaign that, like previous Peruvian presidential campaigns, witnessed the strong challenge of an "outsider," Ollanta Humala. Humala was a controversial figure, not the least because of ideas espoused by his family – most notably his father, Isaac Humala, who was a vocal advocate of a racialist-nationalist ideology known as "*etno-cacerismo*." This is a compound term that came from a celebration of the "copper race" (providing the "etno") and Andres Avelino Caceres, a nationalist hero in the nineteenth-century war against Chile.

Returning to Cotler's comment about a Balkanized future for Peru, he explained in an interview that he is not opposed to Indigenous movements ("that would be absurd"), but rather, "what I am against are those kinds of positions that threaten me physically. This is not simply a theoretical or academic problem. The Humalas [los Humala] wanted to take away my Peruvian citizenship [because of Cotler's Jewish background]. This has been said explicitly" (J. Cotler, interview, 10 August 2006).

Still, in many sectors of Peruvian society, not just Humalismo but all ethnic discourses are tinged with danger. As a former NGO director remarked, "there is the belief among many Limeño elites that Indians will come and kill them in their sleep" (Anonymous, interview, 2006). Another researcher noted that the climate around the time of the election reminded him of the "1960s and 1970s when the Lima elite lived with the fear that the Andean migrants in the shantytowns would descend from the hills and invade the residential neighborhoods of the capital" (Portocarrero, 2006).

The election reached a second round with two candidates: the nationalist Ollanta Humala versus a much reformed, born-again-conservative Alan García (who sought to redeem himself for his disastrous 1985–90 presidency). Ollanta Humala distanced himself from his family and declared himself a nationalist, not an ethno-nationalist. Humala remained characterized as the candidate of the poor, southern Andes, and García was the candidate of the northern coast and Lima. García's slim 52.62 per cent victory is even more dramatic when seen in regional terms. Humala won in a landslide in the strongly Indigenous areas of the southern Andes and the Amazon, whereas García won in the north and along the coast.

As I have suggested elsewhere (Lucero, 2007), the electoral victory of Alan García represents the closing of an opening for Indigenous politics that came with the overlapping end of war and the end of the authoritarian Fujimori years (1990–2000). The interim presidency of Valentín Paniagua not only put into motion the process that would produce the public hearings of the Truth and Reconciliation Commission but also the "*mesas de diálogo*" between the government and Indigenous peoples. Under Toledo, the *mesas de diálogo* gave way to a National Commission for Andean, Amazon, and Afro-Peruvians (CONAPA) that was headed by Toledo's wife, Eliane Karp. Due to severe criticism from both opposition political elites and Indigenous leaders, Karp was forced to resign and CONAPA was restructured as a new governmental body with greater institutional stature known as INDEPA, the National Institute for the Development of Andean, Amazonian, and Afro-Peruvian Peoples (García & Lucero, 2004, 2011).

The Toledo years represent a missed opportunity for a more pro-Indigenous political agenda. The García government, though, openly criticized the findings of the Truth and Reconciliation Commission (TRC)'s *Final Report* (one that was critical of the broad patterns of internal colonialism in Peru) and sent a clear signal of the diminished place that Indigenous issues would have in his government by folding the new state agency for Indigenous affairs, INDEPA, into the Ministry for Women's Affairs. At the same time, to the surprise of many, García travelled in June 2007 to Ayacucho, the department most damaged by the war, and enacted one of the recommendations of the TRC report: the payment of reparations to individuals affected by the violence. He was accompanied by the former president of the TRC, Salomon Lerner. While one can cynically suggest that such a high-profile trip was the stuff of photo-op politics, it did breathe a little life into what many had thought was a moribund set of TRC recommendations.

This historical sketch of Indigenous politics in Peru shows some of the difficult terrain that Indigenous actors and their allies must negotiate. In the next section, I illustrate some of those negotiations by describing the historical evolution of Oxfam America, as it is one of the first agencies to work explicitly with all major Indigenous political organizations in the Andes.

Indigenous Politics: A View from Oxfam America

Support for Indigenous organizations marked a trend that began in the early 1980s when Oxfam America began to fund Indigenous organizations as part of its "rights-based" approach to addressing the social problems of poverty and social exclusion. Oxfam America is one of twelve Oxfam International affiliates, a network of non-profit agencies that trace their beginning to the Oxford Committee for Famine Relief, founded in 1942 in response to the plight of Greek war refugees. In the early 1970s, a group of volunteers founded Oxfam America (with support from Oxfam Great Britain) in response to humanitarian crises that accompanied the struggle for independence in Bangladesh. In the 1980s, under the direction of U.S. anthropologist Richard Chase Smith, Oxfam America's newly formed South American Regional Program focused its humanitarian and political work specifically towards

Indigenous people (anonymous interviews at offices of Oxfam America and IBIS in Lima, Peru, and La Paz, Bolivia, 2006–7).

Smith had conducted much research surveying the landscape of Indigenous politics in the Andean/Amazonian region and presented his view of Indigenous politics in an oft-cited paper titled "Searching for Unity within Diversity." Smith called for an analytical distinction between three types of Indigenous organizations: *campesino* labour unions, *indianista* groups, and ethnic federations.[5] His typology was structured along the dimensions of identity, autonomy, and representativeness. The collective identities of *campesino* and *indianista* organizations operated in terms of ideological oppositions of class analysis, in the case of *campesinos* (workers vs. capital), and of anti-colonialism, in the case of *indianistas* (colonizers vs. colonized). Ethnic federations were less tied to grand theories and sought to articulate local identifications. In terms of autonomy, all organizations responded to "outside" interests to some degree. *Campesino* organizations were often closely connected to political parties of the left, and ethnic federations counted on close NGO ties. While *indianistas* were most vocal in refusing "to make any alliance with outside groups which may be 'tinged' with non-Indian domination," in practice they too often received funds from friendly European NGOs (Smith, 1983, p. 34). Smith's last criteria concerning representativeness suggested that modern Indigenous organizations should be independent from the rigid ideologies and the tutelage of political parties or outside actors, and should connect leaders at the top with communities at the base. Smith saw *indianista* groups as the least representative of all types.

This conceptual view grew out of a variety of negative interactions that Smith had had with members of *indianista* organizations like the CISA (el Consejo Indio Sud-Americano, the South American Indian Council). CISA was seen by Smith as a divisive and overly "ideological" force, and it was already receiving funding from the International Work Group for Indigenous Affairs (IWGIA) in Copenhagen and had already spoken for Indigenous people at the United Nations.[6] At Oxfam America, Smith's interest was "to get more of a community-based approach as opposed to [that of the] ideologues" (R.C. Smith, interview, 6 May 2006). In this spirit, Smith, as a representative of Oxfam America, and in coordination with other advocacy groups like Cultural Survival, convened a foundational meeting between Oxfam America and Amazonian Indigenous leaders from Bolivia, Colombia, Ecuador, Peru, and Brazil in Lima, Peru.

"I went into this meeting with that analysis [of the merits of *campesino, indianista,* and ethnic federations] already made." Thus, this meeting served as a kind of foundational moment in the relationship between Oxfam America and Indigenous organizations. It is important to emphasize that the participants at the meeting were far from blank slates awaiting the wisdom of Oxfam, Smith, or anyone else. All leaders present came from organizations that themselves were products of years of struggles between Indigenous communities, states, and social forces. However, this meeting did represent an important opportunity to find a new articulation of South American Indigenous politics in light of the problems that had arisen with CISA (R.C. Smith, interview, 6 May 2006).[7]

One of the Indigenous leaders at the meeting described some of those complaints as a problem of what he called "*indígenas sueltos*" (literally "loose Indians"): "These are Indigenous people without majority support. Loose Indians or cheap Indians without a clear position. Wherever there is money, there they go. When there isn't they aren't there. They have no real identity, they lack their own identity. They are following their own interests" (Anonymous, interview, 20 May 2006). Speaking of an *indianista* activist in Peru, Smith used similar language. He stated that the *indianista* leader "is not Indian, but as Mestizo as you can get. He was of the school of thought that anyone can be an Indian as long as your heart is in the right place and that sounded very dangerous to me" (interview, 6 May 2006).

Not all accept Smith's view. Javier Lajo, a former member of CISA, recognizes that the organization had its problems, but believes that it should not be up to White, U.S. anthropologists to certify or decertify who can and cannot speak for Indigenous people (Lajo, 2003).[8] While this is an important critique, it should be pointed out that a negative view of CISA was not confined to the head of Oxfam America, but was also voiced often by Amazonian and Andean leaders in Bolivia, Ecuador, and Peru. Moreover, while we should not overestimate the ability of one INGO to dictate the terms of Indigenous recognition, it is important to see the process of "positioning" indigeneity (Li, 2000). It is in this sense that this meeting among INGO and Indigenous leaders in the early 1980s in Lima was instructive.

At this meeting, then, one sees the conflict of two of Smith's "types": ethnic federation against Indianist organization. From an early moment, Oxfam America made a choice to work with ethnic federations.[9] When I asked Smith if it was a political decision to work with ethnic federations rather than Indianist or *campesino* federations, he responded, "It was a political decision not to work with CISA. But it was not a decision against working with *campesino*-based organizations" (R.C. Smith, interview, 5 May 2006).

Thus, from the standpoint of Smith and Oxfam America (at the time), the criterion of representativeness worked against *indianismo*, while that of autonomy worked against *campesino* federations. This left the "ethnic federation" as the remaining organizational alternative, not only by default, but also because it worked best with the remaining criterion: identity. Unlike "*campesino*" and "*indianista*" identities, "ethnic federation" did not impose a broad class or racialized pan-Indian category, but rather encouraged the articulations of various local identities. There is good reason to doubt the adequacy of the "ethnic" modifier in "ethnic federations" (as Indigenous groups continue to debate the utility of "nation" and "nationality" to describe their status), but the kind of "people-centred" actors represented in the 1984 meeting in Lima (Shuars, Aguarunas, and Kichwas) properly illustrates the view Oxfam had of "revitalizing" the traditions of and "restoring pride" in indigeneity.

In addition, this meeting allowed for an extraordinary cross-regional exchange of views on indigeneity. Smith and Oxfam America had invited a legal scholar of Native North America, the late Howard Berman, to join the conversation. Addressing the group of leaders from ONIC (Colombia), CONFENIAE (Ecuador), AIDESEP (Peru), CIDOB (Bolivia), and UNI (Brazil), Berman shared some of his experiences working with the Iroquois Nation – who, at the time, were "setting the tone" for internationalizing Indigenous rights in spaces like the United Nations. As Smith tells the story, Berman provided a masterful discussion of some of the key questions about the keywords of Indigenous politics.

> What was territory, what was people, pueblo, what did it mean? What was self-determination and why was there such a fight over it? [On] all these issues Howard Berman was working academically … It was a master class. I learned a lot from an international law perspective and the Indigenous representatives learned a lot. Then there was an internal debate, are we a nation, nationality, people, tribe? [And the idea of] self-determination was scary, not just to the military but also to Indigenous people. It was less scary as Howard Berman explained that there was a whole range of relationships with the state, [from separation to assimilation], and self-determination meant deciding where you wanted to be. That made it much more palatable. (Interview, 5 May 2006)

In consideration of these ideas, a decision was made to create a new framework for collective action, formalizing the relationship among the various Indigenous people in what became known as COICA (Coordinadora de Organizaciones Indígenas de la Cuenca Amazónica, the Coordinator of Indigenous Organizations of the Amazonian Basin). The success of these efforts lies not in homogenizing Indigenous subjectivities but rather in the creation, dissemination, and socialization of a particular framework which Indigenous people navigate in a variety of ways. (See also Lucero, 2006; Greene, 2001; Warren & Jackson, 2002; Andolina, Radcliffe, & Laurie, 2009.)

I should add one final note about the historical moment during which these ideas and organizations were forged. When Smith presented his views on the importance of ethnic federations (and his critique of class-based organizations) in an academic seminar at the Colegio de México, many critics immediately thought of Cold War–era Nicaragua, where the Miskito struggles against the Sandinista government were taken as an example of the dangers of Indigenous politics – the danger of serving "reactionary" political projects and weakening "revolutionary" ones (R.C. Smith, interview, 2006; cf. Hale, 1994). However, as the 1980s came to a close with the dramatic collapse of "class-centred" projects, the "people-centred" projects that Oxfam America had been supporting in Latin America suddenly found support from a growing number of practitioners of what Colegio de México scholar Rodolfo Stavenhagen coined as "ethnodevelopment," a term that would a decade later be "operationalized" in the policies of the World Bank.[10] Already at this moment, we can see important lessons about indigeneity that have been subsequently elaborated in the growing literature on indigenous movements.

First, there was (and is) a geopolitics of "encountering indigeneity." The Cold War moment in which these early discussions emerged along with the existing connections between *indianista* organizations and European NGOs, and between the Iroquois and the United Nations, served as an important context for actors in Oxfam America and for the Amazonian Indigenous representatives. The international environment created both constraints and opportunities for the elaboration of new partnerships between Indigenous actors and INGOs and helped change the style in which transnational Indigenous politics had operated up until then. It is important to signal that the partnerships between INGO officers and their Indigenous counterparts take place within a network of norms and power relationships that are constantly open to negotiation (Brysk, 1994, 2000; Greene, 2006; Warren & Jackson, 2002).

Second, the process of elaborating Indigenous subjectivities and keywords, such as self-determination and territory, was already subject to the (locally) embedded encounters of such transnational actors as missionaries, anthropologists, development workers, oil companies, and others with local contact to Amazonian populations. For instance, by the time Evaristo Nugkuag, one of the Peruvian Amazonian leaders, arrived at the 1984 Lima meeting, he had already passed through the classrooms of the Summer Institute of Linguistics, attended a university in Lima, lobbied vigorously in Germany against the destructive consequences of filming Werner Herzog's *Fitzcarraldo*, and met a group of U.S. and Peruvian anthropologists who were interested in supporting the efforts of Aguaruna activists to create their own political organization. The important lesson is twofold: on the one hand we must avoid implying that Oxfam America imposed any form of indigeneity on Indigenous people; on the other, we must emphasize that it became an important part of a process already underway to define the shape of Indigenous responses to a wide variety of outside threats, such as transnational mining companies.

Mining Resources, Anti-Mining Identities

The late 1990s saw several changes in Oxfam America. First, Richard Chase Smith left the organization to found a new NGO, the Instituto del Bien Común. Oxfam also restructured its program in ways that departed with its earlier development strategy of working in terms of regions (Amazon/Andean). While it continued to work in Bolivia, Ecuador, and Peru, it developed the following programmatic lines of action: (1) Indigenous peoples; (2) sustainable development; (3) risk management and disaster relief; and (4) extractive industry. The last theme of extractive industry was in many ways the most controversial as it placed Oxfam America in the treacherous terrain between communities on one side, and states and transnational mining and oil companies on the other. Clearly, though, the issue of extractive industry was of vital importance to the livelihoods of the populations with which Oxfam America had historically worked. As it states on its official website (www.oxfamamerica.org), "of the 5,660 Indigenous communities in Peru, 3,200 are now affected by mining." Thus it is not surprising that the first "strategic partner" that Oxfam America worked with under its newly restructured program was a new organization called the Coordinator of Communities Affected by Mining (CONACAMI).[11]

While mining has a long history in Peru, the boom in extractive industry took place during the government of Alberto Fujimori (1990–2000). Fujimori created a legal environment that enabled the skyrocketing of mining claims, which went from about 4 million to over 25 million hectares in the years after Fujimori's reforms. For many communities the effects were (and are) disastrous. Populations have been displaced, productive agricultural lands have been dramatically reduced in size, water sources have been taken over by mining interests, and environmental contamination has provoked the outcry of communities in Cajamarca, Cuzco, Piura, Junín, and many other regions. Extractive industry, remarks activist Miguel Palacín, is part of the "fictitious development" that has trapped Peru. De Echave and Torres (2005) have provided data suggesting that departments with mining activities have higher rates of poverty than departments without them.[12]

In the mid-1990s, Miguel Palacín and others began to organize protests against this unequal exchange in which state and industry profited while highland communities suffered. However, mining companies used the legal system, which was already tilted in their favour, to denounce Palacín and accuse him of criminal activity. Palacín was forced to go into hiding. Emblematic of the double-edged nature of globalization, however, Palacín received unexpected aid from the north. Canadian First Nations formally requested that the charges against Palacín be investigated by the state. The state attorney looked into the Palacín case and found that there was no basis to any of the charges, which were subsequently dropped (though new ones were later reinstated; there are currently over 500 CONACAMI leaders that have criminal charges pending). After this brush with the law, Palacín realized that "the only weapon is organization" (M. Palacin, interview, 2003). Thus, in 1998 he led organizing efforts throughout the Central and Southern Sierra to bring communities together. In October 1999, with the help of the Peruvian NGO Cooperacción, the first congress of a new national organization, CONACAMI, was convened and Palacín was elected president.

At its first congress (1999), CONACAMI did not describe itself as an "Indigenous organization." Many communities do not identify as Quechua nor as Indigenous, but as rural *campesino* communities. Despite this mixed constituency, over time CONACAMI began to adopt a more explicitly Indigenous message using the language of territory and self-determination that had been part of the meeting in Lima organized by Oxfam America decades earlier. In the Second Congress

(2003), CONACAMI explicitly embraced an Indigenous agenda which included espousing the principles found in international agreements, like Convention 169 of the International Labor Organization on the collective rights of Indigenous peoples. Given this change in the discourse of this new organization, it is important to ask how CONACAMI went from a strictly environmental and economic position to incorporating the concerns of Indigenous peoples and collective rights. It is here that Oxfam America (and other agencies) played an important role.

With the help of international agencies like Oxfam America and IBIS-Denmark, CONACAMI participated in a series of exchanges with the Ecuadorian organization ECUARUNARI (the Andean affiliate of the most important Indigenous federation in Ecuador, CONAIE) and the Bolivian *ayllu* confederation CONAMAQ.[13] These exchanges helped integrate CONACAMI into the transnational network and language of the global Indigenous movement.

Within Peru, CONACAMI also contributed to the reconsideration of Indigenous questions. CONACAMI joined a pan-regional effort called COPPIP, the Permanent Conference of Indigenous People, established with the goal of uniting Andean and Amazonian peoples for the first time in the same organization. CONACAMI became the main Andean organization and AIDESEP the main Amazonian actor, and both organizations agreed to rotate the presidency of COPPIP. Though this effort has not (yet?) resulted in a high level of coordination among national Indigenous actors, its existence and CONACAMI's participation in it are important parts of the story of Indigenous politics in Peru.

At the local and regional levels, however, members of CONACAMI debated over the wisdom of embracing an "Indigenous" organizational identity (Anonymous, interviews, 2006; Paredes, 2005). As many communities did not consider themselves to be Indigenous in any way, local leaders rejected the changing position of the national leadership. They also questioned the decision of national leaders like Miguel Palacín to involve CONACAMI in broad coalitions of progressive causes, some of which, like feminist and gay movements, had little support at the community level. At a CONACAMI meeting, one leader remarked angrily, "Miguel Palacín first wanted us to be faggots [*maricones*] and now he wants us to be Indians [*indios*]" (Anonymous, interview, 2007). National leaders admit that there are "two factions" of CONACAMI – one that worries exclusively about mining, and another which incorporates indigeneity – and that these factions have had their encounters and disagreements in the congresses of the organization.

In 2006, the presidency passed from one faction to the other as Miguel Palacín, who took over the leadership of the international Coordinator of Andean Indigenous Organizations (CAOI), was replaced briefly by regional anti-mining leader Luis Riofrío, who was then replaced by "Indigenous" activist Mario Palacio. Of course, it is certainly possible to relate "mining" concerns with "Indigenous" concerns. National leaders note that by using the categories of Indigenous peoples and territory, they move their struggles into the legal terrain covered by international agreements (like ILO Convention 169) that require industries to consult with local communities before the work and damage of extraction is done. Yet, within the funding agencies, professionals are divided as to whether CONACAMI's Indigenous position has won it more allies or enemies (Huber, 2007).

Over the years another debate has emerged, exposing tensions between Indigenous organizations and national NGOs. While agencies like Oxfam America continue to work with both Indigenous organizations and local NGOs, there exists a sense of competition between Indigenous and non-Indigenous development partners for the resources of the international community. This has meant that Indigenous organizations, as they seek to develop and implement their own programs, have had to act more like NGOs in meeting certain legal requirements of the state as well as the expectations of funding agencies. Thus, CONACAMI, in order to qualify for official international (that is, bilateral, state-issued) development aid, registered as an ONGD (Organización No-Gobernamental de Desarrollo, or Development Non-Governmental Organization). As a series of high-profile conflicts between community and transnational mining communities emerged, resulting in the termination of one important mining project in Tambogrande, the Peruvian Agency of International Cooperation (APCI), which was the formal ONGD registry, revoked ONGD status from CONACAMI. The director of APCI at the time, Oscar Schiappa-Pietra, suggested that he was under enormous pressure from the mining companies and that elements in the press had organized an aggressive campaign against CONACAMI and Oxfam.[14] The newspaper *Correo* was especially vocal. It accused CONACAMI of being a source of violence:

> It is in Peru's interest that mining take place in a climate of peace in order to consolidate its growing productivity. This is why we cannot give carte blanche to radicalist [*radicalista* (*sic*)] positions of organizations like Oxfam and CONACAMI. Confrontational and violent situations, like the ones

> that stained Peru with blood in the 1980s and the early 1990s, are not the solution but rather the undermining of national development. (Valencia Dongo-Cárdenas, 2006, n.p.)

The equivalence between anti-mining protests and the bloody war initiated by the Maoist Shining Path has been a recurring and constant theme in the critique of CONACAMI. On 5 June 2007, as President Alan García announced the signing of another mining agreement with the transnational Anglo-American Company, he declared that unlike the mining companies that were "partners" in working for development and the national interest, those who opposed mining were working against the nation. "All those who work against mining in our country have hidden motives and are supported with the financial support of other countries," García declared (field notes, 2007). While he never mentioned Oxfam or CONACAMI by name, there was little doubt that these two organizations were not far from his mind.

CONACAMI continued to be an important point of reference for national opposition to the mining-centre development model that has been a common denominator across the administrations of Fujimori, Toledo, García, and the ostensibly leftist government of Ollanta Humala. In the July 2007 National Strike, CONACAMI, along with historic *campesino* organizations like the CCP, was an important part of the protest landscape even if its declarations were more about economics than about cultural identity (field notes, 2007). Still, CONACAMI (or ex-CONACAMI) leaders continue to find ways to build bridges between economics and culture. Former president Miguel Palacín became the head of the Andean Coordinator of Indigenous Organizations, travelled to the 2007 Indigenous Summit, and delivered what some present regarded as the best exposition of the problems and strategies of Indigenous leaders (Anonymous, interview, Oxfam America, June 2006).

Like Palacín, subsequent CONACAMI president Mario Palacio has also attempted to braid mining and Indigenous themes. In the proclamations during the national mobilization against García's economic policies, however, CONACAMI leaders were less likely to speak of "Indigenous people" and more often invoked the broader "Peruvian people." Thinking about CONACAMI's identity debates, an Amazonian Indigenous leader remarked, "Unfortunately, in Peru, it is better to say '*campesino*' than it is to say '*indígena*'" (Anonymous, interview, 6 May 2006).

The arc of CONACAMI's Indigenous positionings is strangely familiar to the arc of one of CONACAMI's adversaries: former president

Alejandro Toledo who, like CONACAMI, emphasized his Indigenous roots more often when he was outside of the country than when he was at home. Toledo's international links, though, raised questions at home. In the view of his critics, Toledo's Stanford education and advocacy of free market neoliberal policies made him less Indian, giving him what *campesino* leader Hugo Blanco (2004) refers to as the "face of an indio but the brain of a gringo" (p. 167). In the case of CONACAMI, the gulf between the leaders and many local communities' self-identification created doubts that adversaries in the state and the press have sought to exploit. Some observers fear that CONACAMI's best days are behind it as it has played a less central role in the negotiation over mining conflicts and has had a difficult time with leadership transitions and self-identification. In places like Cusco, where one important mining conflict was successfully negotiated, CONACAMI pulled out of the negotiations and there was little secret that there was a lack of support for CONACAMI president Miguel Palacín among the members of the Cusco CORECAMI affiliate. During a research visit in June 2007, CORECAMI Cusco had seemingly vanished. One local observer explained that many local leaders come to work with national organizations like CONACAMI in hope of having access to resources that will help them survive. As CONACAMI brought few resources to the local level, those local leaders also seemed to stop coming (R. Pajuelo, personal communication, June 2007).

CONACAMI has also played a less central role in the most contentious conflicts over extractive industry that have taken place in the Amazonian town of Bagua and the Andean region of Puno. The 5 June 2009 conflict between the Peruvian state and Awajún and Wampis protesters has been characterized (correctly) as a conflict over an aggressive effort on the part of the government of President Alan García to facilitate extractive industry in the Amazon region through a series of business-friendly executive decrees known as the "Laws of the Jungle." This aggressive policy move was meant to weaken the ability of Indigenous communities to gain titles for their lands and also to reverse previous ecological commitments made by the Peruvian government to protect the Cordillera del Condor, promises made in the wake of the peace agreements signed by Ecuador and Peru in the late 1990s (Huaco, 2011). With greater distance from peace accords and the bi-national spirit of environmentalism, the expanding demands from mining companies (and rising commodity prices) have found increasing favour with the Peruvian government. Beginning with Fujimori, Peruvian administrations helped inaugurate a "boom" in extractive industry. The García

"Laws of the Jungle" are the culmination of this policy change, and a clear signal to Indigenous communities that their concerns are very much secondary. In a now infamous article that President García wrote for the Peruvian newspaper *El Comercio,* García (2007) compared Indigenous protesters to the proverbial *"perro del hortelano,"* the dog in the manger that does not eat and does not let others eat. He followed up with a television appearance in which he declared that the Indigenous people protesting these laws were not "first-class citizens," but rather were standing in the way of progress. The government sent police forces into the Amazonian town of Bagua where, predictably, violent clashes unfolded that took the lives of twenty-three police officers and ten civilians, with many more injured. The "Baguazo" became a political disaster for the García government, who tried to frame the conflict, in a controversial television spot, as an encounter between "extremism" and the nation, between law and disorder, civilization and barbarism. As images of Indigenous protesters with spears were juxtaposed with the corpses of killed police officers, a narrator urged Peruvians to not let Indigenous extremism (not to say "terrorism" – though that association was very heavily implied) stand in the way of national progress. The remarkable thing about the ad is that it was widely rejected, as massive anti-García demonstrations took place in Lima, criticizing the government policies of extraction, and forcing the García government to put many of its policies on hold.

Two years after the Baguazo, at the other end of the country in the southern department of Puno, history seemed to repeat itself. As Puno had become one of the more important destinations for extractive industry, many voiced increasing concerns (once again) about the environmental harm caused by both large transnational companies (mostly Canadian, in this case) and smaller-scale informal mining. In 2011, the most socio-environmental conflicts took place in Puno. As in Bagua, extractive industry in Puno has been encouraged and facilitated by the state. The Peruvian constitution (Article 71) actually prohibits the granting of mining concessions to foreign companies in territories within fifty kilometres of a national border, with the caveat that exceptions can be granted if declared by executive decree to be a "public necessity." The García government found many such necessities in the border region of Puno, and once again conflicts ensued. Weeks of mobilization and confrontations resulted in injuries, property destruction, and finally forced the government to annul the executive decree that gave the Canadian firm Bear Creek Mining a concession for the Santa Ana mining project (Salazar & Gomez, 2011).

Across the Andes and Amazon, conflicts related to mining are on the rise. These conflicts are varied and complex. As Arellano (2011) has demonstrated, most of these conflicts do not resemble Bagua or Puno in terms of being a call for the cessation of extractive industries. As well, most are distributional in nature and have to do with the way in which rents and negative externalities are managed. Yet this is what makes Bagua and Puno so striking and important: they go beyond localized conflicts with specific firms, and include the language of Indigenous self-determination and the right to prior consultation (established by international law) in mobilizing broad sectors of society. This has been a pattern that continues with the current, ostensibly leftist government of Ollanta Humala, who declared martial law in the Andean department of Cajamarca in 2012 over another round of anti-mining protests. Again, a specific mining project ("Conga") has led to a region-wide bloc of mobilization. CONACAMI has been vocal in condemning the state's embrace of extractivism, but it is not the centre of the anti-mining movement – a movement which has become increasingly decentralized. While the declining political importance of CONACAMI might be lamented by the organization, the continuing battles over extraction continue to bring attention to the racial, environmental, and social dimensions of colonial legacies that continue to affect Native communities and Native lands.

Preliminary Conclusions

Peru presents a challenge for students of Indigenous politics. Indigeneity is both central and elusive in national politics. This brief exploration of some of the encounters between an international NGO and a variety of local actors has illustrated two of the challenges and lessons of encountering indigeneity. First, regimes of indigeneity involve a geopolitics of recognition that can only be understood across local, national, and global scales. Indigenous people throughout the Americas (and beyond) have found it often inevitable and sometimes useful to explore the political imbrications of a variety of legal, economic, and political systems. Since the first contacts with missionaries, the state, and agents of global capital, Indigenous people have found that new systems of domination are not without points of entry within which they can contest the very terms of domination. The rising importance of non-state actors in the wake of aggressive neoliberal economic reforms (which shrank already weak states) provided an additional set of opportunities that Indigenous people have been able to use.

Second, these global connections often involve risks for Indigenous social movements. As anthropologist Beth Conklin (2002, p. 1052) puts it, "Good global politics do not always make good local politics." In some cases, the lure of international funds creates a perverse incentive in which Indigenous leaders must spend more time attending to the demands and expectations of international audiences than to the needs of local communities. Similarly, the construction of indigeneity can also have a Janus-faced appearance in which some discourses are for external consumption and have little to do with the lived "social fact" of indigeneity at the local level. This is not to say that Indigenous people should exit global civil society (as if this were even possible in the times inaugurated by Internet Zapatismo and international legal recognition of Indigenous rights). However, it is important to note that what Sikkink and Keck (1998) notably dubbed the "boomerang effect" – the ability of local actors to gather strength by going transnational – can lead to unexpected outcomes, as boomerangs do not always land where one intends, especially in transnational fields where NGOs and Native communities work in the shadow of billion-dollar extractive industries. Nevertheless, despite tremendous odds, Indigenous peoples continue to find ways to defend their lands, traditions, and communities. Their struggles are far from over.

Acknowledgments

I am indebted to María Elena García for her insights and suggestions. Erin Korte provided valuable research assistance. Max Forte brought remarkable editorial skill and patience to this project.

NOTES

1 Much of the literature about Latin America has shown how indigeneity is marked by a set of racial, spatial, and socio-economic markers, but gender has received less attention. Gender frequently mediates access to urban labour markets, as it is men who often leave Indigenous communities for work in large cities and acquire stronger Spanish-language skills than the women who stay behind in monolingual Indigenous contexts. Such dynamics help explain why women, as De la Cadena (1995) writes, are "more Indian."

2 In Toledo's case, the slogan might be "*Cholo sí, Indio no*," as he often self-identified as a *cholo*, an interstitial category between Indian and Mestizo

that is shared with many migrants or children of migrants who come from the country to the city. Toledo's administration was considered a disappointment for the standpoint of advancing Indigenous rights and representation. For more on the Toledo years, see García (2005), García and Lucero (2004, 2008), and Greene (2006).

3 For alternative views of the ways class and ethnic identity can coexist rather than being mutually exclusive see De la Cadena (2001), García (2005), Mallon (1998), and García and Lucero (2004). García and I have taken issue with the teleological way that much of the discussion of indigeneity has unfolded (e.g., the view that they have not *yet* reclaimed their real identity). See García and Lucero (2011).

4 Sendero elements, however, remain in parts of the jungle, and occasional attacks against police and military stations still occur.

5 Page numbers are from the original 1983 paper. Smith (2002) has revisited his typology to note the decline of *indianista* organizations and the emergence of two additional ideal-types for the Andean countries: the Indigenous non-governmental organization and the Indigenous political party.

6 Leaders from CISA participated in the first meetings of the UN Commission on Human Rights, based in Geneva (R.C. Smith, personal communication, 2006; Smith, 2002).

7 For Smith's published account of that meeting, see Smith (2002).

8 For a more thorough discussion of Lajo's critique see García and Lucero (2011).

9 This does not mean that Oxfam only funds ethnic federations, as it also supports community-level organizations and even academic groups.

10 According to Smith, Stavenhagen was one of the critics at the seminar at the Colegio de México. A man of the left, Stavenhagen seemed to have his worries about identity politics. If this is so, his transformation into one of the leading scholars of Indigenous rights is quite remarkable.

11 Originally called the Coordinadora de Comunidades Afectadas por la Mineria, it is now the Confederación de Comunidades Afectadas por la Mineria.

12 There is debate over the economic impact of mining. Barrantes (2005) suggests that the department is too big a unit to allow a detailed understanding of the effects of mining activities. Using household data, she has found a slight economic benefit for households that are in mining districts when compared to households in similar districts without mining.

13 *Ayllus* are traditional forms of Andean organization that can link non-contiguous settlements across various ecological altitudes through systems of kinship and a rotating authority structure. For more on contemporary *ayllu* politics see Lucero (2006) and Andolina et al. (2009).

14 Schiappa-Pietra saw his decision as one that was not harmful for CONACAMI, which, as he points out, is not an NGO, and even without being in the ONGD registry can still receive funds from private agencies like Oxfam America. Thus the removal of CONACAMI from the APCI registry, at the time, was largely symbolic. A new law that passed in 2007 has changed the government oversight that accompanies even private international funds, but it remains to be seen how much changes in practice, especially since many have questioned the constitutionality of what people call the "anti-NGO" law (O. Schiappa-Pietra, interview, June 2007).

REFERENCES

Albó, X. (1991). "El retorno del indio." *Revista Andina 9*(2), 299–357.

Andolina, R., Laurie, N., & Radcliffe, S.A. (2009). *Indigenous Development in the Andes: Culture, Power, and Transnationalism.* Durham, NC: Duke University Press.

Arellano, J. (2011). *Minería sin fronteras? Conflicto y desarrollo en regions mineras del Perú.* Lima, Peru: Instituto de Estudios Peruanos.

Barrantes, R. (2005). Minería, desarrollo, y pobreza en el Perú, o de como todo depende del cristal con que se mire. In R. Barrantes, P. Zarate, & A. Durand (Eds.), *Te quiero pero no: mineria, desarrollo, y poblaciones locales* (pp. 17–79). Lima, Peru: Oxfam America and Insituto de Estudios Peruanos.

Blanco, H. (2004). Presentimiento. In G. Portocarrero, C. Rivera, & C. Sagástegui (Eds.), *Arguedas y el Perú de hoy* (pp. 165–7). Lima: SUR.

Brysk, A. (1994). Acting Globally: Indian Rights and International Politics in Latin America. In D.L. Van Cott (Ed.), *Indigenous People and Democracy in Latin America* (pp. 29–51). New York: St. Martin's Press.

Brysk, A. (2000). *From Tribal Village to Global Village: Indian Rights and International Relations in Latin America.* Stanford, CA: Stanford University Press.

Conklin, B.A. (2002). Shamans versus Pirates in the Amazonian Treasure Chest. *American Anthropologist, 104*(4), 1050–61. http://dx.doi.org/10.1525/aa.2002.104.4.1050

Cotler, J. (2005). Existen grupos de interés muy fuertes alrededor del tema minero. Interview by C. Valenzuela. http://www.agenciaperu.com/entrevistas/2005/jul/cotler.htm

De Echave, J., & Torres, V. (2005). *Hacia una estimación de los efectos de la actividad minera en los indices de pobreza en el Perú.* Lima, Peru: CooperAcción.

De la Cadena, M. (1995). Women Are More Indian: Ethnicity and Gender in a Community Near Cuzco. In B. Larson & O. Harris (Eds.), *Ethnicity, Markets and Migration in the Andes: At the Crossroads of History and Anthropology* (pp. 329–48). Durham, NC: Duke University Press.

De la Cadena, M. (2001). Reconstructing Race: Racism, Culture and Mestizaje in Latin America. *NACLA Report on the Americas 34*(6), 16–23.

Escobar, A. (1995). *Encountering Development: The Making and Unmaking of the Third World*. Princeton, NJ: Princeton University Press.

García, A. (2007, October 28). El síndrome del perro del hortelano. *El Comercio*. http://elcomercio.pe/edicionimpresa/html/2007-10-28/el_sindrome_del_perro_del_hort.html

García, M.E. (2005). *Making Indigenous Citizens: Identity, Development, and Multicultural Activism in Peru*. Stanford, CA: Stanford University Press.

García, M.E., & Lucero, J.A. (2004). 'Un País Sin Indígenas'? Re-thinking Indigenous Politics in Peru. In N.G. Postero & L. Zamosc (Eds.), *The Struggle for Indigenous Rights in Latin America* (pp. 158–88). Brighton, UK: Sussex.

García, M.E., & Lucero, J.A. (2008). Exceptional Others: Politicians, Rottweilers, and Alterity in the 2006 Peruvian Elections. *Latin American and Caribbean Ethnic Studies*, *3*(3), 253–70. http://dx.doi.org/10.1080/17442220802462345

García, M.E., & Lucero, J.A. (2011). Authenticating Indians and Movements: Interrogating Indigenous Authenticity, Social Movements, and Fieldwork in Contemporary Peru. In L. Gotkowitz (Ed.), *From Purity of Blood to Indigenous Social Movements* (pp. 278–98). Durham, NC: Duke University Press.

Greene, S. (2004). Indigenous People Incorporated? Culture as Politics, Culture as Property in Contemporary Bioprospection Deals. *Current Anthropology*, *45*(2), 211–37. http://dx.doi.org/10.1086/381047

Greene, S. (2006). Getting Over the Andes: The Geo-Eco-Politics of Indigenous Movements in Peru's Twenty-First Century Inca Empire. *Journal of Latin American Studies*, *38*(2), 327–54. http://dx.doi.org/10.1017/S0022216X06000733

Hale, C.R. (1994). *Resistance and Contradiction: Miskitu Indians and the Nicaraguan State 1894–1987*. Stanford, CA: Stanford University Press.

Hall, G., & Patrinos, H.A. (Eds.). (2005). *Indigenous People, Poverty and Human Development in Latin America: 1994–2004*. Hampshire, UK: Palgrave Macmillan. http://dx.doi.org/10.1057/9780230377226

Huaco, M. (2011). A dos años del "Baguazo": Aportes para una cronología credible. *Revista Ideele*, 209. http://www.revistaideele.com/node/1070

Huber, L. (2007). *Diálogo entre las agencias de cooperación y el movimiento indígena Informe Nacional Perú*. Report Prepared for Oxfam America, Ibis, SNV, and HIVOS.

Lajo, J. (2003). La Invisibilidad Indígena en el Perú: Comentarios a Un País Sin Indígenas. Unpublished manuscript.

Li, T.M. (2000). Articulating Indigenous Identity in Indonesia: Resource Politics and the Tribal Slot. *Comparative Studies in Society and History*, *42*(1), 149–79. http://dx.doi.org/10.1017/S0010417500002632

Lucero, J.A. (2006). Representing "Real Indians": The Challenges of Indigenous Authenticity and Strategic Constructivism in Ecuador and Bolivia. *Latin American Research Review*, *41*(2), 31–56. http://dx.doi.org/10.1353/lar.2006.0026

Lucero, J.A. (2007, February). Decolonizing Democracy: Bolivia and Peru in Comparative Perspective. Unpublished Paper Presented at Woodrow Wilson Center Conference, Santiago, Chile.

Mallon, F. (1998). Chronicle of a Path Foretold? In S. Stern (Ed.), *Shining and Other Paths* (pp. 84–117). Durham. NC: Duke University Press.

Mayer, E. (1991). Peru in Deep Trouble: Mario Vargas Llosa's "Inquest in the Andes" Reexamined. *Cultural Anthropology*, *6*(4), 466–504. http://dx.doi.org/10.1525/can.1991.6.4.02a00030

Méndez, C. (1996). Incas Si, Indios No: Notes on Peruvian Creole Nationalism and Its Contemporary Crisis. *Journal of Latin American Studies 28*(1), 197–225.

Paredes, M. (2005). Conflicto Minería-Comunidades y Discurso Indígena. Paper Presented at SEPIA IX Conference, Trujillo, Peru.

Portocarrero, J. (2006). Opina Javier Portocarrero Maisch*: Elecciones 2006: ¿amenaza del sur andino? Perú 21. http://web.archive.org/web/20091124120702/http://weblogs.elearning.ubc.ca/peru/archives/027972.php

Salazar, G., & Gómez, E. (2011, July). Analizando los decretos de Puno. http://www.actualidadambiental.pe/?p=11234

Sikkink, M., & Keck, M. (1998). *Activists beyond Borders: Advocacy Networks in International Politics*. Ithaca, NY: Cornell University Press.

Smith, R.C. (1983). Search for Unity within Diversity: Peasant Unions, Ethnic Federations, and Indianist Movements in the Andean Republics. Paper presented at Cultural Survival Symposium, Iniciativas Indias y Autodenominación Económica. Cambridge, MA.

Smith, R.C. (2002). *Un Tapiz Tejido a Partir de las Vicisitudes de la Historia, El Lugar y la Vida Cotidiana.* Lima: Oxfam America.

Trivelli, C. (2005). *Los hogares indígenas y la pobreza en el Perú. Una mirada a partir de la información cuantitativa.* Lima: IEP. Documento de Trabajo No. 141.

Valencia Dongo-Cárdenas, R. (2006, April 20). Clima de paz requisito clave para consolidar crecimiento productivo de la minería, Correo (Lima, Peru).

Vargas Llosa, M. (1983). Después del informe: Conversación sobre Uchuraccay. Entrevista a Mario Vargas Llosa realizada por Alberto Bonilla. *Caretas* (738), 7 March.

Warren, K., & Jackson, J. (Eds.). (2002). *Indigenous Movements, Self-Representation, and the State in Latin America*. Austin, TX: University of Texas Press.

Yashar, D. (2005). *Contesting Citizenship in Latin America: The Rise of Indigenous Movements and the Post-Liberal Challenge*. Cambridge, MA: Cambridge University Press. http://dx.doi.org/10.1017/CBO9780511790966

8 The Colour of Race: Indians and Progress in a Centre-Left Brazil

JONATHAN W. WARREN

Since the 1990s a large number of Brazilian Indigenous communities have been federally recognized, successfully acquired land, established their own schools, and achieved a higher degree of autonomy and self-determination. Furthermore, anti-Indian violence is no longer condoned by the Brazilian government; racism has been officially acknowledged; race-cognizant government policies, such as affirmative action, have replaced race-neutral ones; and a number of antiracist commissions and initiatives have been established at federal, state and municipal levels. Finally, the first centre-left politicians in Brazilian history, Luiz Ignacio Lula da Silva (2003–2010) and Dilma Rousseff (2011–present), both of the Workers' Party, have controlled the executive branch of government for almost a decade.

Given these substantial changes, one could be forgiven for expecting a positive report on the state of Indigenous affairs in contemporary Brazil. Unfortunately, the outlook is rather dim. Perhaps most surprising is that many of the culprits are from the centre-left, namely, the Workers' Party, social scientists, and sectors of the *movimento negro*.

In the North American press, much has been made of Brazil's selection as a host of the 2014 World Cup and 2016 Summer Olympics, its "BRIC" status, and President Lula's and Dilma's continuation of the neoliberal monetary, trade, and fiscal policies of the Cardoso administration. On this latter front they compare favourably with the so-called populist leaders and policies in Argentina, Bolivia, and Venezuela. Much less attention, however, has been given to the ongoing social inequalities, forged through centuries of ethnic cleansing, slavery, and European colonialism, which threaten to lay to waste yet another commodity boom.

For hundreds of years, the poor majority who inhabit the urban shantytowns and the countryside have been constructed as impediments to progress. Primarily of African and Indigenous descent, these people (*"o povo,"* or "the people," as they are commonly called) have been viewed as encumbered with biological, moral and cultural deficits. Consequently, when not neglected, these sectors of the population have been treated in very paternalistic ways. Their opinions and concerns have rarely been taken into account, because they have been regarded as childlike subordinates who do not know what is in their own best interests – let alone the interests of the nation. Over the decades, such attitudes have engendered countless modernization projects which have been unsuccessful because, amongst other things, they cut against the grain of local conditions, rather than building upon them. Development has been understood as a process of replacing, rather than working within, the sociocultural and material realities of *o povo*. The resulting development initiatives have been highly inorganic and therefore largely ineffective.

In the municipality of Araçuaí, Minas Gerais, in 2007, to take one example from my fieldwork,[1] the local Bishop sold large tracts of church land to developers planning to establish massive eucalyptus plantations in the region. One of the primary justifications he gave for the sale was that these plantations would improve the economy by adding tax revenues and jobs to a region in desperate need of both. Given the well-documented environmental destruction that eucalyptus trees inflict, such a development project only makes sense if the communities and environment in question are considered of little value: something is being brought to nothing. However, if one were to take into consideration the rich sociocultural landscape, which may be materially poor but is hardly an economic wasteland, then such a project would be ill advised. From this vantage, the obvious outcome is that thousands of communities built around tenant and subsistence farming – including four Indigenous communities in the area (the Arana Indians, Arana Caboclos, Apukare, and Cinta Vermelha) – will experience a significant economic downturn, and may even be destroyed, because the eucalyptus farms will dry up the few springs that exist, decimate the surrounding fauna and wildlife, and badly pollute the waterways.

As a labour leader from a poor family, it was hoped that President Lula would challenge the elitism upon which such a development formula hinges. To his great credit, his government advanced a few redistributive policies, such as *bolsa familia*, against predictably fierce resistance from the middle and upper classes, who regarded such investments as monies wasted on social incompetents. Therefore, unlike previous administrations, this government treated *o povo* as capable of modernity. But the mode of investment continued to be largely predicated on the assumption that these people, their communities, and the spaces that they occupy are deficient. The idea that the popular sectors have practices and perspectives that should be respected, built upon, and invested in as a way of advancing economic development – rather than neglected, dismissed, or violated – has not become part of the centre-left's common sense.

These elitist sensibilities, combined with the tremendous political and economic power of mining, agro-business, and the energy sectors, has led the da Silva and Rousseff administrations to throw their support behind a number of large, locally insensitive development initiatives such as dam construction, urban mega-projects, and mono-agricultural production, to the detriment of the general public and the Brazilian economy. Unfortunately, commodity prices are notoriously fickle, and thus leave economies dependent upon them subject to booms and busts. Furthermore, almost all economists agree that if Brazil is to become a developed economy, it must move from a commodities-dependent economy towards value-added manufacturing and increased productivity, both of which require investments in education, health care, and infrastructure that serve the general public rather than further marginalizing them.

Instead of making these sorts of investments, the centre-left administrations have embraced the top-down development strategies of their predecessors. The megaprojects in Rio de Janeiro typify this age-old tradition. In preparation for the World Cup and the Olympics, billions of dollars have been invested in infrastructure which overwhelmingly favours the elite sectors. The schools, health care, and transportation networks that service the poor majority are not being updated or improved. Instead, the airport is being renovated and existing transportation networks improved, so that one can pass more readily between the airport and elite neighbourhoods without having to notice urban blight. The *povo* are not consulted or included in the decision-making process for these projects. At best they are excluded; at worst, many become victims of the process. In the centre of Rio de Janeiro, for instance, thousands of working-class residents are being displaced by these urban renewal projects. This is an iteration of what occurred a century ago, when Rio underwent renovations to make it more closely resemble Paris, to demonstrate its level of civilization to the European elite. In the process, thousands of servants, vendors, craftsman, and merchants were displaced to the peripheries where they created some of Brazil's first favelas.

Even rhetorically, President da Silva and Rousseff have done little to challenge these development patterns. President Lula, at times, even went so far as to characterize the agricultural oligarchies in utopian terms. For example, he publically praised sugar cane producers as having transformed themselves from villains into the planet's saviors, given their role in producing ethanol. Unfortunately, the reality of sugar cane cultivation is usually the opposite: low-value-added, highly exploitative production that results in profit windfalls for a few landholders at the expense of local ecosystems, communities and economies. The experiences of a sugar cane cutter perhaps best expose how the "new" centre-left development strategy represents a rerun, rather than a break from the past:

> My name is Antonio. I'm 39. I had to leave to work. I left with my two brothers. We went to São Paulo to cut sugarcane … It was necessary because there is little work here. We earn too little. As many here say, slavery ended but only if you put "slavery" in quotation marks. Many work earning only $8 a day. This doesn't pay for anything especially if one has a large family. So people go to cut sugarcane in order to earn more money. I worked fifteen years cutting sugarcane. The first time I went was in 1987 with my dad. That's where I learned to cut sugarcane … It's hard work. One works from four in the morning until six in the evening. The more you cut, the more you earn. The more you work, the more you earn. Since I had little formal education, this was really the only option available. Here one works from seven in the morning until six at night earning $8 or less. I would cut more than one thousand meters of sugarcane each day. The places I worked only employed the best cutters. At the minimum one had to cut ten thousand kilos a day or ten tons. I would cut thirty-three tons a day between March and November including Saturdays and Sundays. That's why I was called "Champion." I would earn up to seven minimum salaries (about $2,000 per month) … It's awful to spend eight or nine months away from one's family. One's whole family is here. It's awful. But it's the only option we have. (Interview by author, n.d.)

The Vanguard of Modernity

As in the past, many Indigenous communities are being victimized by the reanimation of commodities-led "development" strategy. Most infamously there is the Belo Monte dam in the Xingu region, which, like various dam projects throughout the world, is based on dubious economic calculations (Roy, 2001). Despite being marketed as the necessary sacrifice society must make for development, such investments of public treasure are fiscally unwise. Unless several other dams are built in the region – something that has been said will never happen – then the Belo Monte dam will be a massive money pit, and that does not even include the economic costs of environmental destruction. As a totem of modernity, however, dams sell politically.

In rural areas, Indians often find themselves in the vanguard of the opposition to these "modernization" initiatives, even though the projects usually adversely affect many more non-Indians than Indians. The conundrum is that Indians' resistance to these economic plans helps to bolster the position of their adversaries – since they are the "antimoderns" in the Brazilian imagination, their opposition inadvertently lends credibility to the argument that these projects are indeed pro-development (Warren, 1999). This despite the fact that Indians – and not the mega-project advocates – are often at the forefront of development. In Minas Gerais, for example, the Indigenous communities are actively collaborating with non-governmental organizations, such as CPCD (The Popular Center for Culture and Development), to establish permaculture agricultural techniques, reforestation, artisanal farming, and micro-industries based on local knowledge and practices. These development initiatives are much more likely to produce economic growth than the context-insensitive monocultural initiatives, which have historically only brought profit to a few at the expense of economic stagnation and environmental destruction.

Perhaps the biggest irony of these anti-Indian "modernization" projects is that they are driven by governments that have been, in many respects, the most antiracist in the history of Brazil. The Lula and Rousseff administrations have built on the Cardoso administration's break from racial democracy to push the nation further away from colourblindness and class reductionism. The Workers' Party administrations have also had the most racially diverse cabinets ever; supported race cognizance programs, including affirmative action; ratified the Durban protocol (something the U.S., Europe, and India refused); and created a new Special Secretary for the Promotion of Racial Equality, which was turned into a ministry-level position. At the inauguration of the SEPPIR, on 21 March 2003, Lula noted:

> At least half of the Brazilian population is discriminated against because they are black. Not only are they black but they are poor. More than 64% of the poor and 70% of the indigents are black. A majority of the un- and underemployed are also black. This is an unjust and cruel situation and is a product of our history – slavery, which lasted four centuries in Brazil, has left profound marks on our society. The Brazilian state should not be neutral in relationship to the race question. To this end, the new Secretary is given the important responsibility to promote racial equality in our country and open a space for the effective integration of this goal in all the projects and actions in which the government is involved. (da Silva, 2003)

A historic statement from the president of a nation that only ten years earlier clung to the idea that Brazil was a racial democracy. To have a head of state directly call into question race-neutral responses to racism is significant. But there is also a deeply flawed aspect to this statement: race is reduced to a question of Blackness. As I discuss below, this is an articulation of racial politics that a number of social scientists have been nurturing for decades.

Race Is Black

In *Racial Revolutions*, I detailed how within the subfield of critical race studies there has been a pervasive, albeit unexamined, assumption that Black identities are key to antiracism and Indian subjectivities are irrelevant. As a result, the focus has been on excavating African histories and genealogies, encouraging the production of Black subjectivities, generating greater popular support for the Black movement, revalorizing Blackness, and so forth. Absent has been a consideration of Indigenous communities, activists and politics.

For instance, in Howard Winant's (1994, p. 146) analysis of the Brazilian racial terrain, Indianness is overlooked. In outlining what he considers the two aspects of racial politics in contemporary Brazil, Winant argues that the first "is about racial inequality, mobility, and redistribution along lines of race and racially based political action. The second is about the meaning of race, the nature of racial identity, the logic of racial categories, the centrality of African currents in Brazilian culture and history and the links between blacks in Brazil and elsewhere in the African diaspora." Note that the primacy of Indigenous currents in Brazilian culture and history, as well as the links between Indians in Brazil and elsewhere, are not deemed relevant to the racial politics of contemporary Brazil. The politics of race is equated mainly with that of African-centred subjectivities, communities, and organizations. An antiracist project is situated exclusively within Black identities and African cultural streams.

Another illustration of this restricted emphasis on Blackness is Michael Hanchard's (1999) edited volume *Racial Politics in Contemporary Brazil*. None of the chapters in his volume ever mention the flight from Indian subjectivities, anti-Indian stereotypes, or the Indian movement in Brazil. The focus is instead on Black antiracist activists, the state of Black social movements, the efforts of racial subalterns to distance themselves from Black subject positions, the failure of Brazilians to appreciate their African heritage, the negative stereotypes associated with Blackness, and so on. None of this is meant to suggest that a work must cover all aspects of racial politics, or that it should not concentrate on Blackness. Rather, the point is that analyses of race – a subject that the title of this book promises to address – are usually studies of Blackness exclusively.

Such a restricted stress on Black identities, communities, and movements in discussions purported to be about antiracism can be perplexing. For example, although it is five times larger than the Indian community, the self-identified Black population in Brazil is relatively modest in size. That is, this bias in the literature could be better understood if Blacks constituted a large segment of the national population. Yet countless surveys have documented the fact that only a small percentage of Brazilians self-identify as Black. According to data compiled by IBGE in the 2010 census, for instance, 48 per cent of Brazilians self-identified as White, 43 per cent as pardo, and 8 per cent as Black. Furthermore, the Indian population has been increasing rapidly – a rate of 10 per cent per year since 1991 – to bring it to 1 per cent of the national population (Perz et al., 2008, p. 8).

In practice, though, many if not most critical race scholars assume that 51 per cent of the population is Black because they, as Jack Forbes long ago observed, "insist upon translating mestico and pardo as 'mulatto' which … results in a grave distortion of the tri-racial character of the mestico-pardo group" (Forbes, 1993, p. 244). Pardos are not only of African and European descent but also boast Indigenous origins (see Piza & Rosemberg, 1999, p. 51). Yet the fact that most pardos are part-Indian, that "perhaps a third of Brazilians ... are at least part-Indian," is frequently overlooked "by modern writers who choose to emphasize only African and European components" (Buckley, 1999, p. 2; Forbes, 1993, p. 245). As a result, there is a proclivity to "lump all pardos, mesticos and pretos together as a 'colored' people, meaning by 'colored' not non-white but only negro or part-negro" (Forbes, 1993, p. 244).

Indians as Ethnics

Scholars of Indigenous people have also contributed to the restricted focus on Blackness. Although several of these scholars have emphasized how colonial conventions and Indian eradication have been informed by racist ideologies and institutions, none to my knowledge have discussed the potential significance of Indianness for antiracism. That is, Indian researchers have not examined the possible impact of Indian communities on the deracialization of power in Brazil.

This principally has to do with the fact that throughout much of the academic community in Latin America, Indians are not considered germane to race matters (Wade, 1997). Within the social sciences, as Peter Wade observes, "the virtually unquestioned assumptions [prevail] that the study of blacks is one of racism and race relations, while the study of Indians is that of ethnicity and ethnic groups" (Wade, 1997, p. 37). Wade suggests that the principal idea underlying this belief that race and Indians are separate matters, and Indians are inconsequential, "is that the category 'indian' does not depend on phenotypical signifiers ... In contrast, 'black' is often seen as a category defined by more fixed phenotypical criteria that cannot be manipulated in the same way" (ibid.). It is of course incorrect, as Wade notes," to use "race to talk of black identity and 'ethnicity' to talk about Indian identity" as if Blackness were only a matter of phenotype and Indianness only a matter of culture: "Such an opposition separates phenotype from culture, as if the former was not itself culturally constructed" (Wade, 1997, p. 39). Furthermore, the category Indian is dependent on physical signifiers, which is one of the reasons most Indians in eastern Brazil, who are of African and European descent, are viewed as racial charlatans. Their African and European features mark them as inauthentic – as not "real Indians." Conversely, the category Blackness is often contingent on nonphysical markers. As Wade explains,

> The Latin American material shows that, for example, the same individual dressed shabbily and smartly will be identified with different color terms that locate the person on a scale between black and white. These terms are not dependent on phenotype alone, because the context of somatic features alters people's classification – and even perhaps perception – of these features. (Wade, 1997, p. 38)

Another reason that it is inaccurate to conceptualize Indianness as a simple matter of ethnicity qua culture is because "the category Indian was an integral part of the colonial encounters within which the discourse of race emerged ... From a macro historical perspective, then, 'indian' was a racial category and retains strong elements of this history" (Wade, 1997, p. 37).

In my discussion with Indian scholars in Brazil, none of them explicitly stated that Indianness was a matter of culture (rather than phenotype or descent) and that this was the reason why they did not explore the relevance of Indians to the politics of race. Instead, when they defended their analytic position, they did so on the grounds that this was how racial subalterns conceptualized their social world. As one Brazilian PhD candidate of anthropology at the National Museum in Rio de Janeiro remarked:

> When blacks refer to whites they mean another race, but Indians don't mean this. When Indians speak of whites, of the white man, they are referring to a civilized man, and to his system of life, to a different cosmology, to a different mode of thinking, and seeing oneself and the world. To an Indian, the white man could be of the white, black or Asian race. The point here is that he is not an Indian and therefore is an other. This is the only reason that scholars don't think of Indian discourses as racialized discourses.[2]

Rather than claiming that Indianness is a matter of ethnicity (that is, culture) and not race (that is, phenotype and genotype), this young scholar justifies the failure of Indian scholars to deal with race by claiming that Indians imagine the differences between themselves and others in exclusively cultural terms. Although it is certainly true that Indians discern differences in cultural terms, they also take into consideration genotype and phenotype. For example, I found that the more "Indian" an individual appeared to be, the more credibility that person had as an Indian within Indigenous communities. In other words, the more an individual approximates the somatic diacritics of Indianness, the less likely she or he is to have her or his Indianness challenged. Moreover, and more importantly, discourses and other practices are rarely, if ever, "race neutral." Indians are producing different aesthetic hierarchies, narratives, symbolic orders, spatializations, political practices, and so on, that in the Brazilian context have racialized meanings and potentially profound implications for the Brazilian racial order. Thus, even if Indians did not conceptualize differences in racial terms, this would not mean that their discursive and material practices were inconsequential to race matters (Warren, 2001).

The Consequences

The Blackening of mesticos and the deracialization of Indians have helped to engender an antiracist movement that largely sees itself as a Black – or latent Black – movement. In other words, social scientists have played an important role in defining Indians in such a way that antiracist activists and entities do not consider Indigenous communities and their problems germane to antiracism. The result is not antagonism, but rather neglect. The Indigenous question, if considered at all, is treated as if it were largely irrelevant to race matters.

So, for example, SEPPIR, the federal entity mentioned above that was created to reduce racial inequality in Brazil, discusses racism as if were primarily, if not exclusively, a question of Blackness. Its website gives figures for how many Brazilians are of African descent (not of Indigenous descent), presents slavery as if there were only a history of African slavery, and selects pictorial representations that only further highlight its Afrocentrism. Moreover, whenever Edson Santos, one of its directors, summarizes the ministry's objectives, little doubt is left as to its de facto anti-Indian bias. The list includes advocating for quilombos; advancing "The Colour of Culture" program "to promote the teaching of a primary and secondary grade school curriculum that teaches the 'History and Culture of Africa and people of African descent'"; distributing 100,000 education scholarships to "Afro Brazilians" as part of the "University for All" program; and "developing programs for better health care and employment opportunity in Black communities" (Carrillo, 2008). Santos has defended his ministry's prioritization of Blackness using the same logic that critical race scholars invoke to justify their emphasis on Blackness: "SEPPIR is charged with promoting racial equality, but with Afro Brazilians consisting of … some 48 percent (of the Brazilian population) … the ministry naturally focuses the majority of its work on Afro Brazilian issues" (Carrillo, 2008). This statement echos the social scientific literature which, as we have seen, overlooks the fact that most pardos, who as of the last census make up approximately 43 per cent of the population, are of Indigenous decent and are socially, symbolically, and culturally linked to Indians.

The exclusion of Indians from consideration, let alone support, by most antiracist organizations such as SEPPIR has hit Indigenous communities at a particularly difficult time. Since the early 1970s, the Catholic Church had been a powerful advocate of Indigenous communities – the biggest non-governmental entity to act as such. However, in recent years, Popes John Paul II and Benedict XVI have successfully purged or marginalized Brazilian priests and bishops associated with liberation theology. This has meant increasingly diminished support for the Indigenous Missionary Council (CIMI), the entity within the Brazilian Church that has assisted Indigenous communities, because CIMI has historically drawn most of its support from Church progressives.

The construction of raceless Indians, it is important to add, has adversely affected not only Indian communities but also the antiracist movement more broadly. First, Indian communities represent one of the few antiracist counter-public publics in Brazil and should therefore be cultivated rather than neglected. Indian identities, unlike other racial identities, are linked to a different "location," described by Charles Hale as "distinctive social memory, consciousness, practices as well as place within the social structure" (Hale, 1997, p. 568). For instance, in my research with Indigenous people, I found them to be far less prone to adopt White talk than other non-Whites. Antonia Xacriaba's response to anti-Indian racism was typical among the Indian I interviewed:

> Whites see Indians as if they were rebels, savages that don't know anything and are lazy. One time, I got into a discussion with a man on the bus because he was talking badly about Indians. So I asked, "Why are you talking badly about Indians? I'm Indian. Why are you talking badly about Indians?"… He apologized and sat down. (Warren, 2001, p. 277)

This is not the racism-evading, conflict-avoiding behaviour that is so common among other Brazilians. Instead, the language of Indians tends to be that of race-cognizant back talk. Moreover, they commonly engage in a set of practices that represent a break from Whitening. By privileging Indian mates, ancestors, communities, symbolic materials, ceremonies, and spaces, they bring into being alternative symbolic arenas in which Whiteness was not hypervalued as the good, the beautiful, the desired or the deserving (Warren, 2001).

Second, the quilombo movement is one of the most significant dynamics affecting racial politics in Brazil in the past decade. The 1988 constitution ensured land and cultural rights not only for Indigenous communities, but also for quilombos. Historically the term meant African-descent communities that were at one time Maroon, or runaway slave, communities. In that past decade, this has been legally and socially redefined to mean "rural black communities that group together descendants of slaves who live on a subsistence level and where cultural manifestations have strong ties with the ancestral past" (French, 2009, p. 123). Thus, being a former fugitive slave community or demonstrating African cultural survivals are no longer required to be recognized as a quilombo community. Consequently, there are many more communities that can and do fit this definition of quilombo, which is evidenced by the fact that there are now estimated to be 3,524 communities in Brazil with a total population of five million (SEPPIR, 2008).

Most analysts agree that this movement holds tremendous potential for profoundly altering racial-class politics in Brazil. For example, if most of these communities were federally recognized, this would lead to land and education reform – as quilombos are constitutionally guaranteed land and schools (in addition to cultural protection). Furthermore, it would expand antiracist counter-publics, as these communities tend, especially over time, to embrace Black identities, engage in back talk, and foreground very different narratives of history and nation (Arruti, 2006). For example, Jan French, in her study of the Mocambo quilombo in northeastern Brazil, found that the quilombo movement there produced a change in the perceived meaning of "Blackness," led people to "assume" a Black identity for the first time in their lives, and generated new, politically effective collective identities and politics (2009). I have found similar practices among the Bau quilombo in Minas Gerais. One song they commonly sang helps to illustrate the contours of this counter-public: "When the Whites laugh, the Blacks cry. When the Black fights, he wins. When the Blacks celebrate, the Whites cry."

Unfortunately, at least in my experience, this opportunity is not being taken advantage of to the degree it could and should be, in part because of how Indians are defined as external to racial politics. In most instances, the sense of quilombo identity and community is very nascent, tentative and fragile. In this way, their situation strongly parallels identity formation among Indigenous communities in many parts of Brazil. That is, these are often post-traditional, rural peoples, undergoing a process of reclaiming previously hyper-stigmatized identities that draws the ire of locals and the violent responses of those who have something materially or socially at stake. Moreover, their ethnic or "tribal" identities are of equal, if not greater, importance than their "racial" identity as Black. Therefore the pan-quilombo organizational and political structure, as it grows, will likely be much more similar institutionally and culturally to the Indigenous movement than to the *movimento negro*, a largely middle-class, urban movement which to date is built around the primacy of race and a much more homogenous understanding of Blackness (Hanchard, 1994).

Given these parallels, obvious allies of these communities would be those who have been involved in the Indigenous movement. In the Jequitinhonha Valley of Minas Gerais, Geralda Soares and Ivan Pankararu, individuals who had been involved for decades in the Indigenous movement, became key partners in enabling the Bau to secure federal recognition as a quilombo in 2007. The Bau, according to one of the elders, Maria do Carmo, are the descendants of two children who were "hunted down in the forest by dogs" in the mid-nineteenth century and became enslaved on Fazenda Santana. The captive boy learned to make trunks, or Bau, and "so the name stuck, Bau. Everyone who asked, 'Where have you been?' the reply would be, 'I was in the house of the Bau.'" Neuza, one of the leaders of the Bau, explains that the Bau were until recently very isolated:

> We were afraid of the people – especially the Whites. We lived there in the fazenda, only amongst ourselves. We didn't know anyone. If we saw anyone, it was one of us. When we saw a White, we got scared to go near. No one had contact with Whites. It was only Blacks. People only married other Bau. Since we've moved to the city, now you have Bau marrying with others. But before it was only Bau with Bau. (Neuza Bau, interview by author, November 2011)

The Bau recognition movement began in 2003. As Geralda Soares explains,

> [T]he Bau at that time were very closed. So we started to try to get to know the Bau. We organized a week of the black. It was at the Nazare High School. We started to incorporate the Bau into this event. A minister from SEPPIR was at the event. We asked her assistance. Later we had a really big gathering at Nazare [Catholic High School]. There were 200 people. After that the schools started researching the Bau – doing interviews. During

> black week the schools are obliged to deal with black history and culture. So the teachers sent students to interview the Bau. And then things built a certain momentum until they were recognized in 2007. (Geralda Soares, interview by author, November 2011)

Neuza gives a lot of credit to Geralda, the former mayor Caca, and the Indians.

> We like [the Indians] a lot. Ivan helped us a lot. Because of him we started discussing who we are, where we are from, what happened, etc. He was helping us to build courage. Everyone in the family was really afraid. Ivan and Gel [Ivan's wife], thanks to God … they helped us a lot. At any time you could go to Ivan's house to get information and he wouldn't hide. We created a union. They loved our dances because they like to have fun. And whenever we see Ivan we get happy. He's a good person. He talks to everyone. He doesn't discriminate. We were always welcome in his house. Without them … they gave us so much help, support to move forward, to go to Belo Horizonte and petition for recognition. (Neuza Bau, interview by author, November 2011)

Unfortunately, individuals such as Ivan and Geralda are often seen as out of place in the quilombo movement, because it is envisioned as a racial/Black matter and therefore the natural terrain of Black entities and organizations. Consequently, individuals and organizations which have a great deal in common with quilombos – namely, Indigenous people, organizations, and activists – are not encouraged to participate and at times are even discouraged. How many consultants within SEPPIR, for instance, come out of the Indigenous movement? How often are individuals like Geralda and Ivan sought out to assist a quilombo in its attempts at community building and petitioning for federal recognition? A wealth of experience and expertise in building communities and movements around subaltern racial identities in rural Brazil is not being harnessed, because "Indian" activism, community building, and organizations are not seen as germane to quilombos, which are seen as a race/Black matter.

The Country of the Future

Progress in Brazil will likely only happen once the sharp social inequalities that define Brazilian society are softened, if not eroded. As discussed above, these disparities are undergirded by a racially inflected elitism in which the rich believe themselves superior to *o povo*. In the documentary film *Wasteland*, Vik Munoz, the world-renowned Brazilian artist, labelled this elitism "the poison of Brazil," because he understood how it impeded progress. Among other things, it has stymied sufficient investments in research and development, education, health care, and infrastructure, which are vital for boosting economic growth.

As detailed above, Indians represent a kind of vanguard of modernity in that they offer a counter-public, which challenges this elitism and its racist underpinnings. And yet they are being threatened, not only by their traditional foes, but also by the centre-left political regime, through its endorsement of an economic project based in natural resource extraction, monocultural production, and top-down megaprojects. Moreover, and more disappointingly, Indians are not being aided or supported by critical race scholars or antiracist NGOs and activists, because of how these groups have coloured race.

Thus, the construction of Indians as raceless ethnics is no trivial or esoteric matter. This definition of who and what Indians are is not only imperilling Indians and Indigenous communities but is also contributing to Brazil's continuing reputation as a country of the future rather than of the present.

NOTES

1 I have been conducting ethnographic fieldwork in Brazil since 1992. After spending about two years in rural and urban Minas Gerais and Rio de Janeiro between 1992 and 1997, I have continued to return at least once a year and spend between one to five weeks on each visit.

2 Email correspondence with Sonia Travassos on 17 March 1999.

REFERENCES

Arruti, J.M.A. (2006). *Mocambo: Antropologia e História do Processso de Formação quilombola*. Bauru, Brazil: EDUSC.

Buckley, S. (1999). Native Struggle to Keep Identities. *Washington Post*, 21 December, p. 2.

Carrillo, K.J. (2008). SEPPIR: Brazil's Special Secretariat for the Promotion of Racial Equality, 12 September.

da Silva, Lula. (2003). "Medida Provisória N° 111, de 21 de Março 2003." http://www.planalto.gov.br/ccivil_03/MPV/Antigas_2003/111.htm

Forbes, J.D. (1993). *Africans and Native Americans: The Language of Race and Evo-*

lution of Red-Black Peoples (2nd ed.). Urbana, IL: University of Illinois Press.

French, J.H. (2009). *Becoming Black or Indian: Legalizing Identities in Brazil's Northeast*. Chapel Hill, NC: University of North Carolina Press.

Hale, C.H. (1997). Cultural Politics of Identity in Latin America. *Annual Review of Anthropology*, *26*(1), 567–90. http://dx.doi.org/10.1146/annurev.anthro.26.1.567

Hanchard, M. (1994). *Orpheus and Power: The Movimento Negro of Rio de Janeiro and Sao Paulo, Brazil, 1945–1988*. Princeton, NJ: Princeton University Press.

Hanchard, M. (Ed.). (1999). *Racial Politics in Contemporary Brazil*. Durham, NC: Duke University Press.

Perz, S., Warren, J., & Kennedy, D.P. (2008). Contributions of Racial-Ethnic Reclassification and Demographic Processes to Indigenous Population Resurgence. *Latin American Research Review*, *43*(2), 7–33. http://dx.doi.org/10.1353/lar.0.0019

Piza, E., & Rosemberg, F. (1999). Color in the Brazilian Census. In R. Reichmann (Ed.), *Race in Contemporary Brazil: From Indifference to Inequality* (pp. 37–52). University Park, PA: Pennsylvania State University Press.

Roy, A. (2001). *Power Politics*. Cambridge, MA: South End Press.

SEPPIR. (2008). Quilombos no Brasil. Presidência da República: Secretaria Especial de Políticas de Promoção da Igualdade Racial – SEPPIR. http://web.archive.org/web/20080314104723/http://www.presidencia.gov.br/estrutura_presidencia/seppir/copy_of_acoes/

Wade, P. (1997). *Race and Ethnicity in Latin America*. London: Pluto Press.

Warren, J.W. (1999). The Brazilian Geography of Indianness. *Wicazo Sa Review*, *14*(1), 61–86. http://dx.doi.org/10.2307/1409516

Warren, J.W. (2001). *Racial Revolutions: Antiracism and Indian Resurgence in Brazil*. Durham, NC: Duke University Press.

Winant, H. (1994). *Racial Conditions: Politics, Theory, Comparisons*. Minneapolis, MN: University of Minnesota Press.

Conclusion
Seeing beyond the State and Thinking beyond the State of Sight

MAXIMILIAN C. FORTE

The collaboration that produced this volume through much iteration has been focused on what is arguably one of the worst questions to be posed to or against Indigenous peoples – one that ultimately calls on *them* to give an account of themselves for being who they are in the light of foreign invasions and occupations. It's as if being who they are is a problem, and furthermore, a problem that they caused. Worse yet, they may not even be who they think they are.

As with all bad questions, one can expect to get a lot of bad answers. So why did we choose to address such a question, going as far as making it the leading question of this project? The answer is simple: the question, however one may assess its epistemological qualities, is a politically important question (the most important, perhaps). It is an institutionalized question, a governing question that structures people's lives, their access to resources, and even their self-perceptions. It is also a key historical question, one that continues to be asked repeatedly, and one that will inevitably lose relevance. That this question has been raised across the Americas, in different forms (substituting, as the case may be, any number of cognate or tribal labels in the place of "Indian"), is due to a shared history of colonization and state-building, as well as the dominance of European theories of citizenship, nationhood, race, identity, and more contemporary concerns for "authenticity." Here we can start to look beyond the constraints and limitations of that question and begin to see past the constraints imposed by states today.

By producing a comparative framework that makes historical sense – one that derives from the European colonization of the Americas and subsequent forces of U.S.-led imperial globalization – and by bringing to light detailed case studies that deal with both the process of racializing and effectively turning indigeneity into a measurable substance, as well as the wide diversity of outcomes and responses, our collection aimed to therefore provide readers with new conceptual tools for thinking past the dilemmas first imposed by colonization. Equipped with the vocabulary used to analyse the comparative racialization of indigeneity in the Americas, our intention is to move debates past the "bad questions" of Indigenous identity so that we may join wider debates about social transformation, social justice, and post-capitalist political forms.

Looking beyond the Politics of a Bad Question

One way to approach this challenge is to understand the combination of two critical factors in this debate as constructed thus far: where one stands on the issue of Indigenous rights to both self-determination and self-definition; and how one perceives history – that is, issues of continuity and discontinuity. There are at least four schools of thought here, varying on whether they are pro- or anti-Indigenous (i.e., pro- or anti-Indigenous rights and Indigenous self-determination, or whether they even recognize an Indigenous presence), and pro- or anti-essentialism (i.e., upholding or undermining claims to continuity and to key markers of identity).

Hence, one position is *anti-Indigenous anti-essentialism*: this involves disclaiming any effort, of any kind, to even speak of the "Indigenous," as the very identity itself fundamentally and inescapably entails essentialism. To be against essentialism in this case means to believe that no identity that permits ideas of commonality and historical continuity is valid, especially not identities such as Aboriginal, First Nations, and so on, which are loaded with historical connotations of precedence. In anthropology, a leading exemplar of anti-Indigenous anti-essentialism is Adam Kuper (1988, 2003), and Garroutte and Snipp in chapter three of this volume address a few others outside of anthropology.

A second position is *anti-Indigenous essentialism*: this is much more common outside of academia, and can be easily encountered in both popular and official discussions about Indigenous identity and Indigenous rights in places such as Canada, the U.S., and Australia. The idea here is simply that of the "real Indian" or the "real Aboriginal" – to be considered real, depending on the culture in question, one must look, speak, dress, and/or live in an "authentic" Aboriginal manner, which means without any signs of change having occurred in the past 500 years. This approach assumes "correct" standards of identity. "Ethnic passing" is an accusation, and one that assumes clear boundaries between ethnicities. In addition, there is an accusation of calculated manipulations motivating claims to Indigenous identity, reinforcing the instrumentalist "interest group politics" approach (see Field, 1994, and Garroutte and Snipp in chapter three of this volume for more analysis of this approach). It can be anti-Indigenous when this is imposed against the rights of persons to self-identify and self-define as Indigenous, or to reclaim stolen lands that were their birthright, by dismissing the claimants as "not real" descendants or not traditional enough (to meet virtually stereotyped inventories of the traits of this or that Indigenous identity).

A third position is *pro-Indigenous essentialism*: this is much less common, and takes us back into academia as well as advocacy. The position is eloquently represented in the work of Andrew Lattas, an Australian anthropologist, who argued that "it is a mistake to see essentialism as exclusively something which the state imposes upon minorities. What this ignores is the cultural and political functioning of essentialist themes in resistance movements and the empowering role of essentialisms in identity politics" (Lattas, 1993, p. 246). The basic idea here is that representational strategies used *by Indigenous representatives* which adopt essentialist tactics (of perhaps dressing up to meet dominant White expectations of Aboriginal difference, authenticity, and continuity) are in fact valuable and useful if they help Aboriginals to achieve their immediate social and political aims. Moreover, the role of the anthropologist should not be to criticize and dismantle such representational strategies – anthropologists should not feel free to morally authorize themselves to act as expert arbiters of other people's forms of identification, and they should not impose themselves as those authorized to create pristine political positions. This is a strategy that conceives of essentialism as a tactical political tool laden with cultural connotations, and not as a scholarly theory of history. Another school of pro-Indigenous essentialism is what Field called the "cultural survival perspective": "The cultural survival perspective embodies an essentialism in which cultural traits or traditions constitute the 'essences' of being Indian and function as Cartesian coordinates against which the degree of 'Indianness' of a group can be determined by social scientists" (1994, p. 228). The reason why this can be classed – with some difficulty – as a pro-Indigenous rights perspective is that it uses surviving cultural traditions as a basis for defending Indigenous cultural and territorial rights, which can also unfortunately reinforce the position of anti-Indigenous essentialists.

Fourth, there is *pro-Indigenous anti-essentialism*: this is a perspective that one would expect to find clearly articulated as such in the works of academics, but it remains, I think, somewhat muted. To some extent one can find this in the works of two New Zealand anthropologists, Steven Webster (1993) and Jeffrey Sissons (2005), as well as in the work of Les Field (1994) and Jonathan Warren (2001) on "post-traditional Indians" in Brazil. Field might use his term "resistance school" to describe these approaches; this "denotes centuries of varying kinds of struggle that began when Europeans successfully destroyed precontact polities and the positions of authority and control that precontact leaders had maintained over territory and resources," with the result being that "the resistance struggle itself has become the primary characteristic of Indian ethnicity … self-identified Indigenous social groups continuously redefine (and often reinvent) their identities in extremely fluid ways" (1994, p. 230). The main argument of this fourth approach is that reinforcing expectations of continuity, cultural survival, and strong traits of Indigenous difference will work to bolster ideas of "the real Indian" (see *anti-Indigenous essentialism* above), and that this is a flaw of both anti-Indigenous essentialism and pro-Indigenous essentialism. History and colonialism matter significantly here: "ethnicity and ethnic group should be understood as processual terms that signify changing identities in relation to colonialism through history, rather than as a set of more or less fixed social categories" (Field, 1994, p. 231). What can be lost in essentialisms of the kinds outlined above is a notion of culture as resistance, of processual modes of identification, of new ways of being and becoming Indigenous through the adaptation and incorporation of the "stuff" of modernity and cultural creolization. (Lattas might counter that he is depicting essentialism deployed tactically to *resist* further loss, and *in relation* to other agents and institutions, in a *process* of defending Aboriginal rights by adopting *new ways* of representing themselves – i.e., as if they as a people were unchanging. This raises the intriguing possibility that all of the essentialisms we know are ones we have encountered relationally, rooted in both history and contemporary political dynamics.)

While the contributors to this volume seem to mostly represent the fourth perspective – what Field called the cultural resistance school – the lines between that and those who feel more comfortable with the cultural survival school were not always clearly drawn. However, it was evident that none of us were content with the idea that there is one certain, sound, and valid answer to the question of "who is an Indian," and we tended to agree that we must move beyond the current repertoire of answers that are being produced across the Americas.

Another way to approach this challenge is to go beyond inventories, that is, beyond taking stock as if people were themselves *stock*. This also implies going beyond management and control, and towards a situation where self-identification and self-determination can coexist (given that they can also overlap), especially if they do not *compete* for the exact same finite resources (although the question of why resources are *made to be finite* under a capitalist regime can no longer be deferred). As Lawrence argues in chapter two of this volume, Indigenous peoples should avoid "accepting external definitions, with their brutalizing, instrumental, and frequently politically motivated analyses of identity," and instead take "both history and self-ascription into account" and rely on "loose definitions rather than those that emphasize tightness, arbitrariness, and exclusion." This is a perspective against competition and regulation, of legislating identities, and one that moves towards collaboration and a continual process of recouping and remaking Indigenous practices and identities. What at this moment might be termed "resurgence" would instead become the long-term nature of indigeneity. Communities and persons on the margin, whose presence is least recognized and whose rights are least assured, may be the ones with the most answers to these challenges.

Another answer to the question, "Are they Indian?" as related by Garroutte and Snipp in this volume, could be neither yes nor no, but rather *when*, *how*, and *to what extent*. For the time being, "who is an Indian" continues to be a persistent question in everyday life and it ought to always provoke further questions, such as: Who is asking? Why are you asking? Why should this even be a question? And whose answer will count more or most? Given that the question is a fundamentally political one, its passing away as a mode of interrogation, accusation, or evaluation will concomitantly have to be achieved through political struggle.

Self-Determination, Self-Identification, and the Futures of Indigeneity

Indigenous persons in North America are at a crossroads, caught between competing ideas of tribal definitions versus self-definitions – both of which are recognized as rights under the newly promulgated UN Declaration on the Rights of Indigenous Peoples – and caught between forces not of their own making. It seems as if there is an inability to forge new forms of organization, of rights and responsibilities that embrace both the essence of cherished traditional norms and evade the mimicry of contrary Euro-American ones. Few speak of systems of at least "honorary citizenship" whereby those not resident on reserved lands, and without a long-term history of family residence within a specific locale, can be accepted as citizens, but without any implication for sharing limited resources. Another aim could be to expand the resource base to what is not in fact a diminishing population – unlike what the various Eurocentric extinctionists would have wanted and dreamt to be the providential outcome of evolution – but a growing population that should have access to lands to suit its growth (for more, see Churchill, 2004, pp. 70, 71). This would also open the door to challenges to the way we conceive of citizenship and rights to access resources within North American society as a whole, a debate that is long overdue and continues to be muted.

However, indigeneity and territory have become increasingly delinked due to the rise of urban Indigenous populations, producing another challenge, or another set of interpretations of the relationship between tribal self-determination and individual self-identification. Indeed, in many parts of the Americas, indigeneity has also become increasingly delinked from all sorts of signs of tangible visibility, which challenges the governing regimes of trait-listing that include race as a system of categorization. While the idea of land-based indigeneity continues to be resilient, there has also been a resurgence of indigeneity among the land-dispossessed. In facing this situation, we can either resort to ideas of instrumentality and interest in assessing the so-called "new claimants" to Indigenous identity, assuming that they are driven by some agenda of maximizing personal material gain, or we can grapple with affectivity through a desire to rebuild broken connections and with the broader movement of criticizing capitalist notions of progress and modernity. While the perception remains dominant that some sort of "privilege" and "property" is associated with Indigenous identity, there will be a continued effort, both from within and without Indigenous communities, to demand "proof." Exclusivity can help to maintain boundaries, and boundaries matter to those that have experienced historical forces of incursion and expropriation, but one has to be precise about one's targets. For as many "wannabes" as have been derided and ousted, there clearly is not a massive rush from the wider non-Indigenous population to acquire the symbols and identity of indigeneity. In other words, the idea that if everybody is Indigenous, nobody is Indigenous, is largely premised on the fear of a fictional scenario. This situation has not been a threat to indigeneity in those nations where Indigenous peoples are not only the majority, but can maintain their identities with greatly varying degrees of access to material resources in both urban centres and rural areas. The only certainty in all of this is that neither *survival* nor *continuity* can be facilitated by diminishing numbers, or by placing definitional straitjackets that serve to enforce systems of numerical reduction.

Having said all of the above, it was not the intention of the contributors of this volume to either advance academic expertise as the ultimate arbiter of Indigenous identities, to provide an easy-to-follow menu for "accurately determining" who is Indigenous, or to provide advice that caters to the functioning of government bureaucracies and their micromanagement of Indigenous affairs. Our greater concern was with the politics that works to preserve the dominance of a very "bad" and yet historically very important question: "who is an Indian"? Our hope is that readers will come away from this effort with a determination to ask better questions – better in the sense of being more analytically productive and with implications that are more socially just and fair. Among the questions we would like to see posed are those that posit indigeneity as a historically specific type of relationality and those that involve issues of power and affectivity, without searching for the elusive "one size fits all" solution. If, however, we overcome the stigmatization of being Indigenous only to then treat it as a category implying "privilege" and uniquely demanding "proof" of belonging, then we will not have gone far past the point of endorsing extinction.

REFERENCES

Churchill, W. (2004). A Question of Identity. In S. Greymorning (Ed.), *A Will to Survive: Indigenous Essays on the Politics of Culture, Language and Identity* (pp. 59–94). Boston, MA: McGraw-Hill.

Field, L. (1994). Who Are the Indians? *Latin American Research Review*, *29*(3), 227–38.

Kuper, A. (1988). *The Invention of Primitive Society: Transformations of an Illusion*. New York: Routledge.

Kuper, A. (2003). The Return of the Native. *Current Anthropology*, *44*(3), 389–402. http://dx.doi.org/10.1086/368120

Lattas, A. (1993). Essentialism, Memory and Resistance: Aboriginality and the

Politics of Authenticity. *Oceania, 63*, 240–67.
Sissons, J. (2005). *First Peoples: Indigenous Cultures and their Cutures*. London: Reaktion Books.
Warren, J.W. (2001). *Racial Revolutions: Antiracism and Indian Resurgence in Brazil*. Durham, NC: Duke University Press.
Webster, S. (1993). Postmodernist Theory and the Sublimation of Maori Culture. *Oceania, 63*, 222–39.

Contributors

Julia M. Coates (Cherokee Nation, Tahlequah, Oklahoma) is presently at the University of California, Los Angeles. Her title is Senior Writer/ Oral Interviewer in American Indian History for the Center for Oral History Research of the Charles Young Research Library. At the time of writing she was an assistant professor in the Department of Native American Studies at the University of California, Davis. Her research interests cover Native American diasporas, history, identity, women, and politics. She has conducted participant-observation fieldwork with hundreds of Cherokee citizens in California, Texas, and New Mexico. Coates also helped to form numerous Cherokee community organizations throughout California and in other states. For over six years, she was the project director and lead instructor for the award-winning Cherokee Nation history course, which brought her into personal contact with most of the employees of the Cherokee Nation, along with thousands of Cherokees in northeastern Oklahoma communities and throughout the country. She also serves on the Tribal Council of the Cherokee Nation as its "At Large" representative. At UC Davis she teaches the Introduction to Native American Studies as well as classes on race, women, development and history within Native America.

Maximilian C. Forte is an associate professor in the Department of Sociology and Anthropology at Concordia University in Montreal, Canada. He teaches courses in political anthropology, the new imperialism, Indigenous resurgence, and various courses on media and visual ethnographies. He is the author of *Ruins of Absence, Presence of Caribs: (Post) Colonial Constructions of Aboriginality in Trinidad and Tobago* (University Press of Florida), and the editor of *Indigenous Resurgence in the Contem-*

porary Caribbean: Amerindian Survival and Revival (Peter Lang), in addition to numerous other edited volumes, chapters, and journal articles dealing with the Indigenous peoples of the contemporary Caribbean. He was also the founding editor of *Kacike: The Journal of Caribbean Amerindian History and Anthropology* and currently maintains the news and essay blog *Review of the Indigenous Caribbean*.

Eva Marie Garroutte (Cherokee Nation) is an associate professor in the Department of Sociology at Boston College. She has a background of research and publication related to the study of Native American issues, health and aging, racial/ethnic identity, and religion. She is the author of the influential book *Real Indians: Identity and the Survival of Native America* (University of California Press) and various articles in sociological and health-related journals. In collaboration with Cherokee Nation Health Services, she has conducted a series of research projects funded by the National Institute on Aging to examine medical communication needs among American Indian elders using tribal clinics. Her current service on editorial advisory boards includes the *Journal of Native Aging and Health, American Indian Quarterly*, and the University of Arizona Press series *Critical Issues in Indigenous Studies*. She is a past Area Commissioner of Indian Affairs in Tulsa, Oklahoma.

Bonita Lawrence (Mi'kmaw) is an associate professor in the Department of Equity Studies, Faculty of Liberal and Professional Studies at York University in Toronto, Canada, where she teaches Indigenous Studies. Her research and publications have focused primarily on urban, non-status, and Métis identities, federally unrecognized Aboriginal communities, and Indigenous justice. She is the author of *Fractured Homeland: Federal Recognition and Algonquin Identity in Ontario* (UBC Press), *"Real" Indians and Others: Mixed-Blood Urban Native People and Indigenous Nationhood* (UBC Press), and co-editor of *Strong Women's Stories: Native Vision and Community Survival*, a collection of Native women's scholarly and activist writing (Sumach Press). She is a traditional singer who sings with groups in Kingston and Toronto at Native social and political gatherings.

José Antonio Lucero is an associate professor in the Henry M. Jackson School of International Studies, at the University of Washington in Seattle. He is the author of *Struggles of Voice: The Politics of Indigenous Representation in the Andes* (University of Pittsburgh Press) and the editor of *Beyond the Lost Decade: Indigenous Movements, Democracy, and Development in Latin America* (Princeton University Program in Latin American Studies). He teaches courses on government, politics, and social movements in Latin America, among others. His research interests focus on comparative politics, Latin American politics, democratization, social movements, and the politics of race and ethnicity.

Donna Patrick is professor in the Department of Sociology and Anthropology and the School of Canadian Studies at Carleton University in Ottawa, Canada. Her current research focuses on multiliteracies, identity, and community-building among urban Inuit. Her other interests lie in the broader area of indigeneity and urban Aboriginality in Canada, as well as in the political, social, and cultural aspects of language use, with a focus on language endangerment discourse and Aboriginal languages in Canada. Her 2003 book, *Language Politics and Social Interaction in an Inuit Community* (Mouton de Gruyter), examines these issues in Arctic Quebec. She teaches courses in language, culture, and power and in Aboriginal and northern issues, with a focus on the Arctic. In teaching and research, Donna approaches the study of Aboriginal issues, language, and discourse through an interdisciplinary lens, focusing on historical, geographical, and social processes.

C. Matthew Snipp is a professor in the Department of Sociology at Stanford University where, among other positions, he has been the director of the Center for Comparative Studies of Race and Ethnicity. He teaches courses in contemporary and historical American Indian Studies as well as rural sociology. He is the author *of American Indians: The First of the Land* (The Russell Sage Foundation, New York), which was selected as an academic book of the year by CHOICE.

Karen Stocker is an assistant professor in the Department of Anthropology at California State University, Fullerton. She is a scholar of applied anthropology with interests in education, the social constructions of race and ethnicity, language, and Latin American ethnography. She is the author of *"I Won't Stay Indian, I'll Keep Studying": Race, Place and Discrimination in a Costa Rican High School* (Colorado University Press).

Jonathan W. Warren is an associate professor in the Henry M. Jackson School of International Studies at the University of Washington in

Seattle. Within the broad area of critical race studies he has focused on Whiteness, racism literacy, racial identity formations, and the links between everyday practices and racism in the U.S. and Brazil. He is the author of the highly regarded book *Racial Revolutions: Antiracism and Indian Resurgence in Brazil* (Duke University Press).

Index